Yellowstone

YELLOWSTONE

A Visitor's Companion

George Wuerthner

STACKPOLE
BOOKS

Published by
STACKPOLE BOOKS
Cameron and Kelker Streets
P.O. Box 1831
Harrisburg, PA 17105

Printed in the United States of America

Cover design by Tracy Patterson

Thanks to Ruthie Matteson for her help with the illustrations.

First Edition

10 9 8 7 6 5 4

Library of Congress Cataloging-in-Publication Data

Wuerthner, George.
 Yellowstone : a visitor's companion / George Wuerthner. — 1st ed.
  p. cm.
 ISBN 0-8117-3078-6
 1. Yellowstone National Park—Guide-books. 2. Ecology—
Yellowtone National Park—Guide-books. 3. Natural history—
Yellowtone National Park—Guide-books. I. Title.
F722.W89 1992
917.87'520433—dc20   91-29403
                                                                CIP

CONTENTS

INTRODUCTION

The Greater Yellowstone Ecosystem (GYE) is one of the last major, relatively intact, temperate-zone ecosystems in the world. At its heart lies Yellowstone National Park, America's and the world's first national park. The park covers 2.2 million acres in northwestern Wyoming—as well as small strips of Montana and Idaho. The ecosystem as a whole takes in 19 million acres, an area about the size of Maine.

To gauge the extent of the GYE, look at any road map showing the tri-state area around Yellowstone and then find these communities: Cooke City, Gardiner, Red Lodge, Livingston, Bozeman, and Ennis, Montana; Ashton and Driggs, Idaho; and Cody, Jackson, Afton, Big Piney, Pinedale, Lander, and Dubois, Wyoming. These towns are within or on the boundaries of the GYE.

The area is generally mountainous. Most of Yellowstone National Park is a volcanic plateau with an average elevation of more than 8,000 feet. This plateau is surrounded by higher ranges including the Beartooth Mountains to the north, the Gallatin and Madison ranges to the northwest; the Centennials and Lionhead to the west; the Tetons, Salt River Range, Wyoming Range, and Gros Ventre Range to the south; the Wind River Range on the southeast, and the Absaroka Mountains to the east.

These mountains are the rooftop of the Middle and Northern Rockies. The Beartooths contain the highest points in Montana, with 29 peaks over 12,000 feet. Here is Montana's highest summit, Granite Peak, which scrapes the sky at 12,799 feet. The 57 highest peaks in the state are in this range. The adjacent Absaroka Range has more than 166 peaks over 10,000 feet, making it one of the most rugged in Montana. The Madison Range northwest of Yellowstone contains more than 128 peaks over 10,000 feet, making it Montana's second-highest range.

In Wyoming, the highest range indisputably is the Wind River, on the southeast corner of the ecosystem. The "Winds" have 45 peaks of more

1

than 13,000 feet, including Wyoming's highest, 13,804-foot Gannet Peak. Nevertheless, the Winds don't have all the high points in the state. Grand Teton is the second highest at 13,770 feet, and Francs Peak at 13,153 in Wyoming's portion of the Absaroka Range is the highest in the Rockies north of the Winds and Tetons.

Flowing from these uplands are the headwaters of the nation's major river systems. The Yellowstone, Madison, Gallatin, Red Rock, Ruby, Stillwater, Boulder, Shoshone, Wind, and Clarks Fork rivers all drain into the Missouri and eventually the Gulf of Mexico and Atlantic Ocean. The Snake and its tributaries, like the Hoback, Gros Ventre, Henry's Fork, Salt, Grey's, and Falls rivers eventually join the Columbia and the Pacific Ocean. Finally, draining off the Wind River Range are the headwaters of the Green River, which eventually joins the Colorado and flows to the Sea of Cortez (Gulf of California).

Most of the larger rivers run through broad, open valleys like the Centennial, Yellowstone (or Paradise), and Madison, but others are in narrow, forested canyons like the Gallatin, Boulder, and Hoback.

Surrounding the well-watered mountain uplands and covering many of the valley bottoms and lower basins are drier grasslands. Most of these are developed and modified to some degree by humans; most of the mountains and plateaus are little altered except by mining and logging, which can be significant in specific places. Nearly a third of the ecosystem is permanently protected as wilderness.

Ecosystem Features

Though first set aside for its extensive thermal features, which are still the largest and best examples in the world, today greater Yellowstone is recognized as an unparalleled biological preserve and wildlife-viewing area. Here roam grizzly bears, the largest elk herd in the country, the greatest concentration of trumpeter swans in the Lower Forty-Eight, some of the most outstanding fisheries outside of Alaska, and a place large enough for natural processes like wildfires to burn thousands of acres without significant danger to human life and property.

These alone would make Yellowstone stand out, but the area also is unsurpassed for its magnificent waterfalls, some of the largest natural lakes in the West, rugged mountains, and, of course, the most spectacular geysers anywhere.

Because of its universal value to humankind, Yellowstone has been designated a World Heritage site. It also is a United Nations Biosphere

Old Faithful erupts approximately once an hour, sending about 11,000 gallons of water 150 feet high. More than a fifth of all the geysers in the world are found within a mile of Old Faithful.

Preserve—the first designated in the United States. For these and many other reasons, Yellowstone is undoubtedly the best-known national park in the world.

But Yellowstone alone is not big enough to encompass and protect the wildlife, scenery, and geological features for which it is renowned. Other federal lands that constitute the GYE include parts of seven national forests: Targhee and Caribou in Idaho; Bridger-Teton and Shoshone in Wyoming; and Custer, Gallatin, and Beaverhead in Montana. There are three national wildlife refuges—Gray's Lake, Red Rock Lakes, and Elk—and a second national park, Grand Teton. These lands, owned by all Americans, make up the bulk of the Greater Yellowstone Ecosystem.

What Is an Ecosystem?

Actually, "ecosystem" has no precise definition. It is used as a package of ideas. Yet the concept as applied to greater Yellowstone has some scientific justification.

In a satellite view of greater Yellowstone, the central heart, or Yellowstone Plateau, is clear and surrounded by mountain ranges that extend like spokes on a wheel. Within this area are basic similarities in flora and fauna. For example, lodgepole pine, aspen, and subalpine fir are found throughout the area. From the central plateau, these forested highlands and ranges give way to grass- or sage-covered plains and lowlands where different plants, wildlife, and geological features dominate. This transition marks the bounds of the GYE.

The boundaries are not always sharp and in some areas are completely arbitrary, since nature exists in a continuum. Nevertheless, greater Yellowstone has its own integrity, and a peculiar combination of biology and geology makes it unique.

Federal Lands in the Ecosystem

National Parks

To many people, any federal land management employee is a "forest ranger." But there are distinctions among the federal land-managing agencies and their goals and duties. Yellowstone and Grand Teton are managed by the National Park Service, part of the Interior Department. National parks were originally set aside to protect grand scenery or unique features like geysers. More recently, this agency has been increasingly aware and willing to preserve the environment. Industries such as logging, mining, and with a few exceptions, livestock grazing, are not permitted within national parks. As a rule, hunting is also banned. The park service is strong on serving the visitor and emphasizes natural history interpretation, recreation, and nature appreciation.

National Forests

National forests are managed by the U.S. Forest Service, an Agriculture Department agency. The seven national forests encompass most of the higher-elevation federal lands around Yellowstone and Grand Teton national parks. Despite the name, not every acre of national forest land is covered with trees; much may include treeless alpine areas as well as lower-elevation grassland parks and meadows. For example, 52 percent of Shoshone National Forest is treeless, due to its extensive grasslands and alpine areas.

National forests are managed by a multiple-use policy under which commercial activities such as logging, mining, grazing, and oil and gas

drilling are permitted along with recreation and the preservation of wildlife habitat, water quality, and soils.

National Wildlife Refuges

National wildlife refuges are managed by the U.S. Fish and Wildlife
Service. These are the only federal lands set aside primarily for wildlife
conservation. The National Elk Refuge was set aside to provide winter
feeding grounds for elk; Red Rock Lakes Wildlife Refuge was originally set
up to protect the nesting and feeding grounds of the trumpeter swan.
Still, refuge managers permit other activities, such as grazing, oil and gas
development, trapping, mining, and recreation, often to the detriment of
the wildlife they are supposed to protect.

BLM Lands

The Bureau of Land Management is a fourth federal agency that manages
lands within the GYE. Though it manages more federal acres than any
other agency, most BLM holdings lie outside the GYE, so this agency
plays a small role here. As a rule, BLM acres tend to be lower-elevation
grasslands and usually do not contain extensive forest cover. One exception is the Centennial Mountains in Montana, which are largely under
BLM management. Like the forest service, the BLM has a multiple-use
mandate, allowing hard-rock mining, oil and gas development, grazing,
and logging as well as fostering habitat protection and recreation.

Wildlands and Wilderness

The GYE respresents some of the most spectacular wildlands in the
country. Much has been formally protected as part of the National
Wilderness System, authorized by the 1964 Wilderness Act, which seeks
to preserve federal lands that "generally appear to have been affected
primarily by the forces of nature with the imprint of man's work substantially unnoticeable."

Wilderness designation prohibits most road building, timbering, mining (except for valid existing claims), and motorized equipment. A
significant exception to the act allows commercial grazing, much to the
detriment of the environment.

Recreation allowed in wilderness includes hunting, fishing, hiking,
camping, and mountain climbing. Though not part of the original intent
of the Wilderness Act, formally designated wilderness areas have become

important as reservoirs for pure water, biological diversity, wildlife habitat, and scenic beauty, and as areas for scientific study.

Greater Yellowstone has some of the largest wilderness areas in the United States. Because some of these are next to other large roadless areas, their ecological and wildlands values are enhanced considerably. The largest is the 920,310-acre Absaroka-Beartooth Wilderness, just north of Yellowstone National Park in Montana. The eastern flank of Yellowstone is bordered by the 704,270-acre Washakie Wilderness. Other major wilderness areas include the Lee Metcalf in Montana and the Gros Ventre in Wyoming.

Despite these special features, the human hand has not always been gentle. A satellite view of the ecosystem clearly shows the straight-as-a-ruler western park boundary, formed by clear-cuts on forest service land that run right up against Yellowstone's border. Other effects are not so clear. Acid rain has been detected in the Wind Rivers, Tetons, and Beartooths, and more and more summer homes, tree farms, livestock pasture, and oil-drilling pads degrade the ecosystem.

The challenge is the preservation of the natural processes that fuel the system—while allowing people to enjoy the wondrous region we know as greater Yellowstone.

What Will This Book Cover?

This basic overview of the natural and human histories of Yellowstone National Park and the surrounding area includes chapters on regional history, geology, flora, and fauna. Though the focus will be on the park, it is not an island but a part of the greater ecosystem. Information usually will apply to the region as a whole. In fact, a great deal of the ecology described here holds true for the northern and middle Rockies in general.

This book is not a comprehensive field guide, however. It is meant to be used with more narrow texts such as plant keys, guides to birds, and so on. Given the number and diversity of plants and animals found in the GYE, it would be impossible to discuss or even list everything. I selected species that are likely to be seen by visitors as well as ones with more interesting ecological relationships.

History of the Yellowstone Area

The history of greater Yellowstone mirrors that of the American conservation movement. In fact, Yellowstone has very often led the way: This is where preservation of the nation's natural heritage began. The first national park and national forest were created here, the first attempts to rescue an endangered species, the American bison, were made here, and this is where the first effort to manage a tract as an ecosystem rather than a political subdivision is being played out. From its early days, Yellowstone has been controversial and precedent-setting.

Early Humans

The archaeological record for the Greater Yellowstone Ecosystem is relatively limited. More than 1,500 sites are known, but many are only camps, not long-term settlements. Few have been excavated, but from what we do know, humans have lived in the ecosystem for at least 10,000 years. During this time, the climate has changed dramatically—from the end of the Ice Age to alternating periods of wet and dry—and the aboriginal people had to change with it.

The earliest humans were the big-game hunters, Paleo Indians who stalked woolly mammoth and other large mammals at the close of the Ice Age. As the climate warmed, many of these large animals disappeared, either because they could not adjust to the change, or they were over-hunted, or both. Native people had to depend more on plant gathering than hunting, though game was still eagerly sought. By 7,500 years ago, most of the current animal species were established in the GYE.

One of the more interesting finds is Mummy Cave along the North Fork of the Shoshone, which has thirty-eight layers of human occupation from 9,000 to 300 years old. The site is named for the 1,300-year-old human body preserved intact by the cave's dry climate.

At Rigler Bluff along the Yellowstone River near Corwin Springs, an ancient hearth contains burnt wood dated from 2950 BC. This site once perched on the shores of a lake probably created when a landslide dammed the river. Another fascinating find was remnants of western yew, a moisture-loving bush now found only in the Pacific Northwest and occasionally in western Montana, indicating a climate once significantly wetter than today's.

The bow and arrow arrived relatively late for Indians of the region, only during the last 1,000 to 2,000 years. Though it improved hunting efficiency, without the horse (which did not enter the region until the 1700s) Indians still had to hunt on foot. This meant reliance on animals like bighorn sheep, which do not wander far. More nomadic bison were also hunted, but typically as part of organized drives, where animals were forced over cliffs to their deaths.

Historic Indian Groups

At the time of European settlement of North America, many of the tribes that today live near greater Yellowstone, including the Sioux, Crow, and Cheyenne, were farmers in the Midwest and eastern Dakotas. The Crows did not settle in Montana until 1780, while the Cheyenne did not arrive in Wyoming until 1810.

The horse dramatically changed these people's lives, transforming them into mobile bison hunters. They could move rapidly from place to place, accumulate wealth and live in larger groups than could otherwise be sustained by local resources. They also had more time to raid their neighbors.

Around 1720, the Shoshone were the first Yellowstone tribe to acquire the horse. They had inhabited southern Wyoming and Idaho, but with horses they pushed northward, expanding their territory into Canada. In time, their foes the Blackfeet and others also obtained horses and began to push back. By the time Lewis and Clark passed through in 1806, the Blackfeet were the undisputed rulers of the upper Missouri region, and the Shoshones were back in the south.

For a time, the Blackfeet controlled all the land east of the Continental Divide, from Alberta to Yellowstone, including much of central Montana. Speaking an Algonquian dialect, the Blackfeet most likely came to the Great Plains from the lake region of Ontario or Manitoba.

As one of the most warlike Plains tribes, the Blackfeet were one reason Montana was settled relatively late. Though they and most other Plains

Indians hunted on horseback, the Blackfoot war parties preferred to walk, believing it helped them ambush their foes, their favorite tactic.

Trappers always dreaded meeting Blackfeet. One of a number of battles was fought on Trail Creek near Victor, Idaho, in July 1837. Trappers commanded by Milton Sublette (whose brother, William, is the namesake of Sublette County, Wyoming) came upon about 200 Blackfeet. One of the trappers shot a Blackfoot who came forward with a peace pipe. After intense fighting, the Blackfeet retreated, leaving nine dead, while the trappers lost four men plus six of their Nez Perce allies.

Osborn Russell, a trapper who traveled throughout the ecosystem, was attacked by Blackfeet near Yellowstone Lake. He and a companion were wounded in their legs, but managed to limp across the Tetons to Fort Hall by present-day Pocatello, Idaho. They made the trip in ten days, an astounding feat.

The Blackfeet never really lost a major battle. Rather, "exotic" diseases, sometimes even preceding the whites, destroyed the tribe and many others. Smallpox ravaged the Blackfeet in 1781, 1837, and 1869. The 1837 epidemic killed two-thirds of the tribe, more than 6,000 people. In comparison, the greatest number of Indians killed in any clash with whites was 500.

From the time Lewis and Clark entered greater Yellowstone to the last Indian occupations in the 1870s, the major tribes here were the Shoshone-Bannock (also known as Snake Indians, hence the Snake River), the Crow (or Absarkee, hence the Absaroka Mountains), and the Blackfeet. Nez Perce, Flathead, Gros Ventre, and Arapaho Indians would pass through on hunting expeditions.

The Crow and Shoshone-Bannock are most strongly associated with greater Yellowstone. The Crow occupied the Yellowstone River Valley from Livingston to the Tongue River east of Billings, Montana, while the Shoshone-Bannock ranged primarily south and east of the region, controlling areas in southwest Montana and adjacent parts of Idaho. In the 1840s, a subtribe of the Shoshone began ranging farther east into Wyoming's Bighorn and Wind River basin and became known as the Wind River band.

The Shoshone arrived in the region around 1300 AD. They came from the south, speaking an Uto-Aztecan language related to that of the Aztecs in Mexico. The Bannock are another Uto-Aztecan-speaking group related to the Northern Paiutes who wandered into southern Idaho around 1600. Bannock and Shoshone intermarried. Both hunted bison in eastern Idaho and northeastern Utah, but overhunting (likely by the Indians with the aid of horse and rifle) depleted bison west of the Continental Divide by 1840. To obtain the shaggy beasts, the Shoshone-Bannock bands had to travel to the Plains.

The Crow, who spoke a Siouan language, came from North Dakota, where they farmed along the Missouri River. After obtaining the horse, they adopted a Plains lifestyle based upon bison. They moved into Montana perhaps only twenty to thirty years before Lewis and Clark began their expedition in 1803. The Crow were excellent horsemen and exceptional horse thieves. They were very proud of the reputation. Always known to be friendly to whites, they seldom killed settlers or trappers (though they loved to steal their horses) and often scouted for the military in campaigns against other tribes.

Although the Shoshone, Crow, Blackfeet, and others passed through the Yellowstone region and undoubtedly entered the high country to hunt, none remained in the mountains year-round. They lived on the plains or in lower valleys, where the climate was easier and game more plentiful. However, one Shoshone offshoot known as the Sheepeaters (they hunted bighorn) appears to have entered the park region about 1800 and adopted a non-horse lifestyle. The Sheepeaters were considered poor relatives by the other tribes, and even most whites remarked on how different they were from their neighbors. Nevertheless, trapper Osborn Russell, who encountered Sheepeaters along the Lamar River in Yellowstone, described them as wearing neat furs and apparently content and happy. Lacking horses, the Sheepeaters were forced to live in small family groups or risk overhunting the game in their area. Evidence suggests that only a few hundred Sheepeaters lived in the GYE. By the 1880s, most had joined the Wind River band of the Shoshone.

Many tribes that didn't dwell in Yellowstone used trails through it to reach the Plains. The Nez Perce, Flathead, Shoshone, and Bannock Indians took the Bannock Trail to bison grounds in order to avoid the Blackfeet and Crow, who lived mainly to the north. Though probably always used as a natural trail, it was increasingly traveled once bison had been wiped out in southeast Idaho and northern Utah. It began in Camas Meadows south of the Centennial Mountains, went up the Henry's Fork to Targhee Pass, crossed into Yellowstone park near West Yellowstone, ascended the Gallatin Range and passed into Indian Creek, followed the route of the present highway between Mammoth and Cooke City, and went up Colter Pass and down the Clarks Fork of the Yellowstone. Another route went up the Lamar and across the Absaroka Mountains into Sunlight Basin and then out to the Bighorn Basin.

The Bannock Trail gained national attention during the Nez Perce War in 1877. This tribe lived in eastern Oregon's Wallowa River Valley and each year traveled across the Lolo Trail in Idaho and out onto the plains of Montana to hunt bison. Although the Nez Perce had treaty rights to much of eastern Oregon and western Idaho, the discovery of gold along the Clearwater river brought an invasion of whites. A few braves killed several whites; with the Army in pursuit, the Nez Perce traveled the old trail across Idaho and into Montana. There were several skirmishes along the way, plus a major confrontation between General Howard and the Nez Perce on the Big Hole River in Montana.

Afterward, the Nez Perce hurried on to Yellowstone, crossing into the park on August 23, 1877. This was five years after its establishment and tourists already traveled its trails. The Indians captured several tourist parties, killed some other whites, and passed down the Clarks Fork of the Yellowstone in early September, outflanking troops under Colonel Sturgis who had been waiting for them to escape from the mountains. The Nez Perce then fled toward Canada and had nearly got away when they were attacked on September 30 near the Bear Paw Mountains, forty miles south of the border. After six days of intense fighting, the Nez Perce gave up, with Chief Joseph making his tragic and historic surrender: "I am tired; my heart is sick and sad. From where the sun now stands, I will fight no more forever."

Other Indians of greater Yellowstone were put on reservations as well. The Shoshone-Bannock were sent to Fort Hall Reservation in Idaho and the Wind River Reservation near Lander, Wyoming. The Crow reservation has been whittled down from its original 38 million acres to two million along the Bighorn River south of Billings, Montana.

The Name *Yellowstone*

While many people believe that Lewis and Clark explored an unknown wilderness during their trek from St. Louis, Missouri, to the Pacific Ocean and back, they had a lot of information amassed by trappers who had previously ventured into the upper Missouri country. As early as 1776, French trappers were living among the Mandan tribes on the Missouri River in North Dakota. These early Europeans on the Plains knew of the

The Yellowstone River meanders through the Hayden Valley in Wyoming, named for F. V. Hayden, leader of three government expeditions to Yellowstone in the 1870s. The publicity about his expeditions promoted Yellowstone's wonders and led to the creation of the park.

Riviere des Roche Jaune, or the Yellowstone River, named for the golden sandstone cliffs along its middle and lower course. Explorer David Thompson visited the Mandan villages in 1797 and heard about the river from French traders. He first used the name Yellowstone. Lewis and Clark made it official, bestowing the name on this waterway when they arrived at its confluence with the Missouri.

Had Lewis and Clark encountered the stream near its headwaters, they might have called it something else. The Crow Indians called it the Elk River for the many elk that passed along its upper reaches during the spring and fall. When the park was created in 1872, it was not called "Yellowstone"; it was referred to merely as a "public park." Common use of "Yellowstone" eventually assured the name around the world.

The Coming of the Whites

Lewis and Clark were the first whites known to enter greater Yellowstone. On its return, the party split up, some retracing the path down the

Missouri, while William Clark sought out the headwaters of the Yellowstone. The groups later met at their confluence.

Clark's party noted that there were so many beaver dams in the Gallatin Valley that travel was nearly impossible. Elk, antelope, wolves, and deer were abundant, though the Indian guides said recent heavy hunting by the Shoshone had driven the bison from the region. The expeditioners continued east across Bozeman Pass and down Trail Creek. Just east of Livingston, they encountered several elk herds of 200 to 300 each. They also saw much evidence of bison, including well-worn trails, but they didn't kill their first until they reached the confluence of the Stillwater River and the Yellowstone (near present-day Columbus, Montana). Just below this point they built canoes and floated toward the Missouri and out of greater Yellowstone.

John Colter, a member of the expedition, is credited with being the first white to cross present-day Yellowstone park. The evidence is shaky, but if he did not go through the park proper, he came very close. On the homeward leg of the expedition, Colter met two other Americans on the Missouri who persuaded him to return upstream to trap. Though the exact route is disputed, it is believed that in the winter of 1807, Colter, traveling 500 miles through the GYE, went from the Bighorn River to the Shoshone near present-day Cody, crossed to the Wind River, followed it to its headwaters, and descended into Jackson Hole.

From there, Colter crossed the Tetons, circled north toward the Yellowstone Plateau, headed up the Lamar River and through his namesake, Colter Pass, proceeded down the Clarks Fork of the Yellowstone and eventually reached the Bighorn once again. He told stories of the hot springs he encountered during his epic winter journey, leading to the designation "Colter's Hell" in reference to the Yellowstone area.

From these beginnings, the Rocky Mountain fur trade developed into a major force in the exploration of the West. By the 1820s, the trade was at its height. Changing fashions and overtrapping ended the mountain man's era by the 1840s.

Before 1820, the Hudson's Bay Company, long established in Canada, was sending trapping brigades through the American West, including one led by Donald McKenzie from 1818–20 into the headwaters of the Snake River. Brigade member John Grey discovered a lake, now named after him and the site of a national wildlife refuge, on the flank of the Caribou Mountains.

In 1822, William Ashley of St. Louis placed an ad in the Missouri Gazette: "Enterprising Young Men: The Subscriber wishes to engage one hundred men to ascend the river Missouri to its source, there to be employed for one, two, or three years. . . ." Among those answering the ad were Jim Bridger, Jedediah Smith, David Jackson, William Sublette, and Thomas Fitzpatick. Today the names of these men are spread across maps of the ecosystem: the Bridger Mountains, Bridger Creek, Bridger Wilderness, and the Bridger-Teton National Forest; Jackson Hole and Jackson, Wyoming; Sublette County, Wyoming; Fitzpatick Wilderness; Jedediah Smith Wilderness and Smith's Fork. The proliferation is not surprising, for nearly every major river system and valley in greater Yellowstone was explored and mapped by these mountain men.

The first hard evidence of any white entering what is now Yellowstone park is a letter written in 1827 by trapper Daniel Potts, who accurately described traveling over the Tetons into Jackson Hole, up the Snake, and along the shore of Yellowstone Lake. He mentions hot and boiling springs near today's West Thumb Geyser Basin.

Historians believe a party of mountain men was attacked in 1829 by Blackfeet Indians on the Yellowstone River between Livingston and Gardiner. Joe Meek escaped alone, traveling south across the Yellowstone Plateau, where he claimed to have seen hot springs and geysers.

One man, Johnson Gardner, trapped the upper Yellowstone in 1831 and gave his name to beautiful Gardner Hole and the Gardner River. These were the first (white man) names for the future park, after that of "Yellowstone" itself.

In the early years, the mostly illiterate mountain men left few accounts of their travels in the region. The scarcity of place names ensured the vague nature of what records we do have. But the blank spots were being filled in by the 1820s, when large groups of white trappers began to fan out into the mountains. Though the image of the solitary trapper may be romantic, during the height of the trade, most traveled in bands that included Indian wives, children, friends, and relatives. This provided significant protection against Indian attacks.

The "rendezvous" was a much celebrated feature of trapping. William Ashley initiated it so that his trappers could gather to unload furs and pick up supplies instead of having to make the trek every year or so to St. Louis. Ashley brought trade goods to a predetermined site each summer where the mountain men would gather along with various Indians for a few weeks of trading, drinking, storytelling, and horse races. Reoutfitted with ammunition, traps, and a few other necessities, the trappers would head back into the mountains for another year.

The first rendezvous was at the headwaters of the Green in 1825. Other sites included the Pogo Agie River, Pierre's Hole by Driggs, Idaho, and the Henry's Fork near the Uinta Mountains. The last rendezvous was in 1840, a few years before the first settlers came rolling west over the Oregon Trail. Many trappers turned to guiding wagon trains and the increasing military explorations of the West.

Osborn Russell was one of the few mountain men able to read and write, and his accurate journals provide perhaps the best early accounts. From a farm in Maine, Russell came to the mountains in 1834 and went on his first trapping expedition in 1835. He subsequently made five trips across what would later be Yellowstone park, plus excursions to the Three Forks area in Montana and as far south as Utah's Wasatch Range. Russell liked no place better than the Lamar Valley in Yellowstone, which he called Secluded Valley. "For my own part I almost wished I could spend the remainder of my days in a place like this where happiness and contentment seemed to reign in wild romantic splendor," he wrote.

Among his discoveries, Russell and his party found Two Ocean Pass, where the waters of the Pacific and Atlantic divide. They later discovered Shoshone Lake and its geyser basin. Though many outlandish tales were told about the sights in the region, the allure of boiling springs, petrified trees, and rivers that flow two ways would draw new explorers to "Colter's Hell."

One major discovery was not considered a fable. This was South Pass, at the southern end of the Wind River Range. First crossed by Robert Stuart and six companions during an epic journey from Astoria, Oregon, in 1812, it was rediscovered by Jedediah Smith in 1823. The pass offered a gentle, easy crossing of the Continental Divide and provided an overland gateway to the Pacific. By the 1840s, the Oregon Trail and South Pass saw thousands of homesteaders walking, riding, and driving wagons westward.

The trail splits just west of South Pass, with one segment turning south toward Fort Bridger near the Utah-Wyoming line and the other, known as the Lander Cutoff, heading north up La Barge Creek, down the Grey's and Snake rivers to Fort Hall and on to Oregon. The Lander Cutoff was not completed until 1859, but in that first year 13,000 people traveled over it. Interestingly, though thousands traveled the Oregon Trail between 1840 and the late 1860s, few whites ventured into greater Yellowstone except for the area along the Lander Cutoff.

The Miners

After gold was discovered in California in 1848, prospectors spread throughout the West looking for the next big strike. It was not until the 1850s and '60s that miners wandered into Montana, Wyoming, and Idaho, but they quickly hit pay dirt.

As early as 1858, gold was found at South Pass, Wyoming. Several towns, including Atlantic City, South Pass City, and Miner's Delight, sprang up to work the deposits. The first strikes in Montana were in 1863, one at Alder Gulch near Virginia City and another at Last Chance Gulch (Helena). From these and other bases, miners struck out for the unknown, looking for the new El Dorado.

Since the trappers had left so few records and the stories that survived were not very credible, Yellowstone was still a great unknown to the miners. The first of their expeditions set out in 1863. Walter De Lacy, for whom De Lacy Creek in Yellowstone park is named, traveled with 41 others up the Snake River from Jackson Hole, looking for gold rumored to be near its headwaters. Not finding any, several men split from the party near Jackson Lake, returning the way they had come. De Lacy and the others went north, passing Shoshone Lake and working their way to the Firehole River, the Madison River, and Virginia City.

At the same time that De Lacy's party was exploring southern Yellowstone, another group of prospectors traveled up the Yellowstone and Lamar rivers to around present-day Cooke City, where they were attacked by Indians. Retracing their steps to Virginia City, they struck gold on a Yellowstone tributary near today's Gardiner, Montana, which they named Bear Gulch.

The following year, gold was discovered at Emigrant Gulch on the Yellowstone and near Baboon Mountain on the Boulder. Other parties of miners traveled in and around the Yellowstone region looking for new strikes, creating new trails, one of which was the Bozeman. It branched off the Oregon Trail in eastern Wyoming, passed around the Bighorn Mountains, and followed the Yellowstone to Bozeman Pass and into the Gallatin Valley, where the new town of Bozeman sat. Indian attacks were frequent on this trail, and founder and promoter John Bozeman was killed by Blackfeet in 1867, near Mission Creek east of Livingston.

But the Indian threat was not enough to deter gold seekers. Prospectors continued to fan out from towns like Bozeman, searching every stream. They rediscovered many things that trappers had seen, from the Grand Canyon of the Yellowstone to Yellowstone Lake and the geyser basins. Unlike the mountain men, miners were inclined to record their wanderings, helping to publicize and renew interest in the region.

In 1867, gold was discovered on Crevice Creek just east of Gardiner, along the north border of what is Yellowstone park. Jack Crandall was among those who came to find his fortune, but mostly he left his mark by giving his name to a creek off Clarks Fork of the Yellowstone, where he was killed by Indians in 1868.

A prospecting party that included Bart Henderson, for whom Henderson Mountain by Cooke City, Montana, is named, traveled up the Snake River into Jackson Hole and continued into what is now the park. They circled Yellowstone Lake and proceeded past the Grand Canyon of the Yellowstone and Tower Falls, down the Yellowstone, and back to Bozeman. In the northern portion of the park, the party named streams such as Hellroaring, Buffalo, and Slough. In the headwaters of Soda Butte Creek, they noted mineralization, which brought Henderson back in 1870. Here were founded the New World Mining District and Cooke City.

Meanwhile, miners were finding "color" in other parts of greater Yellowstone. There was a minor gold rush in 1870 in the Caribou Mountains of Idaho, where Caribou City temporarily sprang up.

The First Expeditions

Enough of the miners' reports filtered back to the press and government officials to stir considerable interest in the "wonderland" purported to lie at the headwaters of the Yellowstone. Several major efforts were launched. The first was the Folsom-Cook-Peterson expedition, composed of three adventurers from Helena, Montana, who spent a month exploring Yellowstone in the autumn of 1869.

The party traveled along the Yellowstone River to what is now the north entrance of the park, then took the Bannock Trail over the Blacktail Plateau to Tower Falls. They encountered a few Sheepeaters on this segment. Crossing the Yellowstone near Tower Junction, they went up the Lamar Valley, where they reported hearing wolves howling and elk bugling in every direction. They worked their way to the Grand Canyon of the Yellowstone and called its spectacular falls beautiful, picturesque,

The Yellowstone River has cut a canyon more than 1,000 feet into the Yellowstone Plateau. Its V shape indicates that it was carved by water.

magnificent, grand, and sublime. Beholding Yellowstone Lake, they predicted its beauty would someday draw throngs of tourists. Eventually, they made it to Shoshone Lake and the Upper Geyser Basin; then, following the Madison River out of the future park, they returned to Helena.

Folsom and Cook combined their journals and submitted the manuscript to Scribner's Magazine and the New York Tribune. No one believed their story and the article was rejected.

Cook said that on one of their last nights in "wonderland," he and Folsom discussed the idea of preserving Yellowstone for the public. Once the idea was circulated, it struck a chord with many who had visited the area. Fittingly, both men are honored by peaks named after them in Yellowstone's Washburn Range.

News of the Folsom-Cook-Peterson expedition excited others, including Henry Washburn, surveyor general of the Montana Territory, who organized an expedition in 1870. The Washburn-Langford-Doane party followed the same general route, though this group turned south near Tower Falls and passed over what is now Dunraven Pass. Mounts Washburn, Langford, and Doane in Yellowstone park are named for them.

From Dunraven on the flanks of Mount Washburn, the three had a good view of the Yellowstone Basin and the lake beyond. They descended the south slope of the Washburn Range and passed the Grand Canyon of the Yellowstone. Traveling around Yellowstone Lake, they visited the Thorofare country and remarked how it was filled with signs of elk, bear, sheep, and beaver.

In several places, they were misled by the numerous elk trails and became quite disoriented. One man, Truman Everts, became separated from the group and could not be found. The autumn snows forced the expedition out of the mountains; everyone figured Everts was dead. Actually, he had been knocked from his horse and lost his spectacles. Nearly blind, Everts wandered through the Yellowstone wilderness for thirty-seven days, surviving on thistle roots. He was discovered, barely alive, by Jack Baronett and George Pritchett. Mount Everts by Mammoth is named for the lost man, and Baronett Peak near Cooke City carries the name of one of his rescuers.

Many expedition members went on to lecture and write about the wonders they had seen. Nathaniel Langford spent the winter on the East Coast lecture circuit, and at a talk in Washington, his audience included Dr. Ferdinand Hayden. Intrigued by the descriptions, Hayden, director of the United States Geological and Geographical Survey, persuaded Congress to finance the first of what would be four expeditions. The following summer, Hayden, for whom Hayden Valley in Yellowstone was later named, assembled a large group of scientists, including botanists, geologists, and zoologists; an artist named Thomas Moran; and a photographer, William Jackson. Moran and Jackson would have mountains named after them: Mount Moran in the Tetons and Mount Jackson near the Madison River.

Hayden's expedition produced several maps and numerous notes, but perhaps most important were dozens of photographs and sketches that proved to everyone that the wonders of Yellowstone were real. He joined a growing chorus of support in Washington for protection of the Yellowstone region, and in March 1872, President Grant signed into law a bill creating a "public park and pleasuring ground for the benefit and enjoyment of the people."

The Park Idea

Since the park was created, many people have tried to claim credit for the idea of a national park—Yellowstone was the first. Actually, this was just an idea whose time had come. It created its own momentum, once it was firmly on the minds of thoughtful people.

First mention of the park idea is found in the writings of George Catlin, who traveled up the Missouri River in 1832 to draw and paint Indians. He suggested that a great "nation's park" be set aside to preserve the beauty and wildness of the West, including its native people.

In 1864, Congress granted California title to lands surrounding the Yosemite Valley and several groves of sequoias. It stipulated that the lands be preserved for the enjoyment of present and future generations, instituting the idea behind our present management of public lands, particularly parks. Later, the state gave this land back to the federal government, which created Yosemite National Park.

The idea that land should be preserved simply for its scenic or recreational values was revolutionary. It collided with the "use-it-up" attitude of those times. If you couldn't shoot it, graze it, cut it down or dig it up, the land and its wildlife had no value. Sadly, such arguments are still common.

More farsighted visions prevailed. Fredrick Law Olmstead, designer of New York's Central Park, pointed out that in Switzerland, scenery had (even in 1865) contributed to the "larger part of the state revenue and all this without the exportation or extraction from the country of anything of the slightest value to the people." He further argued that a nation had a moral obligation to protect and preserve "natural scenes of an impressive character" for its people. Olmstead and others laid the philosophical foundation for the establishment of a national park.

It would be nice if moral concerns had predominated in the efforts to preserve Yellowstone, but there is much to suggest that avarice was the main motivator. One of the first promoters of the park idea was the Northern Pacific Railroad, whose director, Jay Cooke (for whom Cooke City is named), hoped park designation would increase passenger traffic along his line. In a letter to Ferdinand Hayden in October 1871, a representative of Cooke and the Northern Pacific, A. R. Nettleton, wrote, "Let Congress pass a bill reserving the Great Geyser Basin as a public park forever—just as it has reserved that inferior wonder the Yosemite Valley and the big trees."

Locally, there was some support for establishment of a park, but then as now, there were many who vigorously opposed it. The Helena Gazette said, "In our opinion, the effect of this measure will be to keep the country a wilderness, and shut out for many years the travel that would seek that curious region if good roads were opened through it and hotels built therein. We regard the passage of the act as a great blow struck at the prosperity of the towns of Bozeman and Virginia City which might naturally look to considerable travel to this section, if it were thrown open to the curious but comfort-loving public."

A Need for Rangers

The new park soon began to attract adventurous tourists, who traveled in by pack train. Though it had created Yellowstone, Congress did not provide for its management or protection. It appointed a superintendent but gave him no staff. There were no penalties for violating park regulations. Visitors regularly defaced park features, chipping away at geyser formations, writing their names into the soft rock terraces, and carting away petrified wood. Hunting was still permitted, and market hunters and tourists alike took a toll.

In 1875, a Captain Ludlow led a short expedition to Yellowstone. In his official report, he noted that vandalism and the unabated slaughter of wildlife were rampant. In the Upper Geyser Basin, Ludlow observed more than thirty people prowling about "with shovel and ax, chopping and hacking and prying up great pieces of the most ornamental work they could find; women and men alike joining in the barbarous pastime." Ludlow urged that troops be stationed in the park to enforce the regulations.

Philetus Norris (appointed superintendent in 1877, and for whom Norris Geyser Basin is named) visited Yellowstone in the same year as Ludlow and commented that nearly 2,000 elk had been killed by the Bottler brothers in one winter near Mammoth Hot Springs. These men, who had a ranch in Paradise Valley, sold just the hides and tongues, leaving the rest to rot. An 1875 visitor, William Strong, reported that nearly 4,000 elk had been killed for their hides (worth $6 to $8 apiece) by market hunters the previous winter.

In 1882, a Civil War hero and the leader of all Western military forces, Gen. Philip H. Sheridan, traveled through Yellowstone. Like others, he was appalled at the slaughter of wildlife and the lack of any kind of police force in the park. Sheridan soon realized that Yellowstone's boundaries were far too limited to provide full protection for its wildlife, and he advocated expanding it to the east and south to take in migration corridors and wintering areas. In essence, Sheridan originated the concept of the Greater Yellowstone Ecosystem.

The Railroad Battles

The last spike was driven on the Northern Pacific in 1883. Linking the East Coast with the Pacific Northwest and paralleling the Yellowstone River through much of Montana, the railroad became an important way for tourists to get to the park. Livingston, sixty miles north, became an important railroad town and a transfer point for passengers headed to the park. A spur line was soon built to accommodate these people, running as far as Cinnabar, near Gardiner.

In the same year, a bill was introduced in Congress to extend the park as Sheridan had proposed. The railroad tycoons blocked it, since they wanted the park reduced. They made approval of the expansion contingent on getting what they wanted on the north end, which was a railroad line up through the Lamar Valley to Cooke City. They claimed they merely wanted better access to the Cooke City mines, but others suspected that the Northern Pacific really wanted to control public access to the park and monopolize the concessions.

The battle lasted for almost a decade and included such proposals as putting turbines on the falls of the Yellowstone to generate electricity for the railroad. The Montana and Wyoming congressional delegations strongly backed the railroads, showing early on the prodevelopment bias of politicians from these states.

Fortunately, the park had staunch defenders such as Senator Vest of Minnesota and the Boone and Crockett Club, a sportsmen's group whose leaders included George Bird Grinnell and Theodore Roosevelt. These park enthusiasts saw the great threats posed by the railroad's plans and also worried that other branch line proposals would soon follow. They feared public access would be strictly controlled by the railroad and felt that wildlife, particularly bison, would be hurt by the deletion of the northern range of the park.

The arguments used on both sides in the 1890s are strikingly similar to those of today. Vest urged that Congress "preserve at least one spot of beauty from the rack and roar of commerce and the greed and avarice of selfish men." Congressman Cox of New York suggested that the bill authorizing a railroad across the park was nothing more than "a measure which is inspired by corporate greed and natural selfishness against national pride and natural beauty." On the other side, Montana's delegate to Congress (it was not yet a state) characterized the Lamar Valley and Soda Butte Creek area as "wholly unattractive country." Congressman

Payson of Illinois could not "understand the sentiment which favors the retention of a few buffaloes to the development of mining interests amounting to millions of dollars." In 1892, a bill was introduced by Congressman Thomas Stockdale of Mississippi to abolish Yellowstone park!

While the debate raged, tourists' ability to travel within the park was eased through the construction of a few stagecoach and wagon roads. Rough accommodations were made available. By 1883, the typical visitor followed a trail and road system that closely followed the "loop" layout of today's park highways. The tourist would travel from Gardiner to Mammoth, on to Norris and Old Faithful, across Mary Mountain, down to Mud Volcano, on to Yellowstone Lake, and then back to the Grand Canyon of the Yellowstone, with the final loop going by Tower Falls and across the Blacktail Plateau and returning to Gardiner. Conservationist John Muir toured Yellowstone in 1885 and bemoaned the fact that people "raced" through the park in an average of five days. Today, a park visitor often takes the same tour in five hours.

Spur lines built to Cody in 1901 and West Yellowstone in 1908 completed railroad access to the park, ensuring those communities a portion of the tourist dollars.

The Army Takes Over

By 1886, despite the battle over railroads and park expansion, the calls for effective law enforcement were finally answered. The Army built Fort Yellowstone at Mammoth Hot Springs, where the old parade ground, barracks, and other historical buildings now serve as park headquarters. The Army also prohibited the removal of any minerals, trees, or other park features. Throwing objects into hot springs and geysers was banned, as were hunting, trapping, and commercial fishing. While these rules may seem completely reasonable now, they were extremely unpopular then. Local people in particular had thought of Yellowstone as their pantry; trapping and hunting had been a major income source for some.

To discourage poaching, the Army built cabins throughout the park, manning them all summer and using them for patrol stops in the winter. It made the first methodical records of the park's features, counting wildlife and monitoring geysers, for example. Though the Army controlled the worst abuses by tourists, it had less success with poachers, many of whom knew the backcountry better than the soldiers.

Early Wildlife Management

The plight of bison finally brought the park's wildlife problems to national attention. The head of a bison could bring a poacher up to $300. Usually, poachers would make short forays into the park or make longer trips in winter when the backcountry was seldom patrolled. By 1894, there were estimated to be fewer than 100 bison left in Yellowstone, the last wild herd in the United States. In response, Congress granted greater protection to wildlife and increased poaching penalties. These were some of the first federal efforts in wildlife conservation. In addition, a campaign was launched to try to capture some of the remaining animals and to breed them in semicaptivity.

It was not until 1902, when the remaining bison in the park were estimated at no more than twenty-five, that some animals were rounded up and "ranched," first at Mammoth and later in the Lamar Valley. In 1915, the bison were once again allowed to roam freely in summer, although winter feeding was practiced until the 1930s. The old bison ranch in the Lamar is now a ranger station and educational center.

While park officials were trying to protect "good" species like elk and bison, they were campaigning against predators—the "bad" animals. Even before the park's establishment, wolfers regularly worked the area for hides. The usual technique was to put out a carcass laced with strychnine. Mountain lions and coyotes were trapped or chased with dogs and shot. Beginning in 1895, the Army began poisoning coyotes as part of the first government predator control program. This was soon expanded to include other predators, despite the January 15, 1883, order by the secretary of the interior that prohibited hunting of park wildlife. Since the order had not specifically mentioned predators, the convenient interpretation was that these species did not deserve protection. The killing of predators continued until the 1930s, by which time the wolf was locally extinct and several other species were nearly exterminated in the region.

The First National Forests

When Yellowstone's boundaries were established in 1872, the surrounding lands were virtually uninhabited. The first ranch in the entire Yellowstone Valley between Livingston and Gardiner was not homesteaded until 1864. Settlement south of Yellowstone in the Jackson Hole area came even later. No one had anticipated conflicts between the needs of wildlife and those of livestock. But as the surrounding lands were claimed and became ranches or mines, it grew obvious that the political boundaries were inadequate. By the early 1900s, Sheridan's calls for an expanded park seemed prophetic.

To ease the situation, Congress passed the Forest Reserve Act in 1891 and President Harrison promptly created the precursor of the national forest system, the "Yellowstone National Park Timberland Reserve." It included lands east and south of the park that are now part of the Teton, North Absaroka, and Waskakie wilderness areas, by permanently withdrawing these lands from entry and settlement. President Cleveland expanded upon this in 1897 when he created Teton Forest Reserve, which encompassed much of what is now Jackson Hole and Grand Teton National Park.

These reserves were enlarged further in 1901 after President Theodore Roosevelt took office. This conservation-minded leader took most of the public domain lands that now lie within the Bridger-Teton National Forest and the northern half of the Shoshone National Forest and placed them in the national forest system. In 1905, Roosevelt created the U.S. Forest Service and made Gifford Pinchot its first director. These two men greatly expanded the scope of the national forests and placed many more acres under the agency's management.

National forests, like most early national parks, were largely created by withdrawing land from the federally owned "public domain." With no purpose initially but to be given away to private ownership and no caretakers but the loggers, miners, and market hunters who freely took what they could, the public domain gradually was more carefully managed. For example, when a national forest was created, the "traditional" uses were permitted as before (untrue for national parks), but the government oversaw and regulated these activities.

Western states strenuously opposed the conversion of public domain lands into national parks and forests, though all Americans owned and had an interest in them. Many Westerners saw their fortunes tied to the free and unrestricted development of resources and the expansion of private property. The retention of public lands was not in their dreams of a prosperous future. A Montana editor probably declared the prevailing attitude when he remarked, "The park is already too huge a joke for them [meaning "ignorant" Easterners] to comprehend."

Even though there was no effective agency to monitor the new national forests, their establishment at least assured permanent public ownership of valuable wildlife habitat. This, coupled with a vigorously enforced ban on hunting in the park and strict hunting regulations outside it, allowed elk to increase gradually. By the winter of 1910–11, they were so numerous that many migrated down the Yellowstone Valley and out of the park, where they raided haystacks and tore up fences. The Montana legislature responded by setting aside a game preserve adjacent to the park; similar legislation was enacted in Wyoming. Wyoming also began feeding elk in winter with hay bought from ranchers.

By 1912, the number of elk in Yellowstone and adjacent national forests was estimated at 50,000. There were calls for herd reductions, so the government trapped the animals and freely distributed them throughout the West, where overhunting had led to their extermination.

The Car Arrives

Other changes were coming to the park. The first tourists were well-to-do, given the great expense of traveling to the park and its accommodations. "Sagebrushers," those who adventurously came in wagons or pack trains, camping along the way, were abused by park concessionaires, who often refused to sell them supplies.

The automobile democratized Yellowstone. It became accessible to everybody, to the point where the park may be in danger of being overrun with cars. But when the first cars rumbled into Yellowstone in 1897, the concessionaires did everything they could to keep them out. Fear that the cars would upset horses drawing tourist-laden carriages led to a ban on automobiles in 1902. Probably the greatest fear of the concessionaires was that they would lose the tourism monopoly. Nearly every visitor except a local person had to rent transportation from them. By 1912, the car was welcome at other national parks, so the superintendent asked Congress for funds to upgrade the roads.

Cars were officially permitted in 1915, but drivers had to pay $5 or $10, depending upon the number of seats in the vehicle. Interestingly, visitors pay no more in 1991 than they did in 1915. With the national parks in reach of the ordinary person, support for them swelled around the country.

Though the Army was still managing the park, increasing visitation meant hiring civilian workers. In 1915, the first rangers were hired to man park entrance stations, beginning the tradition of the seasonal ranger. That autumn, two other temporary rangers were hired specifically to kill coyotes, mountain lions, and wolves. In 1916, the National Park Service was created to administer the growing list of sites: Yellowstone, Yosemite, Grand Canyon, Mount McKinley, and others. The military was no longer needed, and in 1918 the Army left Yellowstone after thirty-two years.

The National Elk Refuge
The southern Yellowstone-Jackson Hole elk herd was estimated at 60,000 in the late 19th century. It really was a herd "complex." Different groups would summer in various places in the higher country and migrate to their traditional wintering areas in the fall. Some elk followed the Snake River out to wintering grounds in Star Valley, while others crossed the Gros Ventre Mountains and wintered on the upper Green near Cora, Wyoming. Some 20,000 stayed in Jackson Hole itself during the winter.

Initially, market hunters and then homesteaders took a serious toll on the elk. Beginning in the 1880s, important winter range and migration routes were turned into ranches and hay fields in the upper Green and Jackson Hole. This and heavy snows led to major kills in 1882, 1888, and 1889. Some people suggested that an elk refuge be established for wintering grounds.

In 1907, the area that is now essentially the Teton Wilderness Area was set aside as the Teton Game Preserve, south of Yellowstone park. Hunting was outlawed, and for 28 years the preserve was a safe elk route between Yellowstone and Jackson Hole.

Another severe winter in 1909 killed off many elk and prompted the Wyoming legislature to authorize $5,000 for a feeding program. It also asked Congress to officially protect the elk range. (Wyoming's request that Idaho preserve its elk wintering range was ignored, since sheep raisers wanted to retain their grazing privileges on Idaho public lands.) Congress responded with $20,000, and in 1912 it authorized $45,000 to buy land for a refuge.

In August 1909, the National Elk Refuge was established. In 1925 and 1927, Rep. Winters of Wyoming introduced two bills requesting funds for its expansion. Though these died, the effort was successful in 1933 with money to bring the refuge up to its present size of 23,754 acres. Today, 5,000 to 10,000 elk winter on the refuge. Though they are fed by refuge personnel in severe winters, in many years this is unnecessary.

Greater Yellowstone Takes Shape
Shortly after the National Park Service was created, an old idea resurfaced. In 1917, Interior Secretary Franklin Lane proposed expanding the

park by 1,200 square miles to encompass what became known as greater Yellowstone. The area would have included most of what is today the Teton wilderness, plus most of the Teton Range, now part of Grand Teton National Park.

There seemed to be little opposition to the idea. A bill was even introduced in Congress in 1918 by the Wyoming delegation. Since grazing would not be permitted in the park, however, Jackson Hole cattlemen used their considerable power to attack it via the Wyoming legislature, which was conveniently dominated by ranchers. A resolution was passed to oppose the expansion, forcing Wyoming Rep. Mondell to abandon the idea.

Proponents of the expansion, including Wyoming Sen. John Kendrick and Yellowstone Superintendent Horace Albright, arranged a meeting in Jackson in hopes of reasoning with the local people. The speakers were swiftly "hooted off the platform by the enraged citizens." Guides in Cody also registered their opposition, since the area available for hunting would be restricted.

Expansion proponents reduced the proposal to the Teton Mountains only, thus leaving most of the important rangeland under national forest control, where it would remain open to grazing and hunting. The compromise was signed into law by President Coolidge in 1929, and Grand Teton National Park was born.

Though spectacular, the new park did not include most of the important wildlife habitat in the Jackson area. In addition to forest service lands, private holdings in the valley were vital to wildlife. A park advocate and philanthropist, John D. Rockefeller, Jr., began quietly buying up private ranches, intending to add them to Grand Teton. Meanwhile, a new plan to increase the park by more than 216,000 acres surfaced in 1938. Local opposition was intense, and the reasoning was the same as before—that this would shut down the local economy, put everyone out of work, and leave Jackson a ghost town. Finally, President Franklin D. Roosevelt created the 221,000-acre Jackson Hole National Monument by executive order, sidestepping community resistance. The lands owned by Rockefeller were given to the United States in 1949, and in 1950 all these lands were added to Grand Teton National Park.

Water Wars

The 1893 proposal to dam the Yellowstone in order to power an electric railroad was only the first of many attempts to develop the greater Yellowstone's waterways. Shoshone Dam was completed by the Bureau of Reclamation in 1911 on the Shoshone River near Cody. It provided irrigation water to nearby ranchers and farmers. In 1913, construction was begun on Jackson Dam on Jackson Lake, within what is now Grand Teton National Park, to provide water to marginal farmlands in Idaho. Owen Wister, author of *The Virginian*, visited the Yellowstone region, including the Jackson area, many times, beginning in 1887. He saw Jackson Lake before the dam, when it was still wild, and afterward, when the giant plug at its outlet prompted him to fume, "[Irrigators are] commercial vandals who desecrated the outlet of Jackson's Lake with an ugly dam to irrigate some desert land away off in Idaho." Wister said the "disgusting dam" destroyed the "august serenity of the lake's outlet forever."

Congress received new dam proposals in 1920, including one several times from Sen. Thomas Walsh of Montana, who suggested the Yellowstone be blocked three miles from the outlet of Yellowstone Lake. Another bill that haunted Capitol Hill originated with Idaho's congressman, Addison Smith, who proposed the construction of reservoirs on the Falls and Bechler rivers in the southeast corner of Yellowstone park. But the nation wouldn't hear of it. The editor of *Outlook Magazine* summed up the opposition when he wrote, "Idaho is trying to loot Yellowstone. . . . No state has a right to do it [dam rivers in the park], no special interest has any business there." Smith rebutted that development of these sites was "absolutely essential" to the economy of Idaho and the area was relatively useless for park purposes.

About this same time, another proposal arose in Montana to dam the Yellowstone outside of the park, at Allenspur Canyon three miles south of Livingston. The proposed dam would have flooded most of Paradise Valley. The proposal was reincarnated in the 1970s but again met a well-deserved death.

Not all dams were stopped. Palisades Dam now sits on the South Fork of the Snake near the Wyoming-Idaho line, Island Park Dam plugs the Henry's Fork in Idaho, and the Ennis and Hebgen dams control the flow of the Madison River in Montana.

Wister's words are as true today as they were in 1887, when he wrote, "The would-be exploiter of the park never dies. It may be a railroad, a light and power company—anything. It is a ceaseless menace, invariably supported by plausible argument and political influence."

Wildlife Issues

Though Yellowstone was originally preserved because of its geological wonders, it was soon apparent that its wildlife was a major asset. Most proposals for expansion involved the protection of animals. Nevertheless, by the 1920s some believed the once-overhunted elk were becoming too numerous, particularly on the northern range (from the Lamar River to Gardiner). Critics said the elk were overgrazing their winter ranges, eroding soil, destroying shrubs and aspen, and were responsible for a decline in beavers as well as other herbivores including antelope, white-tailed deer, and bighorn sheep. Some park denouncers even claim elk and bison are not native to Yellowstone but were driven there after the park's establishment by excessive hunting on nearby plains. Because they were never found there, or were very few, so the logic goes, the present herds are "unnatural." Whether today's herds exceed what is "normal" or desirable may be debated, but elk and bison are as unquestionably native to the Greater Yellowstone Ecosystem as any species can be.

One of the earliest accounts of wildlife in the GYE came from trapper Osborn Russell, who recorded many encounters with elk, bison, antelope, and deer from 1834–43. There were few other good records until 1870, when Nathaniel Langford noted "an abundance of the tracks of elk and bear, occasionally the track of a mountain lion," around Yellowstone Lake. That same year, miner Bart Henderson reported "thousands of bear, elk, buffalo, and deer" near the northeast corner of the park near Cooke City, but he may have tended to exaggerate. Nonetheless, thousands of animals were killed just after the establishment of the park. In 1877, Superintendent P. W. Norris wrote that 2,000 hides of elk, plus "nearly as many each of the bighorn, deer, and antelope, and scores if not hundreds of moose and bison, were taken out of the park in the spring of 1875."

Skepticism is aroused because a number of parties reported traveling through the park for days without seeing an elk or killing any game. But remember that even today, it is possible to drive through the park and see few elk or other animals. This does not mean they have disappeared.

Whatever the historical status of elk in the ecosystem, it is undeniable that by the 1920s they were abundant, and by the 1930s park officials were removing them to other Western sites. In 1962 alone, 4,619 elk were removed from the park. This program ended in Yellowstone in 1968, though elk are still hunted in Grand Teton National Park—729 were killed in 1989, for example.

In 1969, Yellowstone began allowing wildlife populations to fluctuate on their own, according to weather, predation, disease, and other natural factors. Since then, elk on the northern range have varied from 5,000 to 20,000, with periodic kills from severe winters.

Many discredit natural regulation, saying that Yellowstone is no longer natural, since humans have manipulated it in some way for so long. For its own good, Yellowstone must be continuously manipulated, they say. Natural regulation advocates concede that Yellowstone may not be pristine, but it is still more natural than a parking lot in Los Angeles or even the surrounding national forest lands, where trapping, logging, and livestock grazing are permitted.

Recent park studies believe that wildlife grazing is not killing off grasslands. Annual variations in climate can actually cause much greater change. Root biomass, one index of grazing, was found to be the same in areas grazed and ungrazed (fenced exclosures) by wildlife. Root development varies, however, with the annual precipitation. One difference between a plot grazed by wildlife and enclosed grasslands was the reduction of biomass shown by standing dead plants and plant litter. The removal of this material does not significantly affect plant productivity.

Willows, aspen, and other species appear to have decreased in size and extent, but this is not necessarily entirely attributable to elk. Many shallow lakes and marshes have dried up during the past 100 years, and some suggest that a climate shift may be responsible. No consensus has been reached.

Supporters of park policy believe that wildlife shouldn't be maintained at some predetermined number. Who can say what is "right" or what is the park's "natural" capacity for elk? Perhaps the park should manage for ecological processes, such as predator-prey relationships, wildfires, and nutrient cycling. As long as these processes are largely free of manipulation, then, some say, park policies are successful. Though nearly everyone agrees on some human control, its nature and degree are hotly debated. Reintroducing wolves into Yellowstone to help control elk numbers is manipulation, but it's far more natural and less intrusive than, say, letting in hunters with pickup trucks.

Conservation Issues
In the 1960s and '70s, logging became a major controversy. Until then, the forest service was largely custodial. But in the '60s, the agency began

to cut timber in greater Yellowstone, usually clear-cutting in a sale area, leaving polygons of nude land blighting the once natural-looking mountainsides.

The clear-cuts were a big problem in a region that depends on tourism, but they also had environmental effects. Soil was disturbed, increasing sedimentation in streams and degrading fisheries. Huge road networks for hauling logs reduced cover for wildlife, forcing the elk from some areas and hurting elk hunting.

The most accessible trees were cut first, of course, and now it is becoming difficult to keep local mills supplied. Some may soon be closed.

Another issue is oil and gas drilling. The Overthrust Belt, a geological formation known to contain fossil fuel deposits, sweeps through part of greater Yellowstone, and gas fields at the GYE's southern boundary have already been developed. It is not known whether deposits in other areas are worth tapping.

Like logging, oil and gas development requires many new roads as well as drilling pads. These can harm scenery, wildlife, and recreation.

A growing issue is livestock grazing. The first ranches were established in the 1860s in some of the lower valleys. Though part of the regional economy for more than 100 years, ranching today contributes to a relatively minor portion of the local economy. Public-land grazing is even less important; according to a 1987 Congressional Research Service Report on the ecosystem, only 144 jobs resulted directly from livestock grazing on greater Yellowstone national forests. The environmental impacts of livestock, however, are significant. Domestic stock compete with native herbivores for forage. Many streams and rivers are diverted to irrigate hay, threatening the ecosystem's outstanding fisheries. Livestock also tramples and consumes streamside vegetation that is so important for stabilizing channels and providing and protecting fish habitat. Because most livestock producers do little to protect their animals, such as using herders and guard dogs, they have created a need for predator control. Coyotes, bears, mountain lions, and even eagles are persecuted every year because livestock is such easy pickings. The ecosystem's premier predator, the wolf, paid the ultimate price for its dietary habits.

Yellowstone's future is uncertain. We know now that we can't simply preserve species by species. If greater Yellowstone is to remain ecologically intact, we also need to preserve processes that shape and maintain its natural itegrity. This is a bigger challenge than was ever imagined, yet if

Cattle concentrate in the riparian zone of a small tributary of the Ruby River in the Snowcrest Range, Beaverhead National Forest. Domestic livestock are responsible for damaging riparian areas throughout the ecosystem.

we are to succeed anywhere, it will most likely be in greater Yellowstone. As with its establishment, Yellowstone will continue to be where new ideas about human relationships to the land are worked out. It's a grand landscape, with an equally grand purpose. May it always be so.

GEOLOGY OF THE GREATER YELLOWSTONE ECOSYSTEM

Recorded in the rocks of the Greater Yellowstone Ecosystem is a history that goes back more than 2.7 billion years, telling tales of continental collisions, the rise and fall of mountain ranges, major volcanic eruptions, and most recently, giant glaciers. This area has a tumultuous past of almost unimaginable violence and destruction.

An outcrop of limestone, a rock that is formed in a warm marine environment, tells of former oceans and a climate that was once mild. Glacial deposits speak of colder weather and events on land. Beyond these simple revelations, the geologic record is often difficult to interpret. A great deal of earth's history lies deep below the surface, where it is impossible to see. Erosion has stripped away many layers of the geologic record—representing millions of years—leaving what geologists call unconformities. Thus, geology is based on conjecture as much as on "rock-solid" evidence. Interpretations are continually changing.

A Few Basic Geological Terms

Geology has its own set of terms and concepts. To fully appreciate the geological history of the Greater Yellowstone Ecosystem, it is necessary to understand these ideas.

Sediments, which are eroded from rock and carried away by water, ice, or wind, eventually settle into areas and accumulate in thick layers. Over time, the layers may be transformed into rock. Because the layers are always horizontal when deposited, we know that sedimentary rock that is not in a flat, smooth formation has been disturbed in some way.

The principle of *superimposition* is also key to understanding geology.

Each rock layer is like a fresh coat of paint, with the last layer being the newest. Thus, in any outcrop of rocks, the youngest will be on top and the oldest at the bottom.

No matter where they are in the rock strata, all rocks are of three basic types: igneous, sedimentary, and metamorphic. All can be found exposed somewhere in the GYE.

Igneous rocks (from the Latin *igneus*, meaning fire) form when molten rock solidifies. They solidify either inside the earth (intrusive) or on the surface (extrusive), as lava or ash from volcanoes. Granite, rhyolite, andesite, and basalt are all igneous rocks.

Granite cools deep below the surface. It is exposed when it has been lifted or overlying rock has been eroded away. Granites make up the core of many mountain ranges in the ecosystem, such as the Wind Rivers, Tetons, and Beartooths.

Rhyolite is basically the extrusive counterpart of granite. It flows onto the surface as lava or is blown out of a volcano as ash. Because volcanoes played such a major role in Yellowstone's heritage, rhyolite is fairly common, making up much of the outcrops in the park.

Granite boulders lie on an old river bench in the Madison River Valley, Montana. Such benches are cut by the river.

At Teton Pass in Wyoming is a fine example of sedimentary layering. Since the sediment was deposited in a horizontal position, the angle at which the strata now lie indicates subsequent uplift.

Sedimentary rocks are composed of particles weathered and broken down from existing rocks, then deposited by erosion in layers. (One of the most exceptional exposures of sedimentary rock still in its original, horizontal position is the Grand Canyon in Arizona.) Among the common sedimentary rocks are sandstone, shale, siltstone, and limestone. Sandstone is composed of particles of sand washed into streams or oceans, then compacted and cemented together. Shale is compacted layers of mud. Limestone is usually the result of a gradual accumulation of the bodies of warm ocean organisms, such as corals and shellfish. Of the three basic types, sedimentary rocks are the most likely to be encountered near the earth's surface.

Metamorphic rocks (from the Greek *meta*, meaning change, and *morphe*, meaning form) are derived from existing rocks that have been changed by heat and pressure. However, they have not been completely melted back into magma. For instance, limestone may be metamorphosed by heat and pressure into marble, while another sedimentary rock, shale, changes to slate. Schists and gneiss are other common metamorphic rocks.

Plate Tectonics—The Big Picture

To understand how the three major types of rock are formed and to grasp the current geology, it is necessary to look at the earth's past. It is largely explained by the theory of plate tectonics, which says that the earth is composed of a dozen or so continental and oceanic plates that "float" on a mantle, rather like ice pans in a river. North America is one of these plates, South America another, and the Pacific Ocean basin a third.

As they move, the plates collide, pull apart, and slide past each other. Ocean basins are created and some continents are joined while others are slowly torn apart. For example, about 205 million years ago North America was joined with Europe, Asia, Africa, and other continents in a "supercontinent" called Pangea. Later, the continents broke up and oceans filled the rifts.

Where one plate collides with another, as along the northwest coast of the United States, the plate margins may be destroyed as one plate slips beneath the other. The descending rock moves closer to the warm mantle and eventually melts to form new magma. The magma rises, and if it reaches the surface, it erupts as a volcano. Mounts Hood, Rainier, and St. Helens owe their origins to the same plate collision. Often, the magma does not completely reach the surface, and the magma slowly cools to form huge granite plugs that later may be exposed as mountain ranges. The granite cores of the Tetons and the Wind River Mountains very likely formed this way.

Most oceanic plates are composed of basalt, which is heavier than the granites in the cores of continents. Thus, in collisions between oceanic and continental plates, the oceanic plate dives into the mantle, melts, and perhaps eventually reemerges as "new" rock. Continental plates, while sometimes broken apart, are almost never subducted. Therefore, the rock at the core of continents is usually ancient.

The motion of wandering plates stresses the earth's crust. Rock layers may actually break, producing faults, or they may merely fold. The results influence much of the landscape of western North America.

The Yellowstone Connection

The oldest rocks exposed in the Greater Yellowstone Ecosystem are called *basement rocks*, which make up continental cores. Usually, one does not see basement rocks because they are covered by younger sedimentary or extrusive igneous rocks like lava. Occasionally, however, lifting of the crust allows erosion to strip away the overlying layers and expose the granites and gneiss of the continental basement rocks.

Within greater Yellowstone, basement rocks outcrop on most of the Beartooth Plateau, seen from the Beartooth Highway between Red Lodge and Cooke City, Montana. Other outcrops of this geological formation are found in Yankee Jim Canyon north of Gardiner, Montana; along the Gallatin Canyon between Gallatin Gateway and Big Sky, Montana; along the Lamar River Canyon in the northern part of Yellowstone National Park; and in the Clarks Fork River Canyon between Cooke City, Montana, and Cody, Wyoming. These rocks are estimated to be 2.7 billion years old and are some of the oldest exposed rocks in North America. Rocks of this age are called *Precambrian* basement rocks, and were originally thought to predate life on the planet. However, we now know that bacteria and algae did exist in the Precambrian era, but due to their lack of hard structures like shells or bones, they left few fossils.

All rock deposited from 2.7 billion to 570 million years ago was subsequently eroded. Therefore, there is no record of this period in the GYE. Just about the time the geologic record returns, however, the planet was exploding with life. This was the beginning of the Cambrian era, during which the first sponges, jellyfish, trilobites, crustaceans, and other animals left their fossils.

Beginning with the Cambrian and continuing almost uninterrupted for more than 500 million years, most of the GYE and much of western North America was washed repeatedly by shallow seas and broad rivers. Mud, sand, silt, and clay collected along ancient shores and in shallow ocean basins, later hardening into immense structures of sedimentary rock.

From the beginning of the Cambrian period and continuing to the Triassic period 245 million years ago, Yellowstone park was centered near the equator and was part of the continental shelf of what would be North America. Warm, shallow seas and swamps inundated this area and sediments accumulated to form sandstone, shale, limestone, and other sedimentary rocks, including Madison limestone and Tensleeps sandstone formations.

The sedimentary origins of Madison limestone are apparent in the horizontal layering in the cliffs above the Gallatin River. The sediment was deposited by the warm, shallow seas that once inundated the West.

Madison limestone, a light-colored, cliff-forming rock, is common throughout the ecosystem, usually fronting on the edges of ranges such as the north face of the Beartooth Mountains between Livingston and Red Lodge, Montana; in the Gallatin Canyon north of Big Sky, Montana; on the top of Sheep Mountain in the Gros Ventre Range seen from Jackson Hole; and along the Shoshone River Canyon west of Cody, Wyoming. It also forms the main rock exposed at the Sinks along the North Fork of the Pogo Agie in the Wind River Range near Lander, Wyoming.

By the beginning of the Triassic period, part of western Wyoming had risen above sea level, and brightly colored sandstones and shales were laid down in river deltas and floodplains. One of these, the *Chugwater Formation*, outcrops as bright red rock along the eastern base of the Wind River Range on the Red Grade seen from state Route 28 south of Lander.

Recorded in these sediments is one of earth's several mass extinctions. Beginning around 290 million years ago, the continents united to form Pangea. Perhaps because of greater competition or changes in climate, one of the largest extinctions in history ensued. By the end of the Permian period, about 240 million years ago, nearly 90 percent of the species on earth had perished. New life began to evolve, and the reptiles flourished in particular. The dinosaurs were part of this expansion.

After the Permian, an inland sea developed along what is now the Idaho-Wyoming line. A thick deposit of phosphate, now known as the *Phosphoria Formation*, was laid down in a shallow sea 200 million years ago. It is one of the largest bodies of phosphate in the United States.

Overthrust Belt

Passing through the same area of western Wyoming and southeastern Idaho as the Phosphoria Formation is the Overthrust Belt, a 5,000-mile stretch of thrust-faulted rock that reaches from Utah to the Brooks Range of Alaska. Geologists believe thrust faults are the result of earth's crust being compressed. In some parts of the Overthrust Belt, oil and gas have been discovered.

The compression that caused the faulting in the affected rock layers of the Overthrust Belt was such that older rocks actually slid on top of younger rocks, subverting the principle of superimposition. The older layers, often thousands of feet thick and sometimes ten or twenty miles across, lie atop younger layers of rock rather like shingles on a roof, overlapping but not totally covering them.

Total movement of rocks along the fault was frequently fifteen or twenty miles. The displaced rock structures typically stand now as parallel ridges with intervening, narrow valleys. In greater Yellowstone, the Caribou Mountains, Palisades, Aspen, Meade, and other Idaho mountain ranges in the eastern Targhee National Forest and Caribou National Forest are all part of the Overthrust Belt, as are the Salt River Range, Wyoming Range, and Commissary Ridge in Wyoming.

In the belt structures near Evanston, Wyoming, large oil and gas deposits have been found. Potential oil development of roadless lands has been an issue and threatens the wilderness ranges of southeast Idaho and western Wyoming as well as places in the Shoshone and Custer national forests.

Absaroka Volcanics

By 100 million years ago, Pangea had broken up and North America had begun its drift north and west toward its present position. The dinosaur reigned supreme. Eventually, the North American Plate, the western edge of which is near today's Idaho-Oregon line, collided with the oceanic

Pacific Plate. The result was the compression of western North America and a great era of mountain building that lasted nearly 50 million years. The ranges of greater Yellowstone resulted. The movement of the Pacific Plate toward and under the North American Plate brought at least two offshore island masses "crashing" into the continent. These land masses stuck and now underlie most of the Pacific Northwest.

The Beartooth Mountains were born during this building episode. They can be seen easily from the Beartooth Highway between Cooke City and Red Lodge, Montana. The range is tilted toward the south and consists primarily of a huge, rolling plateau of granite-gneiss rock. At one time, these igneous rocks had been thickly covered with sedimentary rock, but numerous earthquakes and the lifting of the range apparently jarred it loose. Nearly all the sedimentary rock slid off to the south; it may have happened in minutes. Beartooth Butte, seen along the Beartooth Highway, is an isolated sedimentary formation that was left. The blocks of Madison limestone found at Heart Mountain just outside of Cody are also evidence of this fantastic event.

As described above, the subduction of one plate beneath another often causes volcanism inland from the actual line of contact. Thus, when the western coast of North America lay farther east than it does today, the Yellowstone region saw great volcanic activity. The peak came 38 million to 50 million years ago, when eruptions in the Absaroka volcanoes covered much of the Greater Yellowstone Ecosystem with *andesite* (named for similar rocks found in the Andes of South America) and other volcanic debris.

The Absaroka volcanoes formed in a line northwest from near Dubois, Wyoming, across eastern Yellowstone park into Montana's Gallatin Range. Today, the resulting formation, referred to as the Absaroka Volcanics, makes up a 3,000-square-mile area including nearly all the peaks within the Washakie and North Absaroka wildernesses. Prominent Pilot Peak, seen in the upper Clarks Fork Valley near Cooke City, is one of the best-known summits, built up of Absaroka Volcanics. Within the park itself, the mountains of the eastern boundary, along the upper Lamar and Yellowstone rivers, are also composed of Absaroka Volcanics.

In many areas, these volcanics bury older granite rocks or sedimentary rock strata. Both the Gallatin Range and Absaroka Mountains in Montana are underlain by Precambrian granitic basement rocks. In particular, the Absarokas, which front on the upper Yellowstone Valley north and

The Lewis River, named for Merriweather Lewis, has cut this canyon through the volcanic ash that makes up much of the Pitchstone Plateau in Yellowstone National Park.

east of Gardiner, Montana, are only the western extension of the Beartooth uplift. Technically, they should be called the Beartooth Mountains as well, but common use dictates calling them the Absarokas.

In the upper Clarks Fork Valley between Cooke City and Cody, dark brown Absaroka Volcanics overlie a layer of limestone that stands out as a prominent light-colored cliff on the mountain slope. A good place to see this layering is at Fox Creek below Pilot and Index peaks.

Once a volcano quiets, the vent is often plugged by solidified magma. In a few places, these volcanic necks, as they are called, have been exposed by erosion. Ship Rock in New Mexico is a classic example of a volcanic neck. Bunsen Peak and Mount Washburn, both in the park, are also believed to be volcanic necks, though more massive and rounded than Ship Rock. Despite the immense pile of exposed volcanic debris, however, granite underlies all of these mountains.

As a rule, these eruptions were rather quiet; the volcanoes oozed lava out over the landscape rather than exploding. Landslides and floods carried rubble down slopes to create a chaotic mixture of rocks, ash, and mud that hardened into a rock called breccia. These flows still have a layered appearance and tend to be brown, red, and purple. You can see these rocks clearly on Baronette Peak and other mountains near the northeast entrance of Yellowstone park by Cooke City, along the North Fork of the Shoshone River between Cody and the east entrance, and in the Ramparts by Togwotee Pass on U.S. 287 between Dubois and Moran Junction, east of Grand Teton National Park.

These mountains exceed 12,000 feet and many are flat-topped and plateaulike. They are highly erodible and running water has cut deep valleys and canyons into them. Also, streams draining the highlands, such as the Lamar and Shoshone rivers, are heavily laden with sediment, particularly in the spring or after a heavy rain.

Fossil Trees

Mudflows spawned by the eruptions of the Absaroka volcanoes raced down the mountains and valleys many times. They buried forests, ironically preserving many trees through fossilization. Many fossils were actually upright, while others were toppled and carried along in streams before being buried. The best examples of these fossil forests can be found in the Lamar River Valley, particularly Specimen Ridge, and in the Gallatin Range near the northern park boundary and on nearby forest service lands. In some areas, huge tree trunks remain standing.

Not only trees were preserved, but also leaves, needles, cones, and pollen grains. More than 200 plant species have been identified. There are even places where fossil soil clings to roots of fossil trees! Many consider Yellowstone's fossil forests to be among the finest anywhere. Seeing most of these remains requires a strenuous hike, but the less physically inclined can view a fossilized tree just off the main park loop road west of Tower Junction.

The mix of tree species is unusual. There were spruce, fir, and pine (species you can find in the area today), but also buried were breadfruit, avocado, dogwood, maple, oak, hickory, and redwood. These are usually found in milder climates. Apparently the spruce, pine, and fir lived at higher elevations on the volcanoes where the climate was colder, while species like redwood lived at lower elevations.

No matter where you view fossil remains, please remember not to collect even small pieces. Considering how rare such forests are, it is regrettable that collection is permitted anywhere. Tragically, the Gallatin National Forest still allows the removal of fossil wood, though restrictions apply. In essence, this is legal vandalism of our heritage and poor stewardship. Please leave fossils intact for future generations to enjoy.

Basin and Range

The basin and range geological province lies between the Sierras and Cascades on the west and the Wasatch Front and Tetons on the east. It takes in all of Nevada and parts of Oregon, Utah, New Mexico, Arizona, Idaho, California, and Wyoming. The province has numerous linear, parallel ranges generally lying north-south with broad valleys in between called basins. Faults divide the basins and mountains; mountains were lifted while basins dropped. What caused this remarkable alignment?

Geologists speculate that seventeen million years ago, a giant meteorite slammed into southeastern Oregon. The collision so weakened the earth's crust that molten rock rose from deep in the mantle. This plume melted other rocks, providing a continuing source of heat and molten rock that occasionally spilled across the landscape in giant flows. One result was the extensive Columbia River lava plateaus of eastern Oregon and Washington. The activity also stressed the crust, resulting in faulting that causes the basin and range pattern.

There is evidence that the entire region is spreading apart from what geologists call crustal extension—a pulling of the crust in an east-west direction. From its beginnings in northern Nevada and southeastern Oregon, the faulting has gradually worked its way eastward as the continent has drifted over the rising plume of molten rock.

The Teton Range in Grand Teton National Park marks the eastern edge of the basin and range province. The Tetons are young, less than ten million years. Most other mountain ranges in the Rockies are fifty million to sixty million years old. The Teton fault block is about forty miles long by fifteen miles wide and has been thrust up along a fault visible as the abrupt break in slope at the foot of the range. The adjoining valley of Jackson Hole has dropped. Uplift along the Teton Fault has been as much as 25,000 feet, or about five miles. Today, Grand Teton, the highest peak in the range, rises more than 7,000 feet above Jackson Hole to a cloud-scraping 13,770 feet. Erosion has stripped off most of the sedimentary rocks that once covered the range, exposing the granitic core.

At the same pace that basin and range faulting has moved eastward, there has been a movement of volcanic activity traced by the lava flows that make up the Snake River Plain of southern Idaho. Its easternmost extension now lies in Yellowstone park, explaining the thermal features. The source is what geologists call a hot spot. New research suggests that a column of heated rock penetrates about 125 miles into the earth, a depth that is well into the mantle. A similar hot spot is responsible for the Hawaiian Islands. As continents slowly drift around the globe, they cruise over these spots, leaving lines of volcanos like blisters left by a blowtorch that has been moved over a painted board. The craters that stretch across southern Idaho's Snake River Plain are a good example. Geologists have confirmed that the oldest eruptions on the plain are closest to Oregon, while lava flows and craters become younger the closer you get to Yellowstone. Geologists believe the hot spot is now directly under Yellowstone park.

The Yellowstone Volcanoes

Geologists say that Yellowstone is a bomb waiting to explode—maybe even as you read this book! The more than 10,000 mud pots, hot springs, geysers, and fumaroles all indicate that a major source of heat (molten rock) lies close to the surface. Research has shown that catastrophic eruptions have occurred at least three times in the past at fairly regular intervals of 600,000 to 800,000 years. And it's been 600,000 years since the last one.

The eruptions were unlike any witnessed in historic times. They were cataclysmic, making Mount St. Helens' eruption look like a puff of smoke. Each began with a lava flow, followed by an explosion that drained the magma chamber. This collapsed the volcanic crater. Much the same thing occurred at Mount Mazama, whose caldera is seen at Oregon's Crater Lake National Park. After the volcano fell in on itself, more lava poured out to partially fill the crater.

The first major discharge occurred nearly two million years ago when an explosion threw into the atmosphere nearly 15,000 times the lava and ash as blew from the 1980 Mount St. Helens eruption. Another occurred 1.2 million years ago and another 600,000 years later. Geologists speculate that a hot spot under the Yellowstone Plateau provides the magma for these eruptions.

The first eruption spewed *rhyolite*, which is viscous and does not flow well, and tends to be thrown out of the earth in blasts. Though some rhyolite did ooze onto the surface during this first period, most was blown sky-high in a red-hot cloud of ash. This cloud fell downhill and welded itself into tuff, a rock composed of ash and bits of volcanic debris. In Yellowstone, this material is called the Huckleberry Ridge tuff, after Huckleberry Mountain near the south entrance. Tuffs are abundant there and are widely distributed in and around Yellowstone park. The cap rock on the top of Mount Everts by Mammoth Hot Springs, for example, is Huckleberry Ridge tuff. It covers soft shale and sandstone laid down more than 100 million years ago. The erosion-resistant tuffs protect the sedimentary rocks, creating the steep mountain one sees from Mammoth. Rocks along the highway by Golden Gate, between Mammoth and Norris, also are Huckleberry Ridge tuff.

Though this first eruption was by far the largest and presumably left the

Gibbon Falls spills over a layer of hard, erosion-resistant rock along the rim of the old caldera, or crater, that formed when the Yellowstone volcano erupted about 600,000 years ago.

largest caldera, not much remains of the original crater now buried under debris from subsequent eruptions. Only remnants of the caldera rim can be found, one being near Island Park west of the park and along its southern boundary.

The second eruption was the smallest. It is called the Henry's Fork caldera because outcrops of these lavas are centered on the headwaters of the Henry's Fork River near Island Park, Idaho, just west of Yellowstone park.

The third and last eruption left a twenty-eight-by-forty-seven-mile caldera, part of which is now inundated by Yellowstone Lake. This is one of the largest in the world. The caldera at Crater Lake, for example, is only six miles across. In fact, nearly all of Yellowstone park's central plateau is the collapsed caldera of this last volcano. If you drive over Dunraven Pass in the park's Washburn Range and look south across the vast, level, forested interior of Yellowstone, you will see the inside of this immense crater. Since the last major eruption 600,000 years ago, there have been minor lava flows and eruptions. West Thumb, an arm of Yellowstone Lake, is a four-by-six-mile caldera, the result of an explosion 150,000 years ago. The Pitchstone Plateau in Yellowstone's southwest corner is made up of rhyolite flows less than 80,000 years old. There are no lava flows more recent than these in the park, but geologists speculate that an eruption may be imminent. Measurements show that the surface between Old Faithful and Canyon is swelling an inch per year.

Glaciation

This last volcanic episode in Yellowstone occurred during a major glacial period, during which most of northern North America was covered with ice thousands of feet thick. Caps and glaciers covered most of the mountain ranges in the Greater Yellowstone Ecosystem and left many U-shaped valleys, cirque basins, and glacier-sculpted peaks.

Beginning about two million years ago, the climate changed throughout the Northern Hemisphere to favor the accumulation of glacial ice. Cooler (not severely cold) weather and plenty of precipitation bring ice ages. When more snow falls in winter than melts in summer, glaciers form and advance. The opposite is true as well.

Though geologists suspect a number of glacial advances, there are records of only three in the ecosystem. The oldest is the *Buffalo Glaciation*, named for the Buffalo Fork of the Snake River where the earliest record of glacial activity was discovered. The Buffalo glacial advance occurred 200,000 years ago, but most evidence of it was obliterated by subsequent ones.

The second is the *Bull Lake Glaciation*. It began 130,000 to 160,000 years ago and is named for the lake on the eastern Wind River Range, where geologists first pieced together evidence for it. Most of the Bull Lake features were overridden by the third advance, the *Pinedale Glaciation*, named for Pinedale, Wyoming, on the west slope of the Wind Rivers. It began 70,000 years ago and ended only 13,000 years ago.

At the time of maximum glaciation, ice sheets and large valley glaciers covered most of the higher elevations in the GYE. A huge sheet spread from the Beartooth Plateau across northern Yellowstone park. It converged with three others near Gardiner, Montana, at Yellowstone's north entrance. The other flows were fed by smaller caps on the Gallatin and Washburn ranges and in the Specimen Ridge area. This river of ice continued north, scouring the valley of the Yellowstone River, called Paradise Valley beyond Yankee Jim Canyon. It is thought to have been the longest valley glacier (ninety miles) outside of Canada and Alaska.

Terminal moraines marking the farthest extent of glacial advance are seen around the Eightmile Creek area near Emigrant, Montana. To the west of U.S. 89 between Eightmile Creek and Antelope Butte (about fifteen miles south of Livingston, Montana), the old braided channels of a glacial outwash plain are still clearly visible from the air.

Ice also spread out from the Absaroka Mountains along the park's eastern boundary. At the height of glaciation about 15,000 years ago, nearly 90 percent of the park was covered up to 3,000 feet thick. Only the extreme western edge was ice-free. There are no glaciers left in Yellowstone park, though a few are still found in the higher peaks of the Beartooth Mountains, Tetons, Absarokas, and the Wind River Range.

The sheet that covered Yellowstone joined with ice over the Teton Range. The area south of Jackson Lake known as the Potholes owes its hummocky topography to morainal deposits left by these massive sheets. Cirque and valley glaciers also sculpted the peaks of the Tetons, contributing to the rugged appearance.

Due to its overall height, the Wind River Range was also covered by a major ice sheet that sent valley glaciers out from the mountain flanks and into the surrounding lowlands. Today, the Wind Rivers have the largest glaciers in the U.S. Rockies, even larger than those in Glacier National

Park. There are at least twenty-four named glaciers, with most in the northern portion.

The only other greater Yellowstone mountains believed to have been covered with an ice cap are the Gros Ventre Range. However, smaller cirque glaciers were common in other ranges, including the Absarokas, Palisades, Centennials, and Henry's Lake Mountains, and the Madison, Gallatin, Salt River, Wyoming, and Hoback ranges. The Snowcrest and Gravelly ranges also had modest cirque glaciers, though neither was heavily sculpted.

Glacial Landforms

One of the most common indications of glaciation in mountains are cirques. These high, rounded bowls look as if they were carved with a giant ice cream scoop. Sitting at the head of a valley, a cirque has a relatively flat bottom and is usually walled by steep slopes or even cliffs on three sides. A fine cirque sits on the southeast face of Electric Peak in the Gallatin Range, seen from Gardiner, Montana. The pyramidal Lone Mountain at Big Sky Ski Resort is the result of several cirque basins encircling it. Some peaks that have had glaciers working simultaneously on their flanks will eventually resemble the Matterhorn in Switzerland. Examples of horns found in greater Yellowstone are Pilot Peak and Grand Teton.

The same scouring and scooping power of glaciers also restructures valleys, steepening the sides and flattening the bottoms. In cross-section, glacially carved valleys are U-shaped, and in the ecosystem, almost all of the higher major stream valleys have such a profile. The more prominent glacial valleys are the Boulder, Stillwater, and Rock Creek valleys in the Beartooths; Hyalite Canyon in the Gallatin Range; Cascade Canyon in the Tetons; Bull Lake Creek in the Wind Rivers; Dunoir Creek in the Absaroka Mountains near Dubois, Wyoming; and the Upper Lamar-Soda Butte Creek valleys in Yellowstone park.

As ice scrapes along the ground and sides of valleys, boulders, gravel, and dirt become embedded in the glacier or are pushed in front or along the sides. This rubble is called *moraine*, and once a glacier retreats, the moraine is deposited in piles. The rolling terrain near Horse Butte and the horseshoe-shaped peninsula of Rainbow Point on Hebgen Lake near West Yellowstone are the terminal moraine of a huge glacier that once flowed out of Yellowstone park along the Madison River.

There also are excellent moraines in Grand Teton National Park south of Jackson Lake, where the Potholes area marks the farthest advance of a glacier that once covered southern Yellowstone park.

As a glacier retreats, sediment-loaded streams flowing from its snout meander as they make their way down a valley. This creates a flat, well-drained, gravelly surface called an *outwash plain*. Jackson Hole contains such a plain.

Because moraines are not sorted by water as are outwash plains, they can contain boulders as well as pebbles and even sand. Because of the fine particles spread across outwash areas, shallow-rooted plants like grasses grow well; moraines, which allow water to drain deeply, encourage tree growth. This is easily seen at the foot of the Tetons, where the moraines, appearing as low hills near the mouth of each canyon, all have some tree cover, while the outwash plain farther out from the mountains is covered with grasses and shrubs.

Glacial erratics are yet another sign of glaciation. In places, there are large boulders resting on bedrock of entirely different origins. These are called glacial erratics. A good example is near Canyon Village on the road to Inspiration Point in the Grand Canyon of the Yellowstone. A massive granite boulder incongruously rests upon volcanic soils amid a lodgepole pine forest. It was carried there by glaciers and dropped as the ice retreated.

Sometimes pieces of ice the size of houses and battleships are trapped in the moraine, melting to form ponds and lakes, often with no inlet or outlet. These are *kettle ponds*. There are good kettles and moraines in the Junction Butte area along the highway between Tower Junction and Cooke City and in the Potholes area of Grand Teton park.

Glaciers also create temporary lakes. During the glacial period, tongues of ice occasionally blocked rivers such as the Yellowstone. The flat, swampy meadows in Hayden Valley four miles south of the Grand Canyon of the Yellowstone owe their existence to relatively impermeable silts and clays deposited in the still waters of a glacial lake. This lake filled the area behind an ice dam blocking the Yellowstone. The poor drainage inhibits trees and accounts for the extensive meadows amid an otherwise solid lodgepole forest.

When the dam melted or was breached, floods roared down the Yellowstone Valley. Traces of the floods remain as giant ripples and gravel bars in the upper Yellowstone Valley. Gardiner, Montana, is built on an old gravel bar. Glacial floods also originated in the Lamar River-Soda Butte Creek areas, and old gravel bars are just down from the confluence of the Lamar and Yellowstone rivers.

Less temporary lakes are often created by the retreat of glaciers. As ice moves down a valley, it makes it deeper. Once the ice melts, moraines may form a natural dam. Most glacial lakes have a long, linear outline. Fremont Lake in the Wind River Range east of Pinedale is an example. If you drive up to Fremont Lake, you will see the unsorted debris as a low hill at its mouth. This is an unerring indication of glacial origins. In Jackson Hole at the foot of the Tetons, Jackson, Jenny, Taggart, Bradley, Phelps, and Leigh lakes are all dammed by moraines.

Besides creating morainal lakes in the lowlands, glaciers also formed many of the alpine lakes along the greater Yellowstone high country. Most are in cirque basins.

There also are occasional *rock glaciers*—rock fragments held together by ice. They actually flow slowly and look similar to rock-covered glaciers, which they may be, in some cases. A rock glacier is found on the northeast slope of Emigrant Peak, a prominent mountain seen from Paradise Valley.

Special Geological Features

Faults are cracks or weaknesses in the earth's crust, and nearly all topographic features are tied to their presence. Faults are created by the movement of plates as well as by local disturbances such as rising magma. An easy way to detect faulting is to look for where sedimentary layers are tilted. Remember that all sedimentary rocks were originally laid down horizontally, so any rocks that have shifted must have been moved by faulting. The colored sedimentary layers now tilted nearly vertical in the Devil's Slide, five miles north of Gardiner, illustrate dramatic faulting.

The lifting of mountain blocks such as the Wind Rivers has tilted overlying sedimentary layers on edge. This is apparent in Sinks Canyon outside of Lander, where limestones are stacked like flatirons. Near the top of Teton Pass are sedimentary layers overlying the granite core of the Teton Range that are angled from faulting.

Topographic maps and aerial photos of the Greater Yellowstone Ecosystem show prominent, straight lines marking the edge of mountain uplifts. These abrupt transitions from valley to mountain slope are graphic examples of faults. Such straight breaks in the crust mark the

Palisades along the South Fork of the Snake River in Idaho; the north face of the Centennial Mountains on the Idaho-Montana line; the east and west sides of the Wind River Range in Wyoming; the Madison Range in the Madison River Valley; the northern terminus of the Gallatin Range and Madison Range south of Bozeman, Montana; the north face of the Beartooths fronting on the Yellowstone River Valley; and the dramatic face of the Absaroka Mountains in Paradise Valley.

Faults create weaknesses in the rocks they cut. Water exploits these zones, explaining why most major river and creek valleys parallel fault scarps. The Clarks Fork of the Yellowstone follows a fault separating the Beartooths from the mountains of the North Absaroka Wilderness to the south of the river. The upper Yellowstone and Lamar river systems follow faults. The Hoback River also cuts through the mountains along a fault; this one marks the break between the Gros Ventre Mountains and the Hoback Range. The North Fork of the Shoshone between Cody and the east entrance to the park is yet another river allied with a major fault.

Earthquakes result from slippage along faults. Given the faults in the GYE, it is not surprising that quakes are common here. The most active areas are in the upper Madison River Valley near West Yellowstone and Hebgen Lake. Other earthquake areas include Norris Geyser Basin, Yellowstone Lake, and the Snake River Valley south of Jackson and around Palisades Reservoir in Idaho.

The most famous Yellowstone earthquake was on August 17, 1959, when a tremor registering 7.1 on the Richter scale shook the Red Canyon Fault area. This fault traces the base of the still-rising Madison Range, which jumped as much as fifteen feet. The quake started a landslide in the Madison River Canyon below Hebgen Lake. The rubble killed twenty-eight people in a forest service campground. The new dam backed up the Madison River to form Quake Lake, where trees killed by the rising water still litter the surface and provide nesting for ospreys.

There was a major slide on the Gros Ventre River east of Jackson, Wyoming, on June 23, 1925. Weeks of heavy rain lubricated surfaces between two bedding planes of rock strata, causing part of the mountain to break away. The dam created Slide Lake. Two years later, the dam broke and the flood killed six people. The lower Gros Ventre River still looks "washed out."

Landslides

Sometimes glacial or river erosion will leave a slope unstable and subject to mass failure. One such landslide is visible on the slope of Sepulcher Mountain just south of Gardiner, Montana, at the park's north entrance. Another old slide can be seen in the Lamar Valley. In each case, the slide areas look hummocky and jumbled.

Landslides are not that common, but general soil erosion can be continual. In particular, soils derived from the Absaroka Volcanics are highly unstable and are a major source of sedimentation in the North Fork of the Shoshone and the upper Lamar, drainages that flow from the Gallatin Range, and in other streams that drain unstable uplands.

Volcanic Landforms

Basalt columns form when lava cools and contracts. These six-sided columns are common in the ecosystem, particularly along the South Fork of the Snake Valley and in Yellowstone park. Two of the better places to see basalt columns are Sheepeater Cliffs near Bunsen Peak and along the Yellowstone River Canyon near Tower Falls.

Many of the waterfalls in the GYE originated from erosion-resistant lava flows, which cap softer rock strata. In the park, many waterfalls tumble over the lip of these harder rocks, plunging down on the softer strata. One such is Upper Yellowstone Falls. Others are Undine Falls between Tower and Gardiner, Lewis Falls on the Lewis River along the highway by the south entrance, and Gibbon Falls on the Gibbon River, which marks the edge of the Yellowstone caldera. Lower Mesa Falls in the Targhee National Forest also is water running over hard volcanic rock.

Hoodoos are formed in somewhat the same way. An erosion-resistant rock caps softer layers so that all the material except that directly beneath the hard cap is carried away. A pillar results. The Absaroka Volcanics have produced many hoodoos, due to the easily eroded breccias that make up these formations. Occasionally, overlying strata or even individual boulders protect the breccias beneath, so that formations such as Chimney Rock and the Holy City of Rocks, along the North Fork of the Shoshone River, remain as weird natural sculptures. There are similar formations in the upper Lamar River drainage and by Tower Falls.

Water-created Formations

There are a number of deep river canyons within the GYE that weren't formed by glacial ice. Valleys cut by glaciers are U-shaped; those cut by running water tend to be V-shaped. For instance, though glacial ice overran the Grand Canyon of the Yellowstone, it did not modify the canyon.

This river valley and those of the North Fork of the Shoshone and the lower Gallatin Canyon are narrow and steep-walled, and none were shaped by glaciers.

In fact, the twenty-mile Grand Canyon of the Yellowstone shows the cutting power of water alone. The river sliced down 1,000 to 1,500 feet into volcanic rocks weakened by heating. The golden canyon walls show the chemical change caused by heating.

Thermal Features

Yellowstone was originally set aside to protect world-class thermal features. The hot springs, mud pots, geysers, and fumaroles are unequaled. Not only are they a main attraction, but they are also responsible in part for Yellowstone's famous wildlife herds. During the harsh winters, the thermal features provide snow-free zones that allow a host of wildlife, from geese to elk, to survive.

Geothermal features are relatively rare because they require three ingredients in the same place. The first is water; Yellowstone's high elevation and deep snows ensure an adequate supply. There must be heat, such as the "hot spot" geologists believe sits under Yellowstone. Third, there has to be plumbing: a major network of fractures and faults that allows the circulation of water from the surface to depths and back again. This whole system has to be able to trap steam. The rise and collapse of the Yellowstone volcano left an enormous network of fractures. Also, nearly all geysers are associated with rhyolite, a relatively rare volcanic rock worldwide that is abundant in Yellowstone.

Hot springs and pools are common throughout Yellowstone. The best-known is Mammoth Hot Springs. Hot water dissolves calcium carbonate from limestone formations, so that when it reaches the surface, carbon dioxide is released and the calcium carbonate precipitates out. The result is travertine, which is deposited in beautiful, delicate terraces. Research shows that the water at Mammoth Hot Springs originates in the Norris Geyser Basin and travels nearly twenty miles before flowing out.

Not all the hot springs in greater Yellowstone form travertine; many are clear, beautiful, and deep. The Abyss and Black Pool at West Thumb and Morning Glory Spring at Upper Geyser Basin look more like steaming, inviting swimming pools. But don't jump in! It's illegal, and you'd probably scald yourself to death anyway.

Living in the hot water are lovely "gardens" of red, yellow, orange, and green algae and bacteria. Thermophilic life adapts to hot water, sometimes even boiling water. Bacteria are found in the hottest waters, usually close to the vents, while algae take to the cooler waters at the edges of pools. There is, in fact, a miniature food chain in these springs. The algae and bacteria are eaten by ephydrid flies; the ephydrids, in turn, are food for the dolichopodid flies.

Mud pots and fumaroles are found where groundwater is limited. Steam from fumaroles contains sulfuric acid (accounting for the rotten egg smell), which breaks down rock to form clays. The semi-liquid clays form boiling mud pots.

The most unusual of Yellowstone's geothermal features are its geysers. These springs periodically erupt with steam and hot water. Old Faithful erupts fairly regularly, while others may remain quiet for years, spurt to life briefly, then go back to sleep.

In Yellowstone, a geyser begins with rain or snow. The water works its way through underground conduits, eventually hitting heated rocks, usually a mile or more below the surface, where temperatures are 400 to 460 degrees Fahrenheit. At the same time, the water dissolves the quartz or silica around it. The rock is usually rhyolite, so the mineral is usually silica. It is critical because it coats the walls of the geysers, making them impermeable and allowing the buildup of pressure.

As the water rises along the rock fractures, a bit of pressure is relieved, allowing some of the superheated water to change to steam. As the water rises even higher, it can pass through a narrow space that may force some water out of the geyser. This further reduces pressure on the water below, causing a rapid chain reaction. With less pressure, more water turns to steam, which occupies 1,500 times more space than liquid water. This forces more water out of the geyser, until there is a virtual explosion and jets are pushed skyward. This often empties the geyser's chambers, restarting the process.

The appearance of geysers in Yellowstone is not random. Most are found in a few major geyser basins—Norris, West Thumb, Gibbon, Lone Star, Heart Lake, Shoshone, and Upper, Midway, and Lower on the Firehole. Geysers tend to be concentrated in the center of these basins, where water flow is greater. Mud springs are found toward the fringes.

Don't take Yellowstone's geysers for granted; only three other regions in the world have anything comparable—the Kamchatka Peninsula in the Soviet Union, New Zealand, and Iceland. With its more than 300 geysers, Yellowstone has more than the others combined. Nearly a fifth of the world's geysers (140) are found within a mile of Old Faithful in the Upper Geyser Basin! The most famous geysers in the park are found there: Castle, Giantess, Riverside, Grotto, and Daisy.

Old Faithful is easily the most famous attraction in Yellowstone. It frequently spouts to a height of 130 to 150 feet. It was discovered by members of the Washburn Expedition in 1870. They spent one and one-half days in the basin and were so impressed by the regular eruptions that they named it Old Faithful.

Old Faithful does not erupt every hour, but varies somewhat depending upon how long the previous eruption was. A short one means the next will be sooner than "average," while a long eruption will result in a longer wait until the next. On average, Old Faithful spouts for about five minutes.

Other geysers are less regular but may erupt for much longer periods. For instance, Giantess is very irregular, erupting only a few times a year, but eruptions may last for thirty-six hours.

The Midway Geyser Basin lies along a one-mile stretch of the Firehole River. With only seven geysers, Midway is better known for its hot springs, including Grand Prismatic Spring, more than 370 feet across. It's the largest hot spring in the world.

Norris Geyser Basin is unusual in that its waters are acidic, primarily from sulfuric acid. Acidic water is rare in the other geyser basins of Yellowstone. Additionally, the water is hotter than at other basins in the park.

CLIMATE AND WEATHER

The Greater Yellowstone Ecosystem sits at a climatic crossroads. Air masses from the Arctic and Pacific Northwest meet there. Most patterns originate in the Pacific Northwest, which is characterized by a warm, moist climate. Before any air mass from this direction can reach Yellowstone, however, it must cross several major mountain ranges, including the Cascades and northern Rockies of Idaho and Montana. This wrings out a lot of moisture, so compared with areas closer to the ocean, Yellowstone's climate is cool and dry.

In winter, arctic air masses also slip down from Canada, usually bringing clear weather and subzero temperatures. Cold air usually travels up the major river valleys and along the edge of the plains east of the mountains. The constant alternation of these two air masses splits greater Yellowstone into major climatic regions. The western side of Yellowstone park and adjacent mountain ranges are influenced far more by Pacific Northwest patterns and tend to have higher winter precipitation and milder temperatures. For instance, the Pitchstone Plateau in the southwest corner of Yellowstone receives the greatest annual precipitation (80 inches), most of it as snow.

The eastern portion of the ecosystem such as the Wind Rivers and Absaroka Mountains near Cody and Lander, Wyoming, have more of a Great Plains climate, characterized by arctic cold fronts and drier winters. Precipitation is more evenly distributed, though there is a May-June peak. Occasionally, subtropical air flows in from the Gulf of Mexico via the Midwest, bringing summer thunderstorms and more rain along the mountains.

The most precipitation usually falls in May and June. Locals call this the June Monsoon. While valleys are likely to be lush, visitors are told that rain or even snow is possible during this period. Livingston, Montana, at 4,700 feet along the Yellowstone River, receives 35 percent of its annual precipitation (5.23 inches) in May and June. Cooke City, Montana, at 7,800 feet but in a mountain valley near the northeast corner of Yellowstone park, also receives its greatest precipitation in this period, 4.95 inches. July (2.31 inches) and August (2.17 inches) are also quite wet, reflecting the influence of summer mountain thundershowers.

Mountains and Climate

When Billings, Montana, at 3,200 feet, is sweltering in 100-degree heat, the 11,000-foot summit of the Beartooth Highway may be enjoying 60-degree weather, though it's only eighty miles away. The reason for this is decreased atmospheric pressure, which allows air to expand. Expansion causes heat loss, so for each 1,000-foot gain in elevation, there is a drop in temperature of 3.5 degrees.

Water cools and heats more slowly than air, so moist air moderates temperature changes. Dry air fluctuates more. After sunset, temperatures often drop quickly on cloudless nights, and the spread between the hottest and the coolest times may be as much as fifty degrees. On cloudy nights, the cover acts like a blanket, allowing less heat to radiate back into space, and temperature extremes are narrower.

Elevation also affects atmospheric pressure. At high elevations, pressure is lower, which means a person has to breathe harder just to take in the same amount of oxygen as at a lower elevation. Shortness of breath or sickness can result if you climb too high, too quickly, Altitude sickness—headaches, fatigue, and nausea—can be fatal if ignored.

Mountain and Valley Breezes

Mountains are popular with summer tourists because of their cool, gentle evening breezes. In the evening, as the atmosphere cools, a downslope breeze kicks up as cold air settles into basins and pockets. The air is sometimes funneled by trees, and a road or clearcut may provide a ready path. If the sinking air is frigid, it may prevent the growth of seedlings. This is one reason why reforestation is sometimes unsuccessful—logging changes cold-air drainage patterns. Basins are often blanketed with meadows while trees grow on adjacent benches and knobs.

Some communities, notably West Yellowstone, Montana, lie in high basins surrounded by mountains. Cold-air drainage often makes West Yellowstone one of the coldest spots in the United States in winter. West Yellowstone's 66 degrees below zero, set in 1933, was the national record (outside of Alaska) until a 70-below night in Rogers Pass, Montana, in 1954.

The sinking cold air is often under a layer of warmer air, especially in winter. Mountain valleys around greater Yellowstone, particularly Jackson Hole and West Yellowstone, often experience these inversions, which also trap pollution. Wood smoke and car exhaust can collect in deadly amounts during prolonged inversions and are a major health hazard in winter.

Snow greatly influences temperatures. It radiates heat back into space during long winter nights, decreasing the air temperature. However, the pack also is an insulator and the ground is seldom frozen. Rodents and other mammals survive the coldest winters while remaining active under the blanket.

Elevations and Orographic Effect

Air masses cool as they rise over a mountain range or plateau. Since cool air holds less moisture than warm, the vapor forms droplets, or clouds. This is called the orographic effect. The puffy clouds over mountains in the summer are formed this way. Towns next to mountains may have far greater precipitation because of this. Red Lodge, Montana, snuggled up against the Beartooth Mountains, averages 22.7 inches of precipitation a year. Pinedale, Wyoming, away from the mountain base, gets only 10.1 inches.

Air masses move from west to east, so western slopes get more precipitation from the orographic effect. Three Forks, Montana (elevation 4,080 feet), in the middle of the Gallatin Valley, gets 11.7 inches of precipitation a year, less than Tucson, Arizona! Close to the Gallatin and Bridger Range thirty miles to the southeast lies Bozeman (4,900 feet) with 18.6 inches; just three miles east, at Fort Ellis (5,200 feet) at the base of the Bridger Mountains, precipitation jumps to 25 inches per year.

The winter effects of orographic lift can be dramatic. Cooke City, Montana, near the northeast entrance of Yellowstone in the Absaroka Mountains, got 417 inches of snow in 1977–78. Highlands such as the Yellowstone Plateau receive as much as 150 inches (more than twelve feet) each winter.

Because moisture is wrung out of air masses in crossing mountains, valleys in the lee are frequently arid and dominated by clear, blue skies, even while the mountains may be cloaked in clouds. These are often

Gardiner, Montana, sits in a rain shadow of the Gallatin Range. It receives less than ten inches of precipitation a year, and the nearly snowless winters make this region a refuge for elk and antelope.

big-game wintering areas. Rain shadow areas include the northern Yellowstone park and upper Yellowstone Valley between Gardiner and Yankee Jim Canyon, Sunlight Basin, Taylor Fork in the Madison Range, Porcupine Basin in the Gallatin Range, and the Lamar Valley.

Once an air mass has crossed the mountain and begins to descend, it expands and warms, and thus can hold more moisture. Such air masses may even suck up moisture by sublimation as they descend, drying out the soils. Such drying winds in the winter are called chinooks, which is supposed to mean "snow eater" in some Indian tongues. It is not unusual for a chinook to strip away inches of snow in an afternoon. Surprisingly, the snow goes almost instantly from a solid to a vapor. A major chinook zone extends along the base of the Beartooth Mountains from Livingston to Big Timber. The average winter wind speed in Livingston is twenty-one miles per hour. Snow more than a foot deep, even in the middle of winter, is rare in the lower elevations along this belt.

River corridors, mountain passes, and other openings can funnel these winds into a hurricane force. Winds of sixty to eighty mph are common in Livingston in the winter. The saving grace is that these winds are usually warm. Big Timber and Livingston are the winter "banana belt" of Montana, averaging about 26 degrees. This is warmer than Des Moines, Iowa, or Chicago, Illinois.

The entire region enjoys low humidity; the average in Cody and Jackson is 50 percent, and they are fairly typical. The cold does not penetrate or feel as icy as it might otherwise. Low humidity and abundant sunshine make winters in many GYE towns far more tolerable than in most of the Midwest and Northeast. Low humidity also makes the summer heat more comfortable.

Thunderstorms

Summer thunderstorms and showers are common, especially over the mountains. Thunderheads are produced when air that has been heated over lowland valleys rises rapidly, forming towering anvil-shaped clouds. In some very high mountain ranges like the Beartooths and Wind Rivers, thunderheads may develop almost every afternoon.

The rising thunderheads develop negatively charged bottoms and positive tops. Sometimes the bottom will be grounded to the positively charged earth and you get a lightning strike. (It tends to strike pinnacles, so get off a mountaintop or ridge during a lightning storm. Otherwise, you may be the highest point.) A lightning discharge superheats the air, causing it to expand tremendously, then contract just as suddenly. It "explodes," and we hear thunder.

The rising water vapor eventually reaches cool air, which condenses it into droplets. Rain begins to fall, sometimes in sheets. If the air is cool enough, the droplets freeze, and updrafts shoot them back up, where layers of ice build. Hail continues to grow until it is so heavy that it falls to earth. Hailstones up to five inches wide have been documented, and some have killed animals and people.

When Is the Best Time to Visit?

Spring weather begins in mid-April and continues through early July above 9,000 feet. For those who like everything green, this may be the most attractive time. However, most rivers are muddy with spring runoff. Fishing is not particularly good, except during the famous salmon fly hatch, which begins in late May or early June, depending upon the river or stream. Backpacking in the higher mountains is nearly impossible, since snow still blocks most trails.

Summer begins in early June at the lowest elevations and not until mid-July above 10,000 feet. Except for thunderstorms, most summers are dry. Even if a shower develops, by the next morning, the sky is usually clear and blue again.

Temperatures in the lowlands will often exceed 90 degrees, and occasionally 100. Evenings are almost always cool. At higher elevations, temperatures over eighty degrees are unusual.

Higher meadows remain green all summer and wildflowers bloom right into early September. In the valleys after mid-July, grasslands begin to turn brown, except for irrigated fields. After mid-July, most of the runoff is gone and rivers clear up, improving the fishing. High mountain lakes thaw by early to mid-July in most areas, and the fishing can be good. Most trails are clear of snow by mid-July, but snow lingers into August on some of the highest north-facing slopes.

Autumn begins in early September at the highest elevations and may continue until early November in lowlands. Most meadows are golden brown, while the aspen, cottonwood, and other deciduous trees begin to change color. Fresh snow is possible in the mountains, adding a white backdrop to the golden trees in the valleys.

Fall days have a real magic. The light is so clear that distant mountains stand out sharply. Days can be very warm, while nights are cool or even cold. At higher elevations, snow and temperatures of zero are possible during September. Unlike the winter, such extremes do not last. Within a few days, the warmth and sunshine usually return.

September is a good time to visit because even popular recreation areas are almost deserted. Places to camp and fish are plentiful. This is also the time to try backpacking in some of the more popular wilderness areas like the Bridger, Jedediah Smith, and Absaroka-Beartooth.

Hiking, even at the highest elevations, is usually good up until the end of September or mid-October, but be prepared for extreme temperatures.

Cooler weather increases trout activity, and fall is when elk begin to bugle and waterfowl begin to pass through the region. Depending upon the species and the state, hunting seasons usually run from early September into December or later. Nonhunters are urged to wear blaze orange when afield at this time of year.

Winter begins in earnest around the middle of November and continues till March or April, depending upon elevation. The weather varies considerably throughout the region, but the lowest temperatures are in December, January, and February. Many areas enjoy warm, sunny winter days, though nights will still have temperatures in the 20s or lower. Temperatures of 40 below or more do occur and must be expected at higher elevations.

The best skiing is found from mid-January into April. March or early April is often best for winter camping, since snows are deep and days are longer.

FLORA

There are at least 1,700 plants in the Greater Yellowstone Ecosystem. This is about the major plant communities, their ecology, and some of the prominent species.

Ecological Tolerance

The distribution and number of plants are not accidental. Each plant's community is influenced by soil type, moisture, topography, wind, fire, and animal and human influences. A species' ability to cope with drought, cold, or poor soils determines where it will live.

Lodgepole pine has a great ecological tolerance, being able to grow in well-drained sites or saturated ones. Lodgepole does require a lot of sun, so this is its limiting factor. Take a walk through the lodgepole forest in Yellowstone and you will see few saplings under mature trees. The canopy blocks out too much light. So long as there is plenty of light, lodgepole flourishes. It is the most widespread tree in the ecosystem.

Other plants have narrow ecological tolerances. Often, they are rare and found in specific habitats, such as the algae in some of Yellowstone's thermal springs and basins. They require temperatures between 122 and 140 degrees Fahrenheit.

Factors Influencing Plants

Regardless of ecological tolerance, environmental factors dictate plant patterns. Dry, south-facing slopes are harsh sites for many plants. Only drought-resistant plants are found here, typically grasses that grow while moisture is high but go dormant (turn golden brown) as the soil dries out. At the same time, the cool north slopes at the same elevation are more prone to frost, but the greater moisture permits trees.

Subtle changes in slope can influence vegetation. A gully may trap wind-blown snow or receive sun for a slightly shorter period during the day, allowing moisture-loving plants to grow where they wouldn't otherwise. Timber often marks the damper gullies while grasses blanket the dry, exposed slopes.

The width of a valley also influences timber cover. Because mountains wring moisture from air, narrow valleys tend to receive more precipitation than wide ones at a similar elevation and can support more trees. Compare the broad, grassy valleys of the Yellowstone River south of Livingston and the upper Madison by Ennis, both at about 4,900 feet, to the narrow, timbered valley of the upper Gallatin at about 5,800 feet. The Yellowstone and Madison valleys are six to eight miles across, while the Gallatin Canyon is no more than a mile wide.

Cool-air drainage also affects plants. In many subalpine basins, cold air will sink so that the low ground is often fifteen to twenty degrees cooler than the slopes. This is enough to keep wildflower meadows free of trees while slopes and knolls are forested.

The timberline marks the limit of forest growth on mountainsides. Below the lower timberline (6,000 to 7,500 feet), moisture is too meager to support trees. The upper timberline is at approximately 9,500 feet. Conditions above it generally are too cold for trees. At the extreme limits for growth are stunted trees called krummholz.

Yellowstone is huge but has only nine types of trees. Great Smoky Mountains National Park in North Carolina and Tennessee is one-thirty-sixth its size yet has more than 130 species. Why?

Yellowstone isn't all that hospitable to trees. It has a short growing season. Moisture and temperature vary a lot. Also, 10,000 years ago, most of the GYE uplands were covered with glaciers, and there actually has been little time for new trees to evolve or colonize the area. Yet, glacial periods also contributed to the region's plant diversity. As many as half of the plants in the alpine tundra of the Beartooth Plateau are arctic relicts and remain isolated on the highest mountains.

Soils also influence where plants grow. Pine can grow on sandy soils with as little as twelve inches of annual precipitation, but on the fine glacial loess (soil deposited by wind during the ice ages) of eastern Washington's Palouse Prairie, only grasses grow even where twenty-five inches of precipitation falls. The fine materials inhibit deep water penetration, allowing grasses to capture most of it. Within Yellowstone, the Hayden and Pelican valleys are veneered with fine soils that settled out of glacial lakes, and both are covered with meadows instead of forests.

Another major factor is fire. Only a few plants are adapted to it and they tend to dominate wherever fire is common. Lodgepole pine readily grows back in burned areas and actually thrives from periodic fires.

Plant Succession

Plant succession is the gradual change in flora as growing conditions change. After a fire, an area may be host to plants that require a lot of light, such as lodgepole pine. After thirty to forty years, the canopy reduces the amount of light needed by young pines. Then shade-loving plants, such as subalpine fir, sprout. If there is no fire or other disturbance, the fir dominates the site after 300 to 400 years. After this, change slows and one fir simply is replaced by another. This is a *climax community*. It will perpetuate until a major disturbance starts the process again.

Vegetation Zones

Plants change as elevation increases. Each zone has a different set of growing conditions—temperature, moisture, season, and wind. The lowest valleys are dry and often warm, at least in the summer. They generally are too arid for trees, except for areas next to water. This zone, usually from 4,000 or 5,000 feet to 6,500 feet, is cloaked with grass or sagebrush.

As elevation and moisture increase, the grass generally gives way to closed forests of Douglas fir, often mixed with aspen. This zone lies between 6,500 and 7,500 feet. Douglas fir is a major species elsewhere but grows in a narrow belt in most of the GYE. It is typically the only conifer between grassland and forest, but some areas have scattered stands of Rocky Mountain juniper and limber pine. Juniper and limber pine are not common in the GYE and are usually associated with windy or very dry sites, such as the stretch along the Gardner River between Gardiner and Mammoth, limestone outcrops along the chinook belt between Livingston and Big Timber, and well-drained moraines in Jackson Hole.

The Douglas fir and aspen give way to lodgepole pine around 7,600 feet. It often forms pure stands, particularly at the lower limits of its range, but in the wetter, higher sites, Englemann spruce and subalpine fir may replace the pine and dominate forests up to the timberline at 9,500 to 10,000 feet. In the most severe timberline areas, there are occasional stands of stunted subalpine fir and whitebark pine. At the highest elevations, trees give way to alpine tundra, dominated by sedges, dwarf shrubs, and cushion plants.

Brook saxifrage is a common flower along ungrazed riparian areas in the ecosystem.

Major Plant Communities

RIPARIAN *page 207*

These are thin lines of vegetation, typically along the banks of lakes, streams, rivers, and springs. They are a transition between aquatic communities and drier uplands. Dominated by water-loving plants such as cottonwood, willow, alder, water birch, aspen, sedges, cattails, monkeyflower, saxifrage, monkshood, mosses, and bluegrass, riparian areas are dense with thickets, grass, and sometimes large trees. Though much of the West is arid, riparian areas have much more in common with eastern forests. Water is abundant and most riparian plants never have to adapt to aridity.

One of the most prominent riparian trees is the cottonwood. Mature cottonwoods have a rough, thick, gray bark and large leaves that turn a beautiful gold in the fall. Greater Yellowstone has three cottonwoods: the black, narrowleaf, and plains. Black cottonwood occupies the highest elevations in the foothills and mountains, plains cottonwood grows at the lowest elevations, and narrowleaf is in between. The narrowleaf has lance-shaped leaves, while the others have larger, heart-shaped ones. Narrowleaf dominates the upper Yellowstone River Valley in the park and Paradise Valley north of there. The lower Yellowstone has plains cottonwood. Narrowleaf is also the common riparian tree around Jackson Hole.

Cottonwood has made several riparian adaptations. It produces tiny cottonlike seeds that are shed during the spring flood. These are carried onto a gravel bar or island, where they get established. Cottonwoods also reproduce by sending up shoots that may form new trees. Beavers may assure a supply of this favored food by chewing at branches and shoots and leaving cuttings around to take root.

Cottonwoods grow rapidly, and their large boles are important for wildlife. Many birds nest in them, woodpeckers seek out their large branches for food, and even after the trees die and fall into streams, they provide habitat for fish and other life.

Blue spruce is another riparian tree, found along the Gros Ventre and Hoback rivers in Wyoming and elsewhere in the Bridger-Teton National Forest. More typical of Colorado and Utah, blue spruce reaches its northern range limit in southern greater Yellowstone, where it forms stringers along rivers. It sometimes hybridizes with Englemann spruce.

Common riparian shrubs are buffaloberry, red dogwood, thinleaf alder, water birch, serviceberry, and several willows: Geyser's, Bebb's, blueberry, and Wolf's.

Riparian areas constitute less than 1 percent of the landscape, but their lushness makes them critical to wildlife. Many warblers nest and forage in riparian thickets, small mammals find shelter from weather and predators, and tall trees provide nesting for eagles, woodpeckers, and owls. Studies show that 75 to 80 percent of Western wildlife depends on riparian areas for survival. Moose and grizzly bear may move between mountain ranges through riparian cover, and bats and birds may depend on the food and shelter along streams during migration.

Wildlife found in riparian habitats includes the yellow warbler, MacGillivray's warbler, red-winged blackbird, Brewer's blackbird, belted kingfisher, killdeer, great blue heron, great horned owl, mink, otter, beaver, muskrat, whitetail deer, and moose.

Riparian areas aid the environment. The roots of trees, shrubs, sedges, and grasses bind the soil, stabilizing stream banks and slowing erosion. The vegetation purifies runoff, trapping silt before it can reach a stream. The deep soil stores water for late-season flow.

Sadly, most riparian areas have suffered degradation. Highway construction has diverted stream channels and removed vegetation. Dams have reduced flooding and disrupted peak water flows. The worst offense has been domestic livestock grazing. In the arid West, cattle spend most of their time in riparian areas. They destroy vegetation during the growing season and trample stream banks, pulverize seeps and springs, and compact the soil, reducing absorption and increasing erosion.

The long-term health of the Greater Yellowstone Ecosystem demands protection of riparian habitats. Land managers, planners, developers, and ranchers must recognize that the "thin, green lines" are really holding the ecosystem together.

GRASSLAND AND SHRUB STEPPE   *page 207*

Grass and shrubs dominate the lower elevations, dry, south-facing slopes, and well-drained benchlands and uplands of the ecosystem. Perennial grasses that grow in scattered bunches are prevalent. They include bluebunch wheatgrass, needle and thread grass, Idaho fescue, and junegrass. Great Basin wild rye and thickstem wheatgrass grow in bottomlands.

These are cool-season grasses because they grow in early spring and summer, when moisture is highest. When summer drought arrives, they become dormant. They turn brown, but the roots are still alive and if rain falls in autumn, the grasses will turn green again until winter.

Mixed with the grasses are shrubs such as spiny hopsage, saltbrush, winterfat, and greasewood. Junegrass, bluebunch wheatgrass, Indian ricegrass, and prickly pear cactus also are found.

Moister sites are dominated by Idaho fescue and bluebunch wheatgrass with wildflowers such as balsamroot, wyethia, lupine, and yarrow. Shrubs include rubber rabbitbrush, green rabbitbrush, bitterbrush, and one type of big sagebrush. Great Basin big sage is found on deep soils and may reach six to eight feet. Mountain big sage is found up to 9,000 feet or on

Rabbitbrush bears yellow flowers in the fall. It is typically found with the grassland-sage plant communities, whose diverse grasses and shrubs provide a variety of wildlife habitats.

dry, southwest-facing slopes. Wyoming big sage is common in dry, shallow soils such as in the Green River Valley south of Pinedale.

Rocky Mountain juniper and limber pine are sometimes found in grasslands. The shrubby juniper has scalelike needles and is typically gnarled. Its cones, or "juniper berries," are fleshy and blue. Limber pine has soft, flexible branches and an open, spreading habit. It is often found in dry, wind-swept areas. It is common along the Gardner River in Yellowstone and the zone between the plains and foothills north of the Beartooth Range in Montana.

Grassland and shrubland wildlife include antelope, bison, bighorn sheep, white-tailed jackrabbit, Uinta ground squirrel, badger, sage grouse, western meadowlark, savannah sparrow, vesper sparrow, Brewer's sparrow, kestrel, nighthawk, brown-headed cowbird, golden eagle, prairie falcon, black-billed magpie, and red-tailed hawk.

Grasslands dominate areas where soil moisture is limited for at least a portion of the year and where there is tremendous precipitation variation from year to year. Grasses and wildflowers survive drought by sprouting, growing, and setting seed during the spring and early summer, when soil moisture is high. Then the above-ground portions die back. The seeds are released and pass through the dry season unharmed.

Because of drought, fires used to be common before the days of modern firefighting, often occurring every ten to twenty years. Since fires usually occur after grasses and flowers have gone to seed, there usually is little longterm damage to the grassland ecosystem. In fact, fires remove plant litter and add fertilizing ashes.

Many shrubs also adapt to drought. Big sagebrush can grow several kinds of leaves, so that when moisture is abundant, it puts out large, efficient leaves, and during drought it retains only smaller, more water-conserving ones.

Mountain big sage, the most common sagebrush in the ecosystem, is usually killed by fires, so an abundance of sagebrush may indicate fire suppression or overgrazing. Livestock eats grass, which competes with sagebrush for water. Also, removing the grass and reducing plant litter make it more difficult for fires to spread, further protecting the sagebrush. In fact, fire suppression eventually favors the return of trees into grass- and shrublands. Photos taken in the last century show that many areas now forested were once grasslands. Trees were restricted to rocky sites or other "fireproof" places.

Grass- and shrublands are important to wildlife. They provide 80 percent of the winter diet of elk, 60 percent of the winter diet of bighorn sheep, and all of the bison's forage year-round. Antelope and mule deer depend on sagebrush in winter.

MEADOWS AND PARKS

There are meadows at higher elevations because cold-air drainage and frosts can prevent the establishment of trees. Other sites are too wet to support trees and are dominated by sedges, grasses, shrubs, and wild-flowers. Some meadows, such as those in Hayden Valley, have fine-textured soils that favor grasses over trees. Common meadow species are sedges, tufted hairgrass, slender wheatgrass, mountain brome, oat-grass, and slender Idaho fescue. Shrubs include shrubby cinquefoil in drier sites and dwarf birch, willows, and rushes in wetter areas.

The broad, veined leaves of the false hellebore indicate its membership in the lily family. Lupine, easily recognized by its fingered leaves, belongs to the pea family. It blooms in early summer.

These meadows and parklands are known for the wildflowers that sweep through every summer. Aster, paintbrush, gentian, geranium, glacier lily, lupine, iris, larkspur, marsh marigold, monkshood, grass of parnassus, mountain bluebell, and penstemon paint the uplands in a succession of colors beginning with the melting of snow.

Many people believe grasses are transitory and expendable, but most can live decades, sometimes centuries. There may even be old-growth grasslands, just like there are old-growth forests. Harsh conditions keep grasses from seeding every year, and seedlings don't usually survive. Only under the best conditions can grasslands regenerate. Excessive grazing is no different than clearcutting a forest. The main difference is that it occurs annually instead of once a century. The effects of overgrazing may take centuries to correct, just as severe overcutting can damage forests for generations.

DOUGLAS FIR   *page 207*

This is not a fir at all. One giveaway is that the cones hang down, unlike the upright cones of true firs. Its cones also are distinguished by the three-tipped bracts on their scales. These trees often reach 400 to 600 years of age in Yellowstone and are quite stout. The thick, corky gray-brown bark is fire resistant, an adaption to frequent grassland fires. Many older Douglas firs are fire scarred.

In Yellowstone, Douglas fir grows in a narrow zone between the lower grasslands and the main forest belt. This ribbon of land ranges from 6,500 to 7,000 feet up to 8,000 feet or higher in the Gallatin, Madison, and Beartooth ranges of Montana, and along the Yellowstone and Lamar rivers in northern Yellowstone park. There are extensive stands of Douglas Fir in the Clarks Fork of the Yellowstone Valley, Sunlight Basin, and North Fork of the Shoshone River in Wyoming. The tree is often found growing in savannahlike settings with pinegrass and flowers such as arnica, Oregon grape, and lupine. In some areas, ninebark, snowberry, Rocky Mountain maple, serviceberry, red dogwood, and thimbleberry accompany it.

In some places, Douglas fir appears to replace lodgepole pine and grows up to 9,000 feet in dense stands. Ranges dominated by Douglas fir include the Centennials on the Idaho-Montana line, the west slope of the Teton Range in Wyoming, the Snake River Range (Palisades) in Idaho and Wyoming, and the Caribou Mountains of Idaho. Wildlife seen in these areas includes mule deer, elk, moose, snowshoe hare, red squirrel, brushy-tailed woodrat, yellow-bellied marmot (if there are rocks), red-backed vole, pocket gopher, northern flicker, black-capped chickadee, mountain chickadee, ruffed grouse, great horned owl, mountain bluebird, red-tailed hawk, western tanager, pine siskin, dark-eyed junco, evening grosbeak, tree swallow, and ruby-crowned kinglet.

ASPEN   *page 208*

With its graceful, straight, greenish gray trunks and round, green leaves, aspen is one of the most beautiful and conspicuous trees in the region. It is relatively rare—constituting, for example, only 2 percent of the vegetation on the northern range in Yellowstone park. Because it grows in valleys and foothills where people live and play, aspen seems more common than it is. It is more abundant from the Tetons southward, including areas of the Palisades, Caribou, Salt River, and Wyoming ranges and Yellowstone's foothill fringes.

Aspen is fast growing and short lived. A sapling can grow ten feet tall in three years and mature in 100 years. Most groves in the ecosystem are 100 years old or less and usually are established after a disturbance. For instance, a beaver may gnaw at a tree, prompting the growth of new shoots from the roots. These "suckers" start most aspen groves. Because the parent grove and the new one are genetically identical, the two will have the same bud development and colors. The relationships are most apparent in the fall, when groves turn color at different times.

Few aspens are produced from seeds, which are tiny and require a lot of moisture, a real drawback in many parts of the West. Many biologists believed that nearly all the aspen groves in the Rockies were established at the close of the Ice Age under wetter conditions. These groves persisted, it was thought, by suckering. But after the Yellowstone fires in 1988, many aspen seedlings were found in the park, raising a possible connection between large fires and aspen regeneration. This may not be apparent when fires are smaller or suppressed.

In some areas, wild animals and cattle eat aspen suckers and seedlings, hindering reproduction. In Yellowstone, elk gnaw on lower trunks, causing dark, rough scars around the boles from six to eight feet up. This discourages further trunk munching, and mature aspens probably are not seriously hurt. However, elk also eat aspen seedlings, and some park service critics believe elk browsing may be eliminating aspen from Yellowstone's northern range. Outside the park, cattle have the same effect.

Flowers and shrubs often associated with aspen groves include timothy, cow parsnip, tall larkspur, geranium, wild rose, columbine, fireweed, Queen Anne's lace, and bluebells. In the southern part of the ecosystem, big-toothed maple is mixed with aspen. This small tree's leaves turn bright red or orange in fall. It is most common from the Snake River Canyon southward, including the Salt River Range and Caribou and Snake River mountains.

Wildlife associated with aspen include beaver, white-footed deer mouse, meadow vole, long-tailed vole, elk, ruffed grouse, violet-green swallow, yellow warbler, warbling vireo, yellow-rumped warbler, tree swallow, yellow-bellied sapsucker, American robin, mountain bluebird, mountain chickadee, and Swainson's thrush.

LODGEPOLE PINE   *page 208*

Pollen research shows that lodgepoles grew in the Yellowstone park area 10,000 years ago, after the retreat of the Ice Age glaciers. It remains the region's most common conifer; four out of five trees are lodgepoles. It is particularly abundant from 7,600 to 9,000 feet, where it is often the only tree seen over thousands of acres.

Lodgepole gets its name from its straight boles, which the Indians used in tepees and lodges. This arrowlike growth and its dense stands distinguish lodgepole. It has short, paired, one- to two-inch needles. Other Yellowstone pines have needles in bundles of fives. Its round cones are no bigger than one to two inches wide.

Little may grow under a lodgepole forest. Common wildflowers include lupine, heartleaf arnica, and Indian paintbrush.

This pine demands full sun. It grows in recently burned areas and has several advantages over other species. It can grow rapidly and mature quickly; a lodgepole just five to ten years old can produce cones. Also, because of the density of most lodgepole stands and the sparse undergrowth, there is little fuel for fires until the trees mature. The low light also kills off the pines' lower branches. This self-pruning further protects trees from a fatal fire that could reach up into the crown. At 90 to 150 years of age, the canopy opens enough to allow undergrowth.

Since the dense canopy inhibits the sprouting of seeds, most lodgepole stands are eventually replaced by more shade-tolerant trees such as subalpine fir. Ironically, to remain dominant, lodgepole pine requires a natural disturbance to open the canopy and enable young pines to establish themselves.

Mountain pine beetle provides one source of disturbance. The beetle can only successfully attack older, weaker pines. It lays its eggs beneath the bark. After hatching, the larvae girdle this layer, cutting off the flow of nutrients along the trunk. The beetle also infects the tree with a potentially lethal fungus. Over ten or fifteen years, enough trees will die to relieve the crowding that led to the infestation. The survivors are stronger and better able to resist beetle attacks.

Many foresters attempt to short-circuit the cycle of aging, disease, and renewal by cutting trees at or near the prime beetle infestation age. This rarely works. Look at the Island Park District of the Targhee National Forest, where nearly all the mature lodgepole pines were cut. The beetle didn't retreat until there were no trees left to attack. How can you "save" a forest by wiping it out? An infested forest is not damaged, merely changed. If anything, logging destroys the forest ecosystem, because it disrupts the age-old lodgepole-beetle relationship.

Standing dead trees do not add to the fire hazard. Live trees, with their resins, are actually more likely to burn. What does increase the chance are young lodgepoles or subalpine fir that help ground fires move into the canopy. A crown fire usually kills the dominant trees. In the GYE, a forest is susceptible to crown fires after 200 to 400 years.

Lodgepole forests have been called biological deserts. Indeed, they aren't too diverse, but there is still much to see and hear. Mammals include snowshoe hare, red squirrel, red-backed vole, yellow-pine chipmunk, and an occasional moose, elk, or deer. There are mountain chickadee, sharp-shinned hawk, Cooper's hawk, red-breasted nuthatch, gray jay, raven, ruffed grouse, great gray owl, three-toed woodpecker, Townsend's solitaire, chipping sparrow, and yellow-rumped warbler.

SPRUCE AND FIR   *page 208*

These trees grow above 8,400 feet. The Englemann spruce and subalpine fir like moist environments and are found along stream courses, in cirque basins at higher elevations, or wherever soil is moist.

Englemann spruce may be four to five feet in diameter. Its cones droop from the branches and only grow at the top third of the tree. They are 1½ to 2½ inches long with soft, papery scales. The needles are about an inch long, four-sided and sharp—you'll probably wince if you grab a branch quickly. The bark is often reddish with thin, quarter-sized scales.

Subalpine fir typically has smooth, gray, resin-blistered bark and soft, one-inch needles. Fir cones are two to four inches long, cylindrical, and grow upright off the branches. These purple cones are seldom found on the ground intact because they disintegrate on the tree.

Though spruce and fir branches usually come down the trunk to the ground, the fir's silhouette is linear, almost spikelike, with a distinct narrow crown. The branches of spruce bend away from the trunk closer to a 90-degree angle, more like a Christmas tree than the fir's.

In the GYE, subalpine fir often reaches further up on mountain slopes than Englemann spruce. Stunted and wind-sheared, it can be found near the timberline. Occasionally, snow will force lower branches to the ground. They will sometimes take root, forming a circle around the parent.

Because they are found at higher elevations, few visitors other than backcountry hikers have the chance to see a spruce-fir forest. However, you can see them from the road at Dunraven Pass in Yellowstone, Teton Pass near Jackson, Togwotee Pass between Dubois and Jackson, Sylvan Pass between Cody and Yellowstone, and the Beartooth Highway between Red Lodge and Cooke City.

Because of the deep snows and moist summer soils, wildfires are rare in this zone. Neither species has developed any particular fire protection; in fact, Indians used to torch subalpine fir as we might set off fireworks. Once a fire does begin in these volatile woods, it can spread rapidly.

The undergrowth of the shady spruce and fir forests includes Labrador tea, heartleaf arnica, lupine, western meadowrue, false Solomon's seal, glacier lilies, twisted stalk, Calypso orchid, and mountain bluebells. In the northern Absaroka Range in Montana and portions of southeastern

Old-growth forests, like this stand near Tie Creek in the Gallatin National Forest, are characterized by an abundance of fallen logs and snags, several canopy layers, and large-bole trees.

Yellowstone and the northern Tetons, showy beargrass is often seen.

In summer, deer, elk, moose, and grizzly bear roam the spruce-fir forests. Also common are red squirrel, pine martin, red-backed vole, deer mouse, and yellow-pine chipmunk. Birds include three-toed woodpecker, gray jay, northern goshawk, blue grouse, pine grosbeak, red crossbill, pine siskin, ruby-crowned kinglet, mountain chickadee, Townsend's solitaire, American robin, and Steller's jay.

WHITEBARK PINE   *page 208*

This is a timberline tree, often scattered in groves among subalpine fir. It looks a lot like limber pine and both have needles in bundles of five. However, whitebark has lighter gray bark and its cones are round and two to three inches long. The limber pine has oblong, three- to six inch cones. Whitebark is open and spreading and usually grows on wind-swept ridges or in subalpine basins.

Periodic fires are important for whitebark pine. It requires bare mineral soil and full sunlight for germination. Without fires, subalpine fir forces whitebark from the best growing sites, and pine is eventually restricted to rocky ridges that are less suitable for fir.

It appears to depend on Clark's nutcrackers to disperse its seed. Red squirrels gather whitebark cones and cache them underground for winter food. Grizzlies are fond of the nutritious pine nut, especially in the fall, brazenly snatching the squirrels' supplies.

Whitebark pine is an important species but rare in the GYE. It is most abundant in the Absaroka, Beartooth, and Wind River ranges; unfortunately, it is declining throughout its Rocky Mountain range from fire suppression and disease. The loss would be a severe hardship on wildlife, and the government has recently been petitioned to declare the whitebark endangered.

ALPINE TUNDRA   *page 208*

This is seen at the highest elevations, generally above 10,000 feet. The growing season is short, often less than two months, with frost always possible. In the thin atmosphere, solar radiation is intense during the day and nighttime cooling is extreme. Temperatures may vary as much as fifty degrees in a day. Since many alpine areas have only recently been deglaciated, soils are often poor. Finally, winds are continuous and strong.

Alpine plants cope with the conditions in various ways. Nearly 85 percent of an alpine plant is underground, with only leaves and flowers exposed. This reduces the energy required to grow a stem and numerous leaves. Many plants have evolved into special forms, such as low mats or cushions. These shapes reduce wind-abrasion and water loss. Plants also benefit from warm microclimates, such as pockets or dips in the ground.

Despite their small size, many alpine plants have large blossoms to attract pollinators. In this gusty place, most pollination is done by strong flying insects, in particular bumblebees, butterflies, and flies, not honey-bees. Some plants have parabolic flowers that track the sun, concentrating solar energy in the blossom. This provides a warm retreat for insects, aiding pollination.

Some alpine plants, such as dryas or mountain avens, take advantage of the wind, producing feathery seeds that are often blown great distances. The wind also helps to blow pollen from plant to plant.

Many alpine plants also can photosynthesize at lower temperatures than species from lower elevations. They may also sprout numerous hairs that not only trap warmth but also reduce water losses by blocking wind immediately next to the leaf. Alpine tundra is frozen much of the year and is often rocky and well drained, so some plants have adapted to drought. They develop a thick, waxy coating on the leaves that slows water loss.

Because of the short growing season, most alpine flowers live more than one year. Many may take five to ten years to store enough energy to blossom. This is one reason why alpine vegetation is so vulnerable to disturbance, and recovery is slow.

Alpine areas have dwarf shrubs like arctic willow, glaucous willow, and bog birch that grow no more than a foot or two in height.

Alpine wildflowers include mountain sorrel, American bistort, alpine spring beauty, pygmy bitterroot, alpine sandwort, alpine chickweed, moss campion, pasqueflower, subalpine buttercup, purple mountain saxifrage, mountain avens, yellow avens, alpine milkvetch, mountain heath, alpine shooting star, Douglassia, sky pilot, alpine forget-me-not, elephant's head, alpine speedwell, Parry's primrose, and alpine hawkweed. Typical animals are pika, yellow-bellied marmot, mountain goat, bighorn sheep, golden eagle, water pipit, and rosy-crowned finch.

Alpine tundra is relatively common in the GYE. The most extensive

Beartooth Pass in Custer National Forest, Montana, is above timberline. A low, mat-forming growth habit is one of alpine plants' special adaptations to the harsh tundra environment.

tracts are in the Beartooth Mountains, where nearly three-quarters of the range is above the timberline. The Madison Range, the North Absaroka, Washakie, and Teton wildernesses, the Wind River Range, and the Gros Ventre Mountains of Wyoming also support large alpine areas.

The best place to see alpine tundra from the road is along the Beartooth Highway between Red Lodge and Cooke City. This highway passes over 11,000-foot Beartooth Pass and remains above the timberline for miles.

Most alpine tundras are too high for cattle, but domestic sheep graze in some areas, including the Bridger, Absaroka-Beartooth, and Jedediah Smith wildernesses and the Centennial and Wyoming ranges. In many places, selective sheep grazing has turned flowered meadows into grasslands. No one has studied the long-term impact of sheep grazing on these fragile environments.

FIRE ECOLOGY

The summer of 1988 will be remembered as the season Yellowstone burned. When the last flames flickered out in November, the fire perimeter covered more than 1.4 million acres. A furious debate ensued about the role of wildfire and fire management. Critics argued that federal agencies irresponsibly let the fires rage. Agency supporters and fire ecologists said that, sometimes, nature is still largely beyond human control.

Normally, the forests of the Greater Yellowstone Ecosystem are basically unflammable. Some have called them the "asbestos" forests. The overall elevation, more than 8,000 feet, and the heavy snow cover for seven to nine months of the year create little opportunity for fires. The forests don't dry out enough to carry a large fire until at least mid-August, and by then the first snows are dusting the higher peaks. Computer modeling by the U.S. Forest Service Fire Research Lab in Missoula, Montana, suggest that in most years, Yellowstone is simply too wet to burn.

The region's fire history can be followed by studying fire scars on old trees and snags. Each fire leaves scar tissue on the survivors. By examining tree rings and scars, it is possible to pinpoint the times of major fires. Such studies have shown that there have been fires much larger than those that burned across the park in 1988.

The higher forests generally are swept by a major blaze every 200 to 400 years. The exceptions are the lower grasslands such as the Yellowstone Valley near Gardiner or along the North Fork of the Shoshone near Cody, where fires every twenty years or less appear to have been normal before the time of modern firefighting.

Before 1988, the last major fires in the ecosystem were in 1750 and 1850. Some parts of the park and nearby areas had not burned for 300 to 400 years. Over such a period, dead trees, snags, and litter accumulate on the forest floor, providing fuel. The area was ripe for a fire, but this alone didn't account for the 1988 fire. Another factor was the invasion of Yellowstone's lodgepole pine forests by subalpine fir. Fir can literally burst into flames, and their branching pattern provides a "ladder" by which fires can climb and sweep from tree to tree.

Even with enough fuel, a fire still has to be started. Lightning is the usual way in greater Yellowstone. Tens of thousands of lightning strikes occur annually, but few start a fire. Even among those that do, nearly all the fires fizzle out quickly. Research in other parks and regions of the West and Alaska shows similar patterns. Also, the vast majority of acreage burned in any fire season results from a handful of blazes.

Even during the extreme drought of 1988, 80 percent of the fires burned ten acres or less, but the largest were giants. The North Fork fire burned 504,025 acres; the Clover Mist, 319,575; and the Huck, 227,525. Note that these figures represent the perimeter of a fire's advance, not the actual acres scorched. Most burned in a mosaic pattern, leaving many areas singed or untouched. Less than 1 percent, or 22,000 acres, saw a "hot" fire.

The fire conditions in 1988 were extraordinary. It took hundreds of years for so much deadwood, snags, and litter to pile up, but there was just as much fuel in 1978 as in 1988, so why didn't Yellowstone burn then? Many critics say that park service fire suppression had allowed too much fuel to build up, but those efforts began only thirty to forty years ago, and in most years fires are rare anyway. So it's safe to assume that suppression wasn't a major factor. Fuel and lightning alone will not sustain major fires.

The key factor appears to be severe drought. The summer of 1988 was the driest on record. By the end of July 1988, moisture content of grasses and forest litter was as low as 2 to 3 percent. Kiln-dried lumber is 12 percent moisture.

However, drought was not the reason the fires were so large. A review of all large U.S. forest fires invariably implicates the wind. It drove flames through the forest; more importantly, it carried embers far beyond the fires and started new ones, what firefighters call spotting.

Spotting makes fire suppression nearly impossible. In 1988, winds regularly tossed burning brands a mile or more in front of a fire's perimeter. The fires even jumped the mile-wide Grand Canyon of the Yellowstone. One run of the Storm Creek Fire galloped nine miles in just four hours! On August 20, "Black Saturday," 60-mph winds drove fires through more than 150,000 acres. Nearly half of the acreage that burned during the

Far from destroying Yellowstone, the fires of 1988 created new ecological possibilities: elk now graze on nutrient-rich regrowth, for example, and the abundant snags provide nesting cavities for birds like woodpeckers and bluebirds.

entire season occurred over just four different days.

During the height of the fires, nearly 10,000 firefighters, including military units, were on the job. Some 665 miles of hand-dug fire lines and 137 miles of bulldozer lines were gouged from the Earth, to little effect. Total firefighting costs came to $120 million, yet firefighters generally felt that their efforts had little real impact. Five out of the eight major fires were fought hard from the moment they were reported, and still the flames leapt higher. Snow on September 10, not firefighters, brought the blazes under control.

Ecological Consequences of the Fires

Scientists have long recognized the importance of wildfire for the ecological health of Western ecosystems. Fires cleanse a forest. The heat kills insects and disease, and even the smoke destroys some forest pathogens. Fires also recycle nutrients. Eastern forests are fertilized when dead trees, snags, and leaves molder back into soil, but the West is generally too dry and cold for that. So fire returns important nutrients for new plant growth.

Fires also enrich aquatic ecosystems. Runoff carries ash and nutrients into waterways and may be critical to the health of Yellowstone's fisheries.

Fires typically don't kill all trees, so the survivors gain a larger share of water, nutrients, and light, and are better able to resist insects and infections.

Periodic blazes prevent forests from invading meadowlands, and fires create snags. Nearly a fourth of the birds and a few mammals in greater Yellowstone depend on these, including bluebirds, woodpeckers, nuthatches, owls, bats, and flying squirrels. Since snags may remain upright for a century or more, fires provide a long-term source of wildlife habitat.

Though few animals are directly killed, fires do influence wildlife. Fewer than 300 large mammals died directly from the flames or smoke. Most small mammals burrow into the ground, and birds fly away. However, drought and the loss of forage from the flames contributed to a major kill of big game in the winter of 1989. As many as 9,000 elk are thought to have starved or been killed by hunters. This die-off helped reduce browsing pressure on shrub and aspen communities, however, and provided carrion for scavengers from grizzly bears to wolverines.

Effects on Vegetation

Lodgepole pine has adapted to fire. Its cones may remain closed until heated, when they gradually open to shed seeds a day or two later. Most trees produce a few such cones, which ensures that there will always be some seeds after a blaze.

Lodgepole also grows rapidly and matures early. A five-year-old lodgepole can produce seeds. Subalpine fir may be fifty or more before they can do so. This helps lodgepole reforest recently burned areas and accounts for the many even-aged stands throughout the ecosystem.

Self-pruning is common among fire-adapted conifers. As the tree grows, the lower branches die and fall off. This leaves the bole free of "ladders" to carry flames into the canopy.

Aspen is another fire-dependent species. Most regenerate not from seeds but suckers—stems that grow from roots of a parent. As many as 60,000 suckers per acre have been reported after a fire, ensuring the survival of aspen groves. Willow, rabbitbrush, some sagebrush, and other plants also regenerate quickly after their crowns are killed by fire. Grasses do well after fires remove the litter of past seasons. The lush growth after a fire attracts bighorn sheep, elk, bison, deer, and antelope.

Conclusions

Yellowstone landscapes are nurtured and shaped by thousands of years of periodic fires. Wildfires cannot "destroy" Yellowstone any more than torrential rains can destroy a tropical forest, so Yellowstone is not recovering from the blazes. It is merely in one phase of an endless cycle. A forest full of charred snags is as much a part of the cycle as a mature stand of green timber. One cannot exist without the other. Preserving Yellowstone means preserving the ecological processes that shape its plants and animals.

FISHERIES

Most people do not consider fish to be wildlife. We have "fish and game" departments, and fishery biologists who are not considered the same as wildlife biologists. While scaly, cold-blooded fish don't appeal to most people as do warm, furry critters or colorful, chirping birds, fish are every bit as important to the Greater Yellowstone Ecosystem as bison and bald eagles.

The GYE's trout fisheries are known worldwide. The rivers are a litany of famous trout streams: the Yellowstone, Lamar, Gallatin, Madison, Henry's Fork, Buffalo Fork, South Fork of the Snake, Firehole, and upper Green. These trout waters are some of the best-managed and, not coincidentally, some of the most beautiful rivers in the world.

Twenty-one fish species are found in the ecosystem, though there are a few more on the fringes. Trout get most of the attention, since sport fishing brings in a lot of money. A 1988 study by the Montana Department of Fish, Wildlife, and Parks found the average total outlay for a fishing trip to be $210. Multiply this by the 293,000 trips in Yellowstone National Park alone in 1988 and the figure is $61,530,000. Over the ecosystem, fishing is probably worth several hundred million dollars annually to the local economy.

But Yellowstone's fisheries have other values. Increasingly, fish watching is popular. In the early 1960s, Fishing Bridge at the outlet of Yellowstone Lake was a popular fishing hole in Yellowstone National Park. For a number of reasons, fishing was discontinued there. By 1978, more than 130,000 people were using the bridge annually to watch, not catch, fish. The water is very clear and fish are easy to see. In fact, in 1988, Fishing Bridge was the most popular fishery in the park, used by 800 percent more people than before angling was stopped.

Fisheries are also key to the overall health of the ecosystem. Fish sustain predators, including white pelican, bald eagle, osprey, loon, mink, river otter, and even grizzly bear. White pelicans annually eat more than 300,000 pounds of trout from Yellowstone Lake. And Yellowstone grizzlies feed on spawning cutthroat trout in much the same way that the Alaska brown bear eats salmon.

Yellowstone's Quality Fisheries

Yellowstone's fisheries are in better condition than almost any others in the country. There are many reasons. Greater Yellowstone is the headwaters for three major river systems—the Missouri, Green (Colorado), and Snake (Columbia). Though not totally immune, Yellowstone streams, as headwaters for the entire West, suffer little from farming, pollution, logging, and dams that have degraded far too many Western waterways. Also, the deep snows that blanket the uplands act as reservoirs, melting slowly through the summer and ensuring a flow through this normally dry season. Since water is not diverted for irrigation in Yellowstone park or the surrounding wildlands, rivers can better deal with downstream withdrawals.

Large lakes and springs near the headwaters of many of these streams also make for outstanding fisheries. Yellowstone Lake is the biggest in North America above 7,000 feet and is among the top 100 largest lakes in the world. This helps to moderate temperatures and flows downstream, providing a more stable environment for aquatic life. Other water sources that influence flow and temperature are Jackson Lake in the Tetons; the 480-million-gallon daily flow of Big Springs, source of the Henry's Fork; and the Shoshone and Lewis lakes headwaters of the Lewis River.

Greater Yellowstone's thermal features also contribute. The clear mountain stream for which we all pine may be nutrient poor and unable to support fish life. Hot springs bring nutrients up from deep in the Earth, enriching the streams. Recent research in Yellowstone Lake has demonstrated that hot vents on the bottom support a bacterial community that feeds on sulfur and other elements and enriches these otherwise sterile waters.

Thermal areas also help to moderate water temperatures. Since fish growth slows if temperatures dip too low, the warm water in the winter substantially lengthens the growing season. The increase in fish productivity can be significant. For instance, one-fourth of the flow to the Firehole and one-fifth of the Gibbon's water, both in Yellowstone park, come from hot springs and geysers. Because of this, a rainbow trout in the Firehole River grows to twelve inches in a year and a half, while a trout in a cold mountain stream takes up to four years to reach the same size.

Though greater Yellowstone aquatic systems are intact physically, they are highly manipulated biologically. When the first whites entered the region, there were no fish in many of the upper reaches of the rivers because of barriers created by waterfalls. Most high mountain lakes in such places as the Beartooths, Wind Rivers, and elsewhere that are now known for their superb fishing were once barren.

The only native trout were five subspecies of cutthroat. The brook, brown, rainbow, and lake were stocked in greater Yellowstone to "improve" the fisheries. Other stockings were less successful. Atlantic salmon were introduced in Yellowstone Lake and disappeared. Yellow perch and bass were introduced to the Gibbon River, which later was poisoned out to prevent their spread throughout the park. While these sport fish were often introduced by government agencies, other species such as chub, sucker, and shiner were stocked indiscriminately when fishermen dumped their unused minnows into the nearest lake or stream.

Still, the number of fish species in the GYE is small compared with other regions of the country, where evolution has been ongoing for tens of thousands of years. (Yellowstone's waterways only recently came out from under glacial caps.) There are seventy species of fish in Great Smoky Mountains National Park and only eighteen in Yellowstone park, an area four times as large.

In addition to the introduction of non-native fish, for a while there was commercial fishing in the ecosystem. Trout were caught in Yellowstone park to feed hotel guests until 1917.

For all these early mistakes, the GYE has seen some of the more innovative fishery management in the United States. The park banned all stocking in 1959, and the rule was applied to all Montana trout streams by the 1970s. (Lakes, particularly in high mountain areas, are still stocked in all three states.) Wild trout management is now emphasized on most waters in the ecosystem.

One problem with stocking is that it mixes fish of different genetic backgrounds, allowing genetic dilution. Rainbow trout readily mate with cutthroat in some waters; only 2 percent of the remaining west slope cutthroat in Montana are thought to be genetically pure. Genetic diversity is crucial to the ecosystem's health. For instance, Yellowstone cutthroat in Heart Lake are in two distinct groups. One spawns in mid-June in streams entering the lake, while the other spawns in the outlet a month later. At best, indiscriminate stocking will cause the new fish to fail; at worst, the fish will breed with the natives and erode the traits that are specific to a certain site or environment. Another problem is that some non-native fish will push out natives. The decline in the Montana grayling in many ecosystem waters is partly because of competition with non-native trout.

Perhaps the biggest drawback is that dumping hatchery fish into a wild stream just doesn't work. It doesn't improve the fishing. As a rule, hatchery fish cannot compete against native fish and eventually die. Until they do, they eat food that would support native fish. The result is fewer fish altogether.

Management Techniques

Since widespread stocking has been halted, the fisheries have improved. Catch and size limits have been instituted. Researchers found during the 1960s that the time needed to hook a trout in Yellowstone Lake had increased, while the fishing in general had declined, in spite of a three-fish limit. To curb this trend and give the anglers something to look forward to, the park came up with some innovative regulations. It limited some rivers to fly-fishing only. In 1973, regulations that require anglers to return all fish to the water unharmed were established for many park streams.

About the same time, the park required the release of all fish over thirteen inches. At first this may seem strange, but on many park waters it is possible to fish all day, catch fifty or more, and never get one small enough to keep! The vast majority of spawning is done by more mature fish, those over thirteen inches. Also, the fishing is enhanced because more large fish are caught, and fish watching is improved because larger fish are easier to spot.

The regulations have resulted in some interesting statistics. In 1988 on the 8.8-mile catch-and-release segment of the Yellowstone River between Yellowstone Lake and the Upper Falls, the average trout caught was slightly over fifteen inches, though this is the second most heavily fished water in the park. Perhaps because fishing is so popular, each trout is caught an average of 9.7 times in a season! Some were captured two or three times a day. Interestingly, with proper handling, fewer than 3 percent of the fish died from angling in the season.

Despite all this, it is reasonable to ask whether fishing is proper within a national park. After all, hunting isn't allowed; why should anglers be allowed to keep fish? Yet some even argue that catch-and-release fishing is hypocritical. Would anyone capture ground squirrels or deer and release them?

Trout in Greater Yellowstone

The only native trout, the cutthroat, is named for the red slash under its gills. Within the region are these subspecies: Yellowstone, west slope, Colorado, Bonneville, and fine-spotted. Their distribution provides a fascinating look into the West's aquatic evolution. For instance, the headwaters of the Madison and Gallatin rivers used to be home to the west slope, while just a few miles east across a watershed divide, the Yellowstone ruled.

Before human intervention, cutthroat were the most widely distributed native trout in the West. Their natural range spread from northern California to Prince William Sound in Alaska, and they reached into most streams of the Great Basin and Rocky Mountains. There were 14 subspecies. The cutthroat is believed to have originated on the Pacific coast. During the Ice Age, the early cutthroat migrated up the Columbia River and its tributaries, including the Snake in Idaho and Wyoming and the Clarks Fork in Montana. Fish in the Snake evolved into "large-spotted" cutthroat. Cutthroat in the Clarks Fork evolved into the west slope.

The large-spotted fish ascended the Snake to its headwaters, including Two Ocean Creek in the Teton Wilderness just south of Yellowstone park. This stream splits, with one branch draining toward the Atlantic Ocean via Yellowstone and the other bound for the Pacific by way of the Snake. By swimming up this watershed divide, the fish crossed the Continental Divide about 6,000 years ago. The descendant Yellowstone cutthroat inhabited both the Yellowstone drainage as far east as the Tongue River confluence and probably nearly the entire length of the Snake. Lava flows over the Snake River plain and downcutting of the river (forming falls and rapids) may eventually have isolated the Yellowstone cutthroat upstream of Shoshone Falls, near Twin Falls, Idaho.

The fine-spotted cutthroat is found in the South Fork of the Snake between Palisades Reservoir and Jackson Lake. It is bordered upstream and downstream by the Yellowstone cutthroat, which puzzles biologists. These breeds should mate, but they don't. In fact, their distribution is so

Aspen flourish in the proposed Lionhead Wilderness, a critical biological corridor linking Yellowstone Park with the Centennial Mountains and other large roadless areas farther west.

Above: Much of the Shoshone National Forest, including the Buffalo Plateau, consists of alpine tundra and grasslands.

Left: Fremont Peak, at 13,745 feet, is the second highest peak in the Wind River Range. John C. Fremont first climbed the peak in 1842.

Right: The bison along the Firehole River in Wyoming belong to one of the few wild herds left in North America.

Left: Seeds from the cones of whitebark pine provide food for squirrels, Clark's nutcrackers, and grizzlies. The whitebark pine is declining throughout the northern Rockies.

Caribou Mountain, on Gray's Lake Wildlife Refuge in Idaho, was the site of a gold rush in the 1800s.

Pinnacle Peak, in the Gros Ventre Wilderness, Wyoming, was formed largely from sedimentary limestone.

Left: Blowout Canyon, shown here in spring, lies in the proposed Palisades Wilderness in Idaho. The Palisades are a segment of the Snake River Mountains, which stretch from Idaho to Wyoming.

Right: Slough Creek in Yellowstone National Park is a productive cutthroat trout fishery. The deep, undercut banks indicate a riparian zone in good condition.

Right: Rabbitbrush frames bison grazing deep in the Lamar Valley of Yellowstone Park.

Spring Creek in Paradise Valley flows at the foot of the Absaroka Mountains, which take their name from the Absaroka (or Crow) Indians who once lived in this area.

Steam rises above a hot pool at West Thumb Geyser Basin, an area that is part of a small collapsed caldera of a volcano that erupted 150,000 years ago.

The rich volcanic soils of the Absaroka Mountains produce lush, verdant meadows.

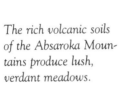

Mount Musumbeah in Wyoming shows a fine example of glaciated rock: its steep cliffs were carved by glacial ice.

*Jules Bowl lies in the Absaroka Mountains,
a range that is composed primarily of
debris from volcanic eruptions between
38 million and 50 million years ago.*

Many of the Taylor Peaks, in the Lee Metcalf Wilderness, exceed 11,000 feet in elevation. The preserve was named to honor the late Sen. Lee Metcalf, one of Montana's staunchest wilderness supporters.

Willows and sedges line Upper Yellowstone Valley near Bridger Lake in the Teton Wilderness, an area approximately 21 miles from the nearest road.

Aspen, one of the few deciduous trees in the Greater Yellowstone Ecosystem, thrive in a grove near Jackson Lake, Grand Teton National Park.

Left: The Beartooth Mountains in Custer National Forest, Montana, contain one of the most extensive tracts of alpine terrain in the United States.

Right: Near timberline, trees like these subalpine fir in Montana's Gallatin Range grow in a low, stunted form called krumholz, German for "crooked wood." Such trees may be hundreds of years old.

Bull elk bugle during the September rut. Elk are the most numerous big game animal in the Greater Yellowstone Ecosystem. An estimated 95,000 are thought to roam the tristate area.

Next page: Balsamroot and other wildflowers bloom along the Lander Cutoff of the Oregon Trail, an alternative route between South Pass and Fort Hall.

The south fork of the Snake River cuts a deep canyon through the Snake River Range east of Alpine, Wyoming. The Snake may have been the original route into the region for the ancestral form of cutthroat trout, from which various subspecies evolved.

odd that on some streams that flow into the Snake between Palisades Reservoir and Jackson Lake, there are Yellowstone cutthroat in the upper reaches and fine-spotted in the lower, which is similar to the distribution in the entire river.

The Bonneville cutthroat is named for Lake Bonneville, a huge body that covered most of Utah and portions of Nevada, Wyoming, and Idaho at the end of the Ice Age. The Great Salt Lake is a remnant. The Bear River, which begins near the Idaho-Wyoming-Utah corner, first flows north, then south into Great Salt Lake. At one time, though, the Bear was a Snake River tributary, and that is how large-spotted trout got into its drainage. Then a lava flow cut off the Bear from the Snake and diverted it to its current flow. During the Ice Age, the Bear would have flowed into Lake Bonneville. As the lake dropped and dried up, it left Bonneville cutthroat isolated throughout its old basin, including the streams in the southwestern portion of the GYE.

The Colorado cutthroat, another descendant of the large-spotted, is native to the Colorado-Green River drainage in Wyoming, Utah, and Colorado. It likely entered the Colorado by crossing a watershed divide between the Snake and the Green, probably between the Hoback River and upper Green or between the Grey's River and La Barge Creek.

The west slope cutthroat is found throughout western Montana and in Idaho, including the Salmon, Clearwater, and Clarks Fork rivers. Despite the name, the west slope also originally was found in the Missouri River upstream of Great Falls, including the Madison and Gallatin rivers. How did this fish work its way across the Continental Divide into the Missouri? It is thought that west slope ascended the Middle Fork of the Flathead River to Bear Creek, and from there to Summit Lake on Marias Pass, just south of Glacier National Park. Summit Lake, like Two Ocean Creek, is squarely on the Continental Divide and drains into both the Clarks Fork via the Flathead River and the Missouri via the Marias. Once in the Missouri River system, the west slope colonized the entire upper drainage.

Today, the west slope is extinct in most of its native range and in Yellowstone park is restricted to the Gibbon River below Gibbon Falls, and Bacon Rind, Fan, Grayling, and Cougar creeks by West Yellowstone.

Tapeworm Cycle

The Yellowstone cutthroat harbors several parasites; the best-known is the tapeworm Diphyllobothrium. This parasite inhabits the other trouts and grayling in the GYE. Birds and mammals also harbor it, including pelicans, grizzly bears, and coyotes. An adult tapeworm may be up to six feet long and lay millions of eggs. These are passed out in the host's feces and into water, where they hatch. The larvae are eaten by crustaceans, which are eaten by trout. The tapeworm encysts in the flesh, where it remains until the fish is eaten by a predator. It is then released to mature into an adult, and the cycle begins again.

The Fish

YELLOWSTONE CUTTHROAT TROUT   *page 208*

Description. Golden yellow on its sides, shading to dark green to steel blue on its back, and white or pale yellow on its belly. Side of head is rose with a red slash on either side of throat. Large black spots on back and tail, diminishing toward head. Typically, two large black spots on gill covers.

Distribution. Yellowstone park is its stronghold. Native to Yellowstone River drainage, including Yellowstone Lake, but stocked widely throughout West.

Natural History. Generally does not eat other fish. Primarily an insectivore. Separated by age class in Yellowstone Lake. Mature cutthroat ascend lake tributaries between mid-May and end of July. Larger fish tend to go farthest up streams. Unlike Pacific salmon, which die after spawning, many mature cutthroat return to lake. Young fish gradually move downstream and into lake at one to two years. Quickly migrate into middle of lake, where they feed on plankton until they reach maturity, eleven to thirteen inches. They then move toward shore and feed on insects and crustaceans. Due to diet, Yellowstones do not usually grow beyond four or five pounds.

Separation of young fish in middle of lake and older ones in shallows may cut competition for space and food.

FINE-SPOTTED CUTTHROAT TROUT

Description. Similar to Yellowstone cutthroat, except covered with fine black spots.

Distribution. Primarily in South Fork of Snake River between Jackson Lake (it is stocked upstream of there) and Palisades Reservoir; all tributaries from Gros Ventre River to Palisades, including Hoback, Salt, and Grey's rivers.

Natural History. Fine-spotted appears to prefer fast water in big rivers like the Snake. Like Yellowstone cutthroat, fine-spotted is primarily an insectivore, though large ones eat other fish. Habitat has been disrupted along Snake. Levees prevent annual flooding, halting flushing of silt from spawning areas. Levees also increase downstream flows, causing channels and islands to erode and decreasing habitat. Fine-spotted is a Category 2 candidate under Endangered Species Act.

COLORADO CUTTHROAT TROUT

Description. Most colorful cutthroat. Small to moderate spots on fish from upper Green River drainage, with yellowish to brassy sides. Belly crimson on mature males.

Distribution. In upper Green River tributaries that drain southeastern Bridger-Teton National Forest.

Natural History. Isolated in small headwaters of upper Green River drainage. Seldom grows to even a foot; early records suggest it occasionally reached twenty pounds. Usually eats insects but takes fish if available. Due to overgrazing, water diversions for irrigation, and competition with other species, genetically pure Colorado cutthroat are rare. A new threat is acid rain, which has been recorded at higher-than-normal levels in the Wind River Range and other areas.

WEST SLOPE CUTTHROAT TROUT

Description. Small, irregular spots above lateral line from anal to pectoral fins. Yellowish green on back, fading to pale yellow on sides and white on belly. Bar marks on smaller fish.

Distribution. Practically extinct in GYE and confined to a few streams in upper Missouri River drainage.

Natural History. Split off evolutionary cutthroat line early and has been isolated long enough that some biologists believe it should be a separate species. Can be highly migratory, ascending streams as much as 200 miles to spawn. Due to restricted distribution, it is unknown whether it does so in GYE. Like relatives, west slope is primarily an insectivore, and young fish in lakes eat plankton. Mating with rainbow trout has been a major problem since stocking has increased range of rainbow.

BONNEVILLE CUTTHROAT TROUT

Description. Similar to Yellowstone cutthroat, except has larger spots more evenly distributed over body.

Distribution. Named for glacial Lake Bonneville. Within ecosystem, known in a few streams, primarily Smith's Fork and Thomas Fork drainages of Bear River on Wyoming-Idaho line.

Natural History. Among rarest cutthroats, once thought to be extinct. Searching has turned up forty-one small, genetically pure groups, mostly in isolated headwater streams. Though once numerous in Bear Lake, commercial netting and dewatering of spawning tributaries had so reduced the Bonneville that in 1940s biologists could not find native trout in the lake. Unlike other cutthroats in GYE, lake-dwelling Bonnevilles switch from insect to fish diet once they mature. Eating other fish spurs growth; Bonnevilles up to twenty pounds or more were reported.

Bonneville has adapted to survive in marginal waters with high temperatures and limited habitat. Probably accounts for persistence in small streams like Thomas and Smith's forks. Stream dewatering, riparian damage, and crossbreeding threaten subspecies, which is a Category 2 candidate under Endangered Species Act.

BROWN TROUT   *page 209*

Description. Generally golden tan or yellow. Belly yellow. Numerous large black and red spots on dorsal half of body. Large mouth, stout head. Lower jaw is hooked in older males.

Distribution. Not native to GYE; not even native to North America. Imported from Europe in 1882 and widely introduced. Common everywhere, but best known in Yellowstone, Madison, Gallatin, Firehole, Gibbon, Gardner, Lewis, and Snake river drainages.

Natural History. Not as sensitive as brook trout to high temperatures, but more so than rainbow. Does not grow well in very cold waters.

Unlike cutthroat, which spawn in spring (which may come in midsummer in high elevations), brown trout is a fall spawner. Will often run up smaller tributaries, but can spawn in main rivers. Browns in the Yellowstone River spawn in side channels—anyplace with enough gravel. Lake dwellers migrate to outlets and inlets for spawning. Fall spawning runs in Lewis Lake and out of Hebgen Lake into Madison River attract many anglers. Feed on insects, but larger ones will feed on fish and can reach twenty pounds or more. Browns up to fifteen pounds caught regularly in Yellowstone River between Springdale and Gardiner, Montana.

RAINBOW TROUT   *page 209*

Description. Named for the pink strip along side. Dotted with black spots, tends to be silvery on sides and steel gray or gun-barrel blue on back.

Distribution. Introduced to GYE; native to coastal streams, rivers, and lakes from Mexico to Alaska, but widely stocked in ecosystem. Henry's Fork and Madison are well-known rainbow streams.

Natural History. Rainbow easily breeds with cutthroat; trout with rainbow stripe and cutthroat slash are common. Rainbow, like cutthroat, is a spring spawner, but some in Madison River have taken to fall spawning. Rainbows, like browns, feed on insects and fish, with twenty-pounders in lakes eating primarily other fish.

BROOK TROUT   *page 209*

Description. Green with reddish belly, particularly during spawning. Distinctive white margins on lower fins. Also known as speckled trout from wormlike black markings on back and red spots on side.

Distribution. Introduced to GYE. Native from Quebec to Georgia. In West, brook trout more numerous in cold, small headwater creeks, especially spring-fed waters. Common in lakes of Beartooth Mountains and Wind River Range.

Natural History. Can't tolerate warm water, so rare in rivers with thermal features. Despite name, is also found in lakes. Prolific, so competition keeps mature fish to no more than eight to ten inches.

A fall spawner. By late September, fish jam by hundreds into tiny creeks feeding some high mountain lakes. Also spawns in gravelly lake shallows. Matures earlier than most trout and may be sexually active at one year and five or six inches in length. Often pushes out native fish, particularly cutthroat and grayling. Indiscriminate stocking of brook trout throughout West has probably led to extinction of native fish more than any other factor.

LAKE TROUT

Description. Gray to blue gray back, fading to white along belly. Light spots, sometimes reddish on sides, with more irregular markings on back. Tail deeply forked. Large mouth. Gets larger than other North American trout; 100-pounders have been netted by commercial fishermen. A 50-pounder would be a record in most places. A 41-pound lake was taken from Yellowstone's Heart Lake in 1931.

Distribution. Found in lakes and rivers connecting them. Prefers cold water more than 100 feet deep. Found from Newfoundland to Alaska, dipping into New England, Great Lakes, and Montana. Introduced into Wyoming. Now found in Grand Teton's Jackson Lake and Lewis, Heart, and Shoshone lakes in Yellowstone park.

Natural History. Beyond twelve to fourteen inches, lakes feed almost exclusively on other fish. Cannibalistic.

GOLDEN TROUT

Description. Looks like a golden rainbow with fewer spots. Rosy lateral band and large black spots mostly on back and tail. Lower pelvic and anal fins have white margin.

Distribution. Rarest trout in GYE. Native to California's Sierra Nevada. Typically found in mountain lakes, usually near or above timberline.

Natural History. Spring spawner. World's record golden trout, an eleven-pound lunker, caught in Cook Lakes in Wyoming's Wind River Range.

MONTANA GRAYLING

Description. Looks like a trout with big scales and huge sailfishlike dorsal fin. Iridescent silver or blue.

Distribution. In North America, primarily in arctic and subarctic regions. Once found in Michigan, limited distribution in Montana. Michigan graylings disappeared from siltation caused by logging; Montana's seem doomed to same fate. Once common in upper Missouri River drainage, now found only in few streams, primarily upper Big Hole River and Red Rock Creek in Centennial Mountains. Transplanted to lakes and rivers elsewhere in ecosystem, including upper Clarks Fork of the Yellowstone and several lakes in Yellowstone. Originally native to Madison and Gibbon rivers in Yellowstone park; nearly all graylings found in these rivers now have moved downstream from Wolf, Grebe, and Cascade lakes.

Natural History. Once coexisted with west slope cutthroat and mountain whitefish with no apparent problem, but introduction of more aggressive non-native trout and habitat degradation have decimated species. Siltation from sheep grazing in Centennials may have caused grayling decline in Red Rock Creek, one of its last river habitats in GYE. Grayling is a Candidate 2 under Endangered Species Act.

KENDALL WARM SPRINGS DACE

Description. One to two inches long. Males, bright purple; females, olive.

Distribution. Smallest range of any fish in GYE. Limited to Kendall Warm Springs and part of its outlet, in the Bridger-Teton National Forest. Springs sit near headwaters of Green River in Wind River Range.

Natural History. Unprotected springs and riparian areas were once trampled by livestock. Often used as bait. Springs are now fenced and population seems to have stabilized. Endangered.

MOUNTAIN WHITEFISH

Description. Yellowstone and Rocky Mountain whitefish once considered two species, but no longer. Gray blue back and whitish belly. Long, with large, loose scales; silvery and slender. Small mouth.

Distribution. Native to GYE. Found in upper Missouri River and Yellowstone headwaters, including Madison and Gallatin rivers. Also found in Snake and headwaters.

Natural History. Grows slowly compared with trout but lives longer. Sixteen-year-olds have been captured. Seems to attain greatest size (sixteen to eighteen inches) in lakes. Not prized for sport, whitefish do rise to fly and can be harder to catch than trout.

LONGNOSE SUCKER

Description. Resembles mountain whitefish. Body nearly cylindrical, with large, flattened head. Back grayish, fading to yellow or white on sides. Pectoral and anal fins whitish.

Distribution. Native. Found in park in Yellowstone River drainage below Lower Falls, including both the Gardner and Lamar rivers. Introduced to Yellowstone Lake and is now found in several streams draining into lake.

Natural History. Prefers quiet, deep waters where it feeds on vegetation, bottom-dwelling insects, and crustaceans. In lakes will often cruise in large schools. Very slow growing. May live 25 years or more, growing more than 20 inches. Sexual maturity reached at five to seven years.

MOUNTAIN SUCKER

Description. Fleshy, suckerlike mouth. Adult usually less than ten inches. Back gray blue, fading to white on belly. Reddish lateral line. Lower fins orangy.

Distribution. The former flatnose sucker of Snake River drainage and Jordan's sucker of upper Missouri both now called mountain sucker. Found throughout West, and in Greater Yellowstone Ecosystem lives in clear, cold streams and rivers wherever there is algae, its major food.

Natural History. Frequently found in fast riffles and shallows, flashing side to side as it grazes on plants.

UTAH SUCKER

Description. Suckerlike mouth. Lower lip divided by groove. Large scales. Dark gray back, bronze sides, whitish belly. Length to twenty-four inches. Breeding males have bright red lateral line.

Distribution. Native to Snake River above Shoshone Falls and old drainage area of glacial Lake Bonneville. Reaches into Yellowstone park at Heart Lake.

Natural History. Slow growing. Lives up to twenty years. Bottom feeder.

UTAH CHUB

Description. Chubby, small mouth, slightly forked tail. Reaches twenty inches. Back is dull gray, brown, green, or bluish with bronze sides and silvery belly.

Distribution. Snake River above Shoshone Falls and old drainage of Lake Bonneville. Introduced in upper Colorado and upper Missouri drainages by careless bait anglers.

Natural History. Prefers quiet water with much vegetation. Young chubs eat plankton but switch to insects and other animals.

REDSIDE SHINER

Description. Deeply forked tail. Back dark green or brown, fading to silvery belly. Black lateral line with red stripe below it. Up to five inches.

Distribution. Throughout old Lake Bonneville drainage as well as Snake River. Indiscriminate dumping of leftover bait introduced it into many other waters, including Yellowstone Lake, where it is now well established.

Natural History. Primarily in lakes, redside confines movement and feeding to shallows, perhaps to avoid predators. Eats plankton and small insects. Diet overlaps Yellowstone cutthroat's.

SPECKLED DACE

Description. Color varies, generally grayish to brownish on back, fading to white on belly. Black irregular blotches on sides and dark stripe from head to tail. Mature fish less than four inches.

Distribution. Native. Primarily in Snake River drainage and Bonneville Basin. Has several habitats, including warm springs with temperatures up to 90 degrees.

LONGNOSE DACE

Description. Long head with overhanging snout. Color olive to brown, with whitish belly. Maximum length five to six inches.

Distribution. North America. In GYE, found in Snake and Yellowstone river drainages. Prefers cold, rapid streams.

Natural History. One of two fish in the Gibbon River above Gibbon Falls; sculpin is the other. Why these fish surmounted the falls while whitefish, grayling, and trout did not is a mystery.

MOTTLED SCULPIN

Description. Wide, stubby; largest at head and compressed toward tail. Usually a few inches long. Oarlike pectoral fins. Darts from place to place among riffles and rocks, hiding from predators.

Distribution. From southern Appalachians to British Columbia. Within Yellowstone, in the Snake River drainage, including Falls River, as well as upper Gallatin, Madison, and Yellowstone.

Natural History. When anglers use a "muddler" fly, they are often attempting to imitate the mottled sculpin. The muddler, made of deer hair, has a large "head" and tapered body. It is often used with a darting motion.

AMPHIBIANS AND REPTILES

Amphibians and reptiles are *poikilotherms*, or cold-blooded animals. Unable to generate much heat on their own, they absorb heat from the environment. Because most poikilotherms cannot function in the cold, they are not well represented in the Greater Yellowstone Ecosystem, and all species found here hibernate during the winter months. Nine amphibians and eight reptiles may be found in the ecosystem.

Amphibians

Amphibian means "two lives": living both in water and on land. Salamanders, frogs, and toads evolved from fishes, pioneering land with two evolutionary innovations—the ability to breathe air, and legs. Amphibians lay their eggs in water, and the young of most species develop in a watery environment. In their aquatic phase, amphibians have fishlike gills, which allow them to breathe under water. Most adults lose these gills and live on land, where they absorb oxygen through their skin or primitive lungs. To keep their skins moist, many amphibians live in moist habitats or are active after a rain or at night, when humidity is higher.

Because they depend upon both land and water, amphibians are a very sensitive indicator of environmental quality. In recent years, there has been a noticeable and widespread population decline among amphibians worldwide. Many biologists believe pollution is the cause.

Acid rain, which has been recorded in the Tetons, Wind Rivers, and Beartooths, is one such threat. The eggs of some species die when exposed to acidity levels just slightly higher than normal; in other cases the tadpoles are born deformed. Acid water can also slow development, delaying the transformation from tadpole to adult among species already living at the limits of their ranges.

Frogs and toads may be even more vulnerable than fishes to acid rain. The acidified snow that has collected all winter melts and is flushed into ponds and lakes in spring, creating an acid pulse just when most frogs and toads are laying their eggs and their young are developing.

And because many amphibians breathe through their skins, they are extremely susceptible to airborne pollutants as well.

Salamanders

Salamanders are very secretive. They typically have tails and four legs. Unlike toads and frogs, salamanders are voiceless. They must keep their skin moist, so they are typically found hiding in moist environments.

TIGER SALAMANDER (*Ambystoma tigrinum*)   *page 209*

Description. Six inches long. Chunky body with bold yellow and black stripes or marbled markings.

Distribution. Ranges from the lowest valleys up to 10,000 feet, where it can be found in rodent burrows, under moist vegetation, or anyplace it can avoid drying sun. Adults migrate to ponds to breed and remain there part of the summer. River otters may sometimes be seen feeding on tiger salamanders that line the shore by the hundreds in certain pothole ponds near Junction Butte in Yellowstone park.

Remarks. The tiger salamander is the only salamander found in the GYE. Under certain conditions, the larval form, known as an axolotl, remains an immature form of the adult and never fully develops. It is typically green or gray with external gills.

Frogs and Toads

Adult frogs and toads lack tails. They have large hind legs designed for leaping and hopping. They also possess conspicuous eardrums. In the spring, most frogs and toads use expandable throat sacs to peep and croak.

Frogs are distinguished from toads by their generally longer legs, smoother skin (few or no warts), excellent swimming and leaping abilities, and less well developed horny tubercles on their feet. Male frogs have vocal sacs in their throats that, in most species, expand like balloons during calling. Male frogs also possess specially adapted thumbs for clasping females during mating.

Toads are stockier and chunkier than frogs, and they hop rather than leap. The conspicuous warts or skin glands secrete toxic chemicals to inhibit predation (but will not give you warts or harm you in any way). The toad's bony cranial crest helps it burrow into soil and mud to avoid desiccation. Breeding takes place in the spring. Toads migrate to water and begin chorusing to attract mates. The calls of males are loud and distinctive for each species. Only two toads are found in the GYE, although the plains spadefoot toad may be present on the very eastern fringe near Cody, Wyoming.

BOREAL CHORUS FROG (*Pseudacris triseriata*)   *page 209*

Description. Up to 1¹/₂ inches long. Pads or discs on the tips of its toes help it cling to vertical surfaces (though it does not live in trees). Usually has two to three dark stripes, sometimes broken into several segments, against a lighter green or brown background. Males have dark throats. Both sexes have light bellies.

Distribution. Found throughout the ecosystem to timberline.

Remarks. Appears as early as April, congregating near water sources. Loud, birdlike trill is repeated 30 to 40 times a minute. Breeding occurs throughout spring.

SPOTTED FROG (*Rana pretiosa*)   *page 209*

Description. Male is 2.4 inches, female slightly larger. Wartier than other frogs, with bumps (skin glands) apparent on its back. Hind feet are webbed. Named for the black irregular spots that cover its generally brown back. Light upper jaw stripe. Upper belly and throat are speckled with black. Undersides of the legs and belly are reddish or orange red—the only frog in the region with a reddish belly.

Distribution. Most common frog in the GYE. Found along beaver ponds, marshy areas, sloughs, and small streams.

Remarks. Emerges from hibernation in early May on the Yellowstone Plateau. Breeding call of short croaks is fainter and weaker than that of the boreal chorus frog. Breeding occurs by June. Larvae reach adult size by the end of summer in late August or September.

NORTHERN LEOPARD FROG (*Rana pipiens*)

Description. About 2.8 inches long, but may grow to 4 inches. Smooth skinned. Has 12 or 13 large black spots with faint white margins set on a green to dark brown background. Belly is white. Hind feet are only moderately webbed. The vocal sacs do not swell.

Distribution. Not particularly common in Yellowstone or Grand Teton national parks and other higher-elevation areas. Found at lower elevations, but occasionally up to 9,000 feet. Associated with cattail ponds and beaver ponds in foothills.

BOREAL TOAD (*Bufo boreas boreas*)

Description. Up to 3 inches long. No cranial crest, perhaps because this toad is typically associated with moist habitats and does less burrowing than other species. Hind feet are webbed. Back is typically black, brown, or olive with a prominent white or eggshell mid-dorsal stripe running nose to tail. Throat is light. Black spots on the belly and sides. Immature individuals may have orange or yellow dots on belly and feet. Glands on the back emit a characteristic musky odor.

Distribution. Well distributed throughout the GYE. Common near water in subalpine settings up to 10,000 feet, this toad ranges some distance to forage on moths, beetles, and ants.

Remarks. Breeding occurs as soon as ice leaves the ponds, where the toads hibernate.

GREAT BASIN SPADEFOOT TOAD
(*Scaphiopus intermontanus*)

Description. About 2 inches long. Light in coloration. Has a vertical elliptical pupil. Feeds at night on ants, beetles, moths, and other insects.

Distribution. Not common in the GYE; its northernmost range is the southern part of the ecosystem. Not usually found above 6,500 feet.

Remarks. Has adapted to arid environments by burrowing into soil to avoid desiccation. Emerges in summer after heavy rains and seeks temporary water holes, where the loud calls of males attract other males as well as females. Breeding, egg laying, and development of young are all accelerated and must be completed before the water sources dry up.

Reptiles

Reptiles are less dependent on water than amphibians. Two reptilian adaptations reduce moisture losses: a scaly skin, and hard, leathery eggshells that seal moisture in and can therefore be laid on dry land. Some reptiles, however, live in aquatic environments.

Turtles are the most primitive of the reptiles. In the GYE, the painted turtle may occur on the very northern fringes in Gallatin County, Montana.

Lizards

Lizards are small, usually less than 8 inches long. They can regulate their temperatures somewhat through behavior. In early morning, when it is cool, lizards lie in the sun to soak up warmth; when it's too hot, they seek out the shade. One evening a lizard approached my campfire, looked right and left, then dashed up close and held its forefeet toward the fire, as a person might position his hands to warm them. The lizard shared the fire with me for about five minutes, then scurried off.

Most lizards feed on insects. Like snakes, they use their tongues to smell; some lizards flick their tongues while hunting, hoping to get a scent of prey.

NORTHERN SAGEBRUSH LIZARD (*Sceloporus graciosus*)

Description. Body (minus tail) is less than 2¼ inches. Scales on the back are keeled, giving the appearance of parallel ridges. Brown with faint blotches on the back fading to light brown on the sides with stripes. Males have blue on the sides of the belly; the belly of the female is white.

Distribution. Inhabits sagebrush deserts, mostly below 6,000 feet. Found in the lower elevations of valleys on the fringe of the ecosystem, including the upper Green River Valley, along the Shoshone River near Cody, along the Clarks Fork east of Cooke City, and along the northern fringes of the Beartooth Mountains in Montana. A remnant population is found in the Norris Geyser Basin of the park, where thermal features allow it to live at much higher elevations.

SHORT-HORNED LIZARD (*Phrynosoma douglassi*)

Description. Flattened, squat lizard up to 3 inches long, minus the tail. Has short, blunt horns along the sides of its body, as well as on the back of the head. Brown or gray—usually matching the ground where it lives—with irregular dark blotches on either side of its midline. Belly is white.

Distribution. Ranging from eastern Montana south into Colorado, this lizard inhabits the eastern fringes of the ecosystem in the Bighorn Basin and along the valley floor on either side of the Wind River Range, including the upper Green River Valley. Also seen along lower tributaries of the Snake River in Idaho, usually in grasslands and sagebrush desert country below 6,500 feet.

Remarks. Usually active from May until early October. Feeds on insects, primarily ants, beetles, and grasshoppers. When attacked, the short-horned lizard squirts blood from its eyes, apparently in an effort to startle predators. It bears 12 live young.

Snakes

Snakes are legless reptiles. They move by contracting muscles for a side-to-side motion. Adapted to preying upon small mammals, insects, and other animals, snakes can easily enter burrows and climb into shrubs and trees. The unhinged jaw allows a snake to swallow large prey. Its body also expands to allow the passage of food. With the exception of the garter snakes, most snakes in the ecosystem are found only at low elevations.

RUBBER BOA (*Charina bottae*)   *page 209*

Description. Seldom exceeds 2 feet in length. Brown with a yellow belly. Looks and feels like rubber.

Distribution. Found near water with shelter in the form of rocks and logs. Secretive and seldom seen, even where common. Ranges throughout Yellowstone and Grand Teton national parks, but its eastern range extension includes only the area north of the Shoshone River, excluding the entire drainages of the Wind and Green rivers in Wyoming.

Remarks. What little is known about its natural history suggests that this snake eats small rodents and lizards. It bears live young, usually fewer than a dozen.

WANDERING GARTER SNAKE (*Thamnophis elegans*)   *page 209*

Description. Less than 30 inches long. Three longitudinal stripes with rows of dark spots set against a brown to greenish background. The belly is gray to light blue.

Distribution. Occurs up to 10,000 feet. One of the most widely distributed snakes in the GYE.

Remarks. This aquatic snake swims readily and preys upon tadpoles, small frogs, rodents, birds, fish, and worms. During mating, five or ten male snakes wrap themselves around a female, attempting to impregnate her. The young are born live.

In September or October garter snakes gather in communal dens, sometimes with other species, including rattlesnakes, where they remain huddled together until the following April.

VALLEY GARTER SNAKE (*Thamnophis sirtalis fitchi*) page 209

Description. Dark head. Bright yellow and red blotches form lateral stripes.

Distribution. Ranges mostly west of the Continental Divide from western Wyoming to California. In the GYE, it has been seen in the Snake River drainage in Wyoming, including Grand Teton National Park, and in the Idaho portion of the ecosystem along the Snake and its tributaries. Usually associated with water.

BULL SNAKE (*Pituophis melanoleucus sayi*)

Description. Up to 7 feet long, with a thick, heavy body. The largest snake in the GYE. Sandy colored with numerous dark brown black blotches on its back that become rings toward the tail.

Distribution. Found below 6,000 feet, along the lower river corridors. May be seen along the Yellowstone near the park's north entrance, along the Snake below Grand Teton National Park, and along the Clarks Fork and Shoshone rivers near Cody.

Remarks. Hunts by day, capturing and killing victims by crushing them. Preys on small rodents, rabbits, and occasional birds and eggs. If frightened, imitates rattlesnake by hissing, rattling its tail, and pretending to strike; it has no poison or rattle.

PRAIRIE RATTLESNAKE (*Crotalus viridis viridis*)

Description. Reaches 4 feet. Large-bodied snake, but shorter than bull snake. Dark blotches on a brown background become rings toward the tail, which ends in a rattle.

Distribution. Associated with rock outcrops, cliffs, and other areas where it can den during weather extremes. Largely confined to the lower river valleys, below 7,000 feet, such as the lower Yellowstone River near Gardiner.

Remarks. The only poisonous snake in the Greater Yellowstone Ecosystem; its poison, however, is usually not fatal to an adult. A terrestrial hunter, but is occasionally seen in water. Preys on small birds and rodents, including prairie dogs, ground squirrels, and rabbits. Young are born live in August or September.

YELLOWBELLY RACER (*Coluber constrictor*)

Description. Slender snake up to 6 feet, although most are half that size. Blue to green back with a yellow belly and white throat.

Distribution. Reaches its westernmost extent on the eastern fringe of the GYE, most notably in the vicinity of Lander, Wyoming, and perhaps near Cody and north into Montana.

Remarks. Eats primarily insects, but sometimes takes rodents and birds.

BIRDS

Evolution and Adaptations

Birds evolved from reptiles about 150 million years ago. Their feathers evolved from modified scales. Flight was possible, and feathers are also excellent insulation, allowing for warm-bloodedness. This lets birds live in many more environments than reptiles. Forty-two bird species remain active year-round in Yellowstone park because of this.

Other evolutionary changes include the development of a light beak instead of heavy teeth. Bones in the skull, legs, and wings are thin, with internal struts to give strength without additional weight. Wings evolved from upper legs, with finger bones dramatically reduced while the forearm lengthened.

Birds are streamlined to reduce drag during flight. They have large flight muscles, and their digestive systems are efficient enough to provide the energy needed for such strenuous exercise. Some birds eat up to a third of their body weight daily just to stay warm and active. Herbivorous birds typically have a crop, where food is stored and ground up before digestion.

Songs

Birds communicate through behavior, coloration, and song. The last is how many people enjoy birds.

Birds can produce complex sounds, up to eighty notes per second. They are so rapid that they sound like a single note or a few notes, while birds, whose auditory responses are ten times as fast as humans', may hear dozens of notes in a single burst.

Though some birds sing year-round, the most intense time is breeding season. Songs attract mates and warn competitors of territorial bounds. Birds are more likely to sing in the early morning and in good weather.

While we may not recognize it, each bird sings slightly differently. A bird learns to tolerate a neighbor's call but reacts violently when an unfamiliar song signals the presence of an intruder. There are also dialects.

Calls are also used to communicate among a flock. The pine siskin, chickadee, and others that forage in flocks tend to make short "location" calls as they move about in dense vegetation. In the open, their calls may stop.

Ravens may even communicate among themselves, establishing calls that are used only with a "friend" or partner. They may call each other by "name," using a cry only to locate another bird.

Low sounds carry farther in dense vegetation than high ones, so some forest species like the blue grouse have a booming call. Marsh birds tend to have loud calls for the same reason. Many grassland birds have high-pitched songs.

Migration

Birds migrate, usually according to season. They seldom migrate because of food shortages; in fact, most birds begin migrations when they are fat. Clues such as length of daylight determine movement. Migration allows birds to exploit food that is not being eaten, and they may find better nesting or fewer predators in their new location.

There are risks, however. First-time migrants frequently fly over territory where food, cover, and other necessities are unfamiliar. There is a greater chance of attack and starvation. Flying over large water bodies such as the Gulf of Mexico exhausts terrestrial birds since there is no place to rest. Some never make it.

Some birds make astounding migrations. The tiny Wilson's warbler breeds in Yellowstone and winters in Africa, an air distance of more than 7,000 miles. Warblers fly at night, when predators are less of a threat and currents are more stable. Large raptors frequently fly in the day, when thermals help them glide.

Diet

Birds' behavior, body shape, habitat, and other characteristics are largely determined by what they eat. Few eat only one thing, but many specialize in specific foods.

Seeds are nutritious and abundant. Seed eaters in the GYE include the red crossbill, American goldfinch, Clark's nutcracker, house finch, pine siskin, evening grosbeak, pine grosbeak, gray crown rosy finch, and others whose stout bills enable them to crack the shells. Most seed eaters have a crop that allows them to store food while foraging and digest it later in safety. Though adults may eat seeds, the young of many seed eaters are fed insects, probably because they are easier to digest and provide more protein. Since seeds keep well, some birds store them. The Clark's nutcracker caches the seeds of the whitebark pine.

There are numerous insect eaters, especially songbirds. Many insectivores, such as warblers, eat other foods during part of the year and thus aren't especially adapted to an insect diet. But swifts, swallows, nighthawks, and flycatchers eat insects nearly year-round. They tend to have small bills with wide, gaping mouths that enable them to catch insects on the wing. They are extremely agile, diving, swooping, and changing direction with remarkable speed and precision.

Swallows and flycatchers typically catch lunch on the wing while warblers glean it off of foliage. Nuthatches and brown creepers climb up and down trees, foraging on bark.

Woodpeckers are among the most specialized insectivores. They drill into trees picking out bark and wood larvae and other insects. They have reinforced skulls designed to absorb the pounding; pointed, stout bills; and stiff tail feathers to balance the force of the head as the bird hammers on a tree. Woodpeckers also have long, sticky, or barbed tongues to grip their prey.

Even some birds of prey may feed largely on insects. Kestrels, for instance, eat grasshoppers in summer.

Another major group feeds largely on fish. The GYE is home to grebe, loon, merganser, bald eagle, osprey, kingfisher, great blue heron, white pelican, California gull, and others. (No songbirds feed upon fish.) Fish eaters have serrated bills, such as in the merganser, which help these ducks hold slippery prey; or pointed bills like the heron and kingfisher to spear fish. The eagle and osprey capture fish with talons. The loon chases fish underwater and uses its webbed feet and streamlined form to overtake its prey.

Cavity Nesters

Many of the birds in the GYE nest in cavities. Though there have been no definitive studies, one survey in western Montana found that more than 25 percent of the species were cavity nesters. GYE cavity nesters include common goldeneye, Barrow's goldeneye, bufflehead, common merganser, merlin, kestrel, pygmy owl, boreal owl, saw-whet owl, northern flicker, yellow-bellied sapsucker, Willison's sapsucker, hairy woodpecker, downy woodpecker, black-backed woodpecker, three-toed woodpecker, western flycatcher, violet-green swallow, tree swallow, black-capped chickadee, mountain chickadee, white-breasted nuthatch, red-breasted nuthatch, brown creeper, mountain bluebird, starling, and house sparrow.

These birds excavate holes in dead trees or snags or use openings resulting from decay. There are some real advantages to cavity nesting. Compared with birds that nest in branches or on the ground, cavity nesters are safer from predators. Their young are less exposed to the elements.

So why don't more birds nest in cavities? Because there are disadvantages as well. In open country, suitable trees may be limited. Even in forests, cavities are common only in large, old trees, which themselves are rare in many areas.

The loss of snags from timbering has seriously reduced the number and quality of large, old trees. One study in Arizona found that the harvest of some live and dead trees reduced cavity nesting by 50 percent. Only ignorant foresters assert that forests with many dead trees and snags are "decadent," "overmature," and worthless. Such forests are essential to many animals, from cavity-nesting birds to flying squirrels to pine martens.

Natural snag producers such as pine beetles, spruce budworms, and wildfires are really allies of many species. To protect bluebirds, you have to protect pine beetles. To ensure plenty of three-toed woodpeckers, you need some wildfires. If mountain chickadees are to nest and eat, you need spruce budworm epidemics.

Birds of the Ecosystem

The Greater Yellowstone Ecosystem has more than 300 species of birds, nearly half of those found in the continental United States. Such inland diversity is startling, but the ecosystem has so many habitats that it's easy for a variety of birds to make a living.

The major habitats include marshy lakes such as Red Rock Lakes and Gray's Lake, where waterfowl like the cinnamon teal, western grebe, and gadwall might be found as well as waders like the great blue heron. Other aquatic habitats include faster-moving rivers and streams, where the harlequin duck and dipper are found. Along these are found various riparian species such as MacGillivray's warbler, yellow warbler, chipping sparrow, and killdeer.

Grasslands and shrublands dominated by sagebrush are home to the sage grouse, sage thrasher, and meadowlark and are patrolled by the northern harrier, Brewer's sparrow, red-tailed hawk, and Swainson's hawk.

In forests, you'll find the goshawk, ruffed grouse, Townsend's solitaire, red crossbill, great gray owl, Steller's jay, gray jay, Clark's nutcracker, mountain chickadee, ruby-crowned kinglet, blue grouse, hermit thrush, robin, mountain bluebird, and hairy woodpecker.

The treeless alpine zone is home to the golden eagle, water pipit, horned lark, rosy finch, raven, and white-crowned sparrow.

Not all birds found in the ecosystem are described below. Rather, these meet one of the following criteria: (1) They are common and widely distributed, like the raven and the mountain bluebird; (2) They are uncommon but nest in the GYE, like the trumpeter swan; (3) They are rare but of special interest, like the whooping crane.

COMMON LOON   *page 209*

Description. Black head with striking black and white stripes.

Distribution. Found at larger lakes, as it requires a long "runway" to become airborne. Common in ecosystem during migration. No more than several dozen pairs nest here in summer.

Remarks. Has a distinctive falsetto wail, a yodeling call, and "laugh." Primarily a fish eater. Designed for diving, its heavy bones act as ballast while its feet are set far back on the body for swimming. Cannot walk. Wing beats are rapid with no gliding flight. Holds head slightly lower than body when flying.

WESTERN GREBE   *page 209*

Description. Slender neck (white below, black on top); white cheeks; thin, yellowish bill. Like loon, holds head lower than body when flying.

Distribution. Common in shallow, marshy lakes such as Red Rock Lakes and Gray's Lake.

Remarks. A fish eater and excellent diver. Rather poor flier and, like loon, needs running start to get airborne. Breeds in colonies.

WHITE PELICAN   *page 210*

Description. Large; white with black-tipped wings. Wingspan nearly 9½ feet. Large yellow bill can be distended.

Distribution. Rivers and lakes. Nests on isolated islands. Of twenty-three colonies west of Rockies, only eight are still active, including one in Yellowstone Lake.

Remarks. Graceful flight alternates between flapping and gliding. Nests in colonies and frequently flies in formations of a dozen or more.

Plume hunting and loss of breeding habitat nearly wiped out the pelican. In the 1920s, an egg-stomping campaign began when the bird was found to be host to a trout parasite. In 1932, nesting colonies were protected; in recent years, there have been 400 nests in Yellowstone. Pelican does not dive; it chases prey into shallow water, then scoops it up in its bill. Pelicans herd fish, making a meal easier for all members of the flock.

TRUMPETER SWAN   *page 210*

Description. Large, white, long neck, buglelike call and graceful flight. Trumpeter similar to tundra swan, but latter is in ecosystem only during migration.

Distribution. May be 1,000 trumpeters in ecosystem. Most abundant at Red Rock Lakes, but also found in Grand Teton park, National Elk Refuge, Yellowstone park, on Henry's Fork, and elsewhere.

Remarks. Largest waterfowl in the world. Trumpeter once found across North America, but habitat destruction and hunting nearly wiped it out. A 1932 survey found sixty-nine remaining. (Several groups were discovered later in Alaska and Canada.) Red Rock Lakes National Wildlife Refuge established in 1935 as haven for dwindling swan population. Warm springs keep small ponds open in winter, when birds are also fed grain.

Trumpeter's existence remains precarious. During winter 1989, nearly 200 starved during prolonged cold snap. (Feeding areas froze over.) U.S. Fish and Wildlife Service and other agencies are moving swans to new areas to establish other populations.

Trumpeter first nests when four or five years old, mating for life. Muskrat houses and beaver lodges are nesting platforms. Young hatch in June and remain with parents through summer and following winter.

Trumpeter swans, almost extirpated in the Lower Forty-eight because of plume hunting and habitat changes, have made a partial comeback in Yellowstone.

CANADA GOOSE *page 210*

Description. Large, long black neck, white cheek patch, gray brown back, light breast and belly. Has distinctive honk. Migrates in V-formations.

Distribution. Most abundant waterfowl in ecosystem. At home in water, but also spends much time on land, particularly when grazing. Grass is primary food.

Remarks. Goose mates for life, which can be up to thirty-three years in the wild. Builds nests of grass and sticks on ground (particularly on islands without predators) or occasionally in trees.

MALLARD DUCK *page 210*

Description. Male: green head, white collar, chestnut breast, white belly. Female: drab brown.

Distribution. Rivers, ponds, marshes.

Remarks. Eats vegetation from water's surface rather than diving. Feet directly under body, so it can walk. Also can leap directly from water into flight.

In midsummer, males gather to molt. They lose bright feathers and wear a temporary, dull, "eclipse" plumage. Unable to fly during molting, ducks dive to escape enemies.

BARROW'S GOLDENEYE   *page 210*

Description. Small duck. Male has greenish black head that appears shiny purple under certain light. White crescent in front of the eye; belly and chest also white. Similar common goldeneye has only a white spot in front of eye; white wing patches found on both species, but Barrow's is segmented by a dark band. Musical whistling of wings heard when a flock takes off.

Distribution. On fast-moving rivers in ecosystem.

Remarks. Dives for crustaceans and insects. In Yellowstone park in summer, it is more numerous than common goldeneye, but in winter common goldeneye migrates into region, often outnumbering Barrow's. Nests in hollow trees or occasionally on ground near water. The nine or ten ducklings are able to keep up when following their mother within a day or two of hatching.

COMMON MERGANSER   *page 210*

Description. Fish-eating duck, with serrated bill for grasping slippery prey. Male has narrow red bill, long green head, white body, dark back with distinctive white wing bars. Female similar but has reddish head, white breast, grayish belly.

Distribution. Rivers and lakes with fish.

Remarks. Sometimes nests in tree cavities; otherwise, will nest on ground. Ducklings trail mother in line. Canoeists and anglers are often amused by a startled family of merganser swimming away. While mother paddles rapidly along, youngsters resemble tiny motorboats as they struggle to keep up.

Merganser is a diving duck, with feet set far back on body. It chases prey underwater and needs running start to get into air.

## GREAT BLUE HERON											*page 210*

Description. Blue gray, whitish head, long legs, and pointy, yellow bill. Call is a hoarse squawk.

Distribution. Rivers and banks of shallow lakes and ponds.

Remarks. The great blue heron eats fish, frogs, and other vertebrates. Builds huge platform nest in riverside cottonwoods, often in colonies. Though usually migratory, it sometimes winters.

AMERICAN COOT

Description. White bill, grayish black plumage. Looks like a duck, is actually a rail. Coot has partially lobed, rather than webbed, feet.

Distribution. Lakes and marshes like Red Rock Lakes, Yellowstone Lake, and other bodies of water.

Remarks. Often gathers in large, noisy flocks. Must "run" on water before becoming airborne. When swimming, pumps its head, which helps identify bird at great distance.

## KILLDEER											*page 210*

Description. A plover with two black neck rings, white belly, brown back, rusty rump.

Distribution. Fields, gravel bars, other open terrain.

Remarks. Named for its repeated call, which sounds like "kill-dee-deer." Nest is merely a scrape in the ground. To defend young, it feigns a broken wing. This distracts intruder.

## WILSON'S PHALAROPE											*page 210*

Description. Shorebird with broad vertical neck stripe that is black near eye and reddish toward base of neck.

Distribution. Marshes and wetlands.

Remarks. In this case, female pursues male. Female sports the bright plumage, unlike most birds, and has a higher level of testosterone than male phalarope. Female defends territories; male incubates eggs and cares for nest. Phalarope twirls in tight circles in the water, creating whirlpools that bring food to surface.

WHOOPING CRANE   *page 211*

Description. Elegant white bird stands nearly five feet tall. Red crown, black legs. Large white wings with black tips.

Distribution. Occasionally seen at Gray's Lake National Wildlife Refuge; rarely anywhere else in ecosystem.

Remarks. Once ranged from Mexico to Arctic, from Rockies to Atlantic. Shot by market hunters for feathers and meat. By 1941, just fifteen left.

A slow reproductive rate has limited recovery. Crane matures at three years and produces only two eggs annually. Typically only one chick survives. About 130 cranes live in the wild today. Nearly all summer in one small area in Northwest Territories of Canada and winter on Texas coast. All are therefore vulnerable to a single catastrophe like a storm or wildfire. As protection, chicks are "cross-fostered" with adult sandhill cranes at Gray's Lake. If all goes as planned, this will lead to new breeding population in Idaho. Thus far, many have died from collisions with power lines, shooting, and other causes. This has cast reintroduction in doubt.

Whooping crane feeds on frogs, rodents, and other small vertebrates in wetlands and grasslands.

SANDHILL CRANE   *page 211*

Description. Uniformly gray with long neck, long legs, red crown. Has distinctive, loud, musical rattle.

Distribution. Wet meadows and mountain parks. Island Park and Red Rock Lakes are good places to see them.

Remarks. Sandhill hunts for frogs, rodents, insects. In spring, large migrating flocks are often seen spiraling upward on thermals.

CALIFORNIA GULL

Description. Gray with black wingtips and white belly. Yellow bill with red spot.

Distribution. Inland breeder, forming colonies on islands and gravel bars. There's a major colony in Yellowstone Lake.

Remarks. Most common gull in ecosystem. Has plumages that vary with season and age. California gull takes four years to mature, going through two plumage phases.

NORTHERN GOSHAWK

Description. Steely gray back, light gray or white belly. White, fluffy undertail coverts. White slash above red eye.

Distribution. Old-growth forests.

Remarks. Swoops and screams if you get too close to its nest. Builds stick nest in old snag or crotch of tree. As with many birds of prey, male is smaller than female and is more agile. May allow male, which does most of the hunting, to capitalize on small prey. He feeds chicks; female broods young and defends nest.

Often preys on grouse, rabbit, and other small to medium-size animals. Does not soar, but weaves and darts through timber. Short wings give it speed while long tail helps in maneuvering.

NORTHERN HARRIER   *page 211*

Description. Relatively large, with long tail and characteristic white rump patch. Flight also unique—looping, dipping, gliding a few feet above ground.

Distribution. Grasslands, wetlands, other open country, sometimes moving into mountain meadows in late summer.

Remarks. Formerly called the marsh hawk, harrier is common in ecosystem. Primarily a rodent eater.

ROUGH-LEGGED HAWK

Description. Black belly against lighter, streaked chest; black tail band; black at bend of wing. Light wings with black-edged tips. Dark and light color phases. Light dominates in this region.

Distribution. Open country in winter.

Remarks. Rough-legged nests in Arctic and spends winter in "balmy" Rockies. Often roosts in groups at night in winter for warmth. Hunts in grasslands, preying on voles and other small mammals. Techniques include hovering, and has even followed foxes, waiting for mice and voles to be flushed out. Arrives in GYE in early October and remains until March.

RED-TAILED HAWK   *page 211*

Description. Broad wings and reddish tail. Light belly marked by dark band.

Distribution. Lower mountain areas and grasslands.

Remarks. Most common hawk in GYE. Shrill "keeerrr, keeerrr" is distinctive. Hunts rodents and rabbits by soaring on thermals. Nests in trees.

SWAINSON'S HAWK

Description. Broad, dark band across chest; white belly.

Distribution. Grasslands and other open country. Particularly common in Red Rock Lakes National Wildlife Refuge, grasslands of Yellowstone park, Jackson Hole, other open valleys.

Remarks. Migrates annually to pampas of South America, but returns to GYE in early May. Stalks small mammals and birds on foot; will wait at entrance of burrows to nab curious rodents.

AMERICAN KESTREL
page 211

Description. Longish tail, sharply pointed wings. Rapid flight. Robin-sized, with rusty-red back and black and white face.

Distribution. Abundant in GYE, particularly at Red Rock Lakes.

Remarks. Hovers as it hunts over meadows and fields. Eats small mammals, grasshoppers, birds. Has unmistakable "killy-killy" call. A cavity nester, unusual for a falcon.

BALD EAGLE
page 211

Description. Wingspan of more than seven feet, white head and tail set against large, brown body. Immature bald eagles are typically brown with white-speckled underwings and tails.

Distribution. Yellowstone Lake area; Snake River and tributaries like the Henry's Fork; and upper Madison and Yellowstone rivers outside of Yellowstone park. Eagles from farther north congregate in GYE during winter, so numbers may be higher then.

Remarks. Once found in every state and Canadian province, bald eagle suffered a severe decline with the widespread use of pesticide DDT, which caused thin eggshells. Since DDT was banned, there has been a dramatic increase in eagles in the region, with eighty-four occupied nests in 1989.

Largely a fish eater, though in winter will sometimes attack ducks and rabbits, and even eats carrion. In GYE, first breeds at six to seven years. Nests used year after year and may be five feet across by six feet deep. Eggs produced between February and April, with hatching a month or so later. Young disperse to northern California and western Oregon their first year, return to Yellowstone area in summer, where they usually remain once they achieve breeding age.

GOLDEN EAGLE page 211

Description. Lacks white head and tail feathers of bald eagle and is uniformly brown. Immature golden eagle has white tail with dark band and white patches under wings. A full-grown golden eagle has a broad tail and seven-foot wingspan.

Distribution. Open country.

Remarks. Swoops over hillsides, mountains, and plains looking for jackrabbit, ground squirrel, marmot, and prairie dog. Because some occasionally kill a lamb, sheepmen persecuted it, killing more than 20,000 before species was protected in 1962. Many sheep owners still shoot on sight, but enough respect for the law has allowed golden eagle to slowly recover.

Mates for life and typically nests on cliffs in bed of sticks. Sometimes builds additional nests that are never or seldom used, though no one knows why. Moves north to nesting grounds as early as February and March, laying eggs while snow is on ground.

GREAT HORNED OWL page 211

Description. Large, with "ears" (feather tufts) on head. Gray brown with finely barred belly.

Distribution. Throughout GYE. Nests on cliffs or in trees.

Remarks. Hooting more frequent on midwinter nights; this is mating time. Nests earlier than any other North American bird, laying two to four eggs in mid-February. Timed so that chicks hatch about when small mammals start stirring in spring.

Preys on small mammals, particularly rabbits. Can fly silently. Primary feathers are serrated, which breaks up flow of air over wing and eliminates noise. Asymmetrical ear openings receive sounds at slightly different times, enabling bird to pinpoint prey.

GREAT GRAY OWL

Description. Third-largest owl in North America. Large, round face; generally gray.

Distribution. Not common, though found in coniferous forests in GYE, the southern edge of its range. Associated with lodgepole pine forests interspersed with meadows.

Remarks. Preys on voles and gophers. Nests in cavities of large, old trees, old northern goshawk nests, or on platforms created by dwarf mistletoe brooms. Since foresters now eliminate dead trees and mistletoe, extensive timbering may be hurting this species.

BOREAL OWL

Description. Dark brown, not more than nine inches long.

Distribution. Boreal forests of Canada; only recently discovered in GYE, where it appears in high elevations. Still relatively rare, but has been found nesting in Grand Teton National Park. Other confirmed sightings in Lionhead area near West Yellowstone and near Henry's Lake.

Remarks. Cavity nester. Favors old-growth spruce-fir forest with many snags. Likes voles, which are common in such forests. Old growth may also be necessary to reduce heat loading in summer.

BLUE GROUSE

Description. Chickenlike. Male has gray plumage, yellow orange eye patch, and purple neck patch that inflates during mating call. Female dull brown.

Distribution. Found year-round in ecosystem's coniferous forests.

Remarks. Has unusual habit of spending summers at lower elevations and winters on subalpine slopes and ridges, where it feeds on buds and needles. In spring, male makes a deep, booming hoot. Like a ventriloquist, a calling grouse is often difficult to locate.

RUFFED GROUSE   *page 211*

Description. Chickenlike, brown; banded tail has black terminal band. Black patch on shoulder.

Distribution. Throughout forests in ecosystem, partial to aspen groves.

Remarks. Male's drumming is distinctive spring sound. Created by fluttering wings on hollow log; sounds like a lawn motor starting up. Can be heard a quarter-mile or more away. Females are treated to a display by the male, who puffs up feathers, spreads tail, and struts about.

Ruffed grouse nests on ground, making young vulnerable to predators. To compensate, many chicks are produced—up to a dozen or more. They are alert, able to see, and move about within a day of hatching. Mother has four calls to communicate with young. One tells them to freeze, another to scatter, a third keeps them motionless, and the fourth means "all clear."

DIPPER *page 212*

Description. Stubby, gray, smaller than robin, bobs up and down. Flies with rapid beat.

Distribution. Found year-round by rivers and rushing mountain streams.

Remarks. Forages for insects on bottoms of fast-moving creeks. Even walks underwater on creek bed or uses tiny wings to swim, even in streams too rapid for people to stand in or wade across. Nests are built of moss under crevices or ledges next to streams. Has adapted to watery existence with oil glands that waterproof its feathers, transparent eyelids, and little flaps to seal nostrils.

BELTED KINGFISHER *page 212*

Description. Loud, rattlelike call often heard before bird is seen. Big head, large, daggerlike bill, ragged, bushy crest, blue gray.

Distribution. Along rivers and lakes throughout GYE.

Remarks. Often perches on branches or hovers over water, ready to plunge in after a minnow or other small fish, its chief prey. Other than terns, kingfisher is the only small bird in area that dives in headlong after fish.

Nests are in burrows bored three to six feet into riverbanks. The female belted kingfisher produces five to eight eggs each May. Young birds learn how to fish by lining up on a branch over water and retrieving dead fish that parents drop. Except when raising a family, kingfisher is solitary and defends territories fiercely.

NIGHTHAWK   *page 212*

Description. Not a hawk, but a member of the goatsucker family, which includes whippoorwill. Large eyes, small bill, and large mouth— ideal for capturing flying insects. Looks like a large, gray swallow, with long, pointed wings that bear distinctive white bar. Changes speed and direction suddenly when flying in order to capture moths or other insects.

Distribution. Near lower-elevation rivers and open fields throughout ecosystem.

Remarks. One of the unforgettable sounds of summer evenings is the "beer-beer" of nighthawk as it feeds. Male also makes whirring sounds during mating displays. Flies and dives toward ground, pulling up suddenly at last moment.

RUFOUS HUMMINGBIRD

Description. Small with reddish back.

Distribution. Common in mountains in mid to late summer, where it seeks red flowers for nectar.

Remarks. The amazing ability of hummingbirds is hovering, which requires tremendous energy. Because of small size, there is much surface area compared with volume; hummingbird loses a lot of heat this way, and for both reasons must consume energy-rich food. Nectar is largely sugar and water, so it's important. Cannot survive on sugar, though, and requires fats and proteins from insects.

To get enough sugar, hummingbird must drink a lot of nectar, enough to force bird to pass water equal to nearly 85 percent of body weight daily. This would be like a human eliminating twenty gallons in a day!

Hummingbird defends territories of flowers against bees, moths, and anything else that might threaten its nectar. Since peak blossoming time varies with elevation and latitude, bird migrates accordingly. Most rufous hummingbirds travel up the Pacific coast in spring as blossoming moves northward and then circle over to the Rockies to move southward as mountain meadows reach peak period.

Hummingbird reduces body temperature at night by entering a torpor. This cuts heat loss. While in torpor, hummingbird may reduce its heart rate from 1,200 beats per minute to as few as thirty-six.

BLACK-BACKED WOODPECKER

Description. Back is black, head has yellow cap in males. White belly.

Distribution. Rare. Associated with lodgepole pine forests, particularly those with dead and dying trees.

Remarks. Attracted to recently burned areas, where it feeds on wood-boring insects. Round patches of fresh bark lining otherwise burnt trunks indicate a black-backed has been feeding. After the 1988 fires, black-backed numbers increased in burned areas. Male drums on trees during mating season to attract females. Nest chiseled out of snags; cavity is later used by other animals.

HORNED LARK

Description. Brown, about size of a sparrow, with two pointed, black feathers ("horns") protruding from top of head. Black breast mark.

Distribution. Along with water pipit and rosy finch, is most likely to be encountered in alpine areas of ecosystem. Unlike other two, horned lark is also common on prairies.

Remarks. Ground nester; distracts predators by behaving as if wing is broken. While it flutters and flops about (always safely away from jaws of pursuer), it draws danger away from nest. Unlike most songbirds, horned lark walks rather than hops when feeding.

VIOLET-GREEN SWALLOW   *page 212*

Description. Robin-sized, with pointed wings, short bill, white patches on side of rump that nearly meet at base of forked tail.

Distribution. Higher-elevation forests.

Remarks. A cavity nester, frequently forming loose colonies of up to twenty birds. Feeds primarily on insects taken on the wing.

CLIFF SWALLOW

Description. Rust-colored rump, square tail, dark throat patch.

Distribution. Abundant near cliffs and buildings where nests of mud are built under ledges or eaves.

Remarks. Like the violet-green swallow, cliff swallow captures insects on the wing.

GRAY JAY   *page 212*

Description. Robin-sized, gray body, white head. Flaps, then glides.
Distribution. Found year-round, often in lodgepole pine forests.
Remarks. Familiar "camp robber" is rather tame, particularly at campsites and picnic areas. Nests early, usually laying eggs in late March or early April while snow is on ground.

BLACK-BILLED MAGPIE   *page 212*

Description. Only large black-and-white land bird in ecosystem. Long, greenish-black, iridescent tail; white patches on wing.
Distribution. Found year-round in aspen and cottonwood groves.
Remarks. Nest looks like a big, messy pile of sticks. Forms loose colonies; usually mates for life.

CLARK'S NUTCRACKER   *page 212*

Description. Stout bill, white patches on black wings, gray body.
Distribution. Mostly high elevations, in limber and whitebark pine.
Remarks. Named for William Clark of the Lewis and Clark expedition, this bird has a raucous call. Mainly eats seeds gathered from whitebark pine and other trees; stores communal caches for winter. As with other corvids (jays, ravens, magpies), nutcracker appears to have a good memory. One study showed that 86 percent of the time, a nutcracker could find caches buried in snow. Sublingual pouch can carry up to 95 pine seeds; handy when the nutcracker stores as many as 22,000 seeds a summer. Tends to be right- or left-footed when handling seeds. Distribution and germination of whitebark seeds is thought to depend significantly on nutcracker. Nests early, usually in February or early March.

COMMON RAVEN   *page 212*

Description. Large, glossy black, with stout bill. Tail wedge-shaped (crow's is square).

Distribution. Common throughout ecosystem (crow found only in lower elevations).

Remarks. Often seen gliding and soaring on summer thermals. Intelligent and can "count" in experimental situations. Extremely adaptable, can survive from tropics to Arctic. Feeds on small mammals as well as carrion, which it may be very dependent on in winter. Reintroduction of wolves may increase raven survival. In Arctic, ravens follow wolves, waiting to clean up kills. Also hunts cooperatively. Very vocal, with large "vocabulary" and individual calls for "friends" or partners.

MOUNTAIN CHICKADEE
page 212

Description. Small, gray, with dark cap, black bib, white cheeks and belly. White line over each eye.

Distribution. Lives year-round in conifer forests.

Remarks. Rather tame. Song is a "fee-bee-bee." Usually forages in small flocks and nests in tree cavities.

BLACK-CAPPED CHICKADEE

Description. Similar to mountain chickadee, except no white line above eye.

Distribution. Very common in GYE, typically at lower elevations in mixed woods.

Remarks. Sings a familiar "chick-a-dee-dee-dee."

RED-BREASTED NUTHATCH

Description. Small, with gray back, white belly, rusty sides. White line through eye.

Distribution. Cavity nester in conifer forests.

Remarks. Climbs down sides of trees while it searches for insects. Nasal voice sounds like a tin horn: "ank."

AMERICAN ROBIN
page 213

Description. Reddish breast, brown back.

Distribution. Found everywhere from suburban yards to alpine tundra.

Remarks. This most familiar of birds has a flutelike song and a varied diet. Favors earthworms, which studies have shown the robin locates by sight, not sound or touch. If winter is mild, some may remain in lower elevations of ecosystem, but most head south and don't return until March. Robins living above 10,000 feet have been shown to have lungs averaging 41 percent larger than those of robins at sea level.

TOWNSEND'S SOLITAIRE

Description. Gray with white eye ring and white sides, long tail.
Distribution. Throughout ecosystem, but more common in higher-elevation coniferous forests.
Remarks. Ground nester. Eats berries and worms, will also grab insects in flight.

SWAINSON'S THRUSH   *page 213*

Description. Brown. Distinguished from other thrushes by buff eye ring and dark spots or streaks on breast.
Distribution. Common in summer, but seldom seen. Prefers moist canyons in coniferous forests.
Remarks. A food generalist, eating insects, worms, berries. Unlike the related robin, it forages in trees, not ground.

MOUNTAIN BLUEBIRD

Description. Males have beautiful turquoise blue backs and white bellies. Females brownish.
Distribution. Aspen and conifer forests next to meadows, where it finds insects.
Remarks. Nests in tree cavities. Abandoned woodpecker holes are natural homes, but bluebird boxes are increasingly important. Over much of its range at lower elevations, bluebird has declined because starlings, introduced from Europe, have taken over so many nesting cavities.

RUBY-CROWNED KINGLET

Description. Small, very active. Nondescript brownish gray, with reddish crown. By far, more common of two kinglets found in GYE.

Distribution. Coniferous forests generally near water, primarily spruce-fir stands.

Remarks. Often forages in winter with other small birds, like chickadees.

WATER PIPIT

Description. Slightly smaller than robin. Drab with white outer tail feathers and a bobbing habit.

Distribution. Alpine tundra.

Remarks. Nests among rock slides, creating sunken nest lined with grass. Feeds on insects and seeds.

EUROPEAN STARLING

Description. Short-tailed black bird with yellow bill.

Distribution. Introduced from Europe and now widespread across continent.

Remarks. Competes with bluebirds and other natives for nesting sites; may be responsible for decline of some species, particularly near towns and cities.

WARBLING VIREO

Description. Small, olive brown, undistinguished light belly. If it looks like a vireo but lacks wing bars, eye rings, or other markings, it is probably a warbling vireo.

Distribution. Common among aspen, though sometimes found in pines in foothills and lower mountains.

Remarks. Tends to forage high in trees on caterpillars and other insects.

YELLOW WARBLER

Description. Only small warbler that is bright yellow over entire body, with reddish streaking on breast.

Distribution. Common warbler in GYE. Found in riparian areas in alder and willow thickets, from lower valleys into mountains.

Remarks. One of the most frequent hosts of the parasitic cowbird, one factor leading to its decline.

YELLOW-RUMPED WARBLER   *page 213*

Description. Black and white, with conspicuous yellow patch at base of tail and on head.

Distribution. Coniferous forests.

Remarks. Audubon's warbler and myrtle warbler were once considered separate species; now lumped together as yellow-rumped. Like other warblers, it forages for insects.

COMMON YELLOWTHROAT   *page 213*

Description. Yellow throat and breast with broad, black cheek stripe across eye. Back is olive brown.

Distribution. Wetlands and irrigation ditches. Only warbler likely to be found in such habitats.

Remarks. Flits through low shrubs and grasses, catching dragonflies and other insects.

MACGILLIVRAY'S WARBLER

Description. Small, olive back, yellow belly, grayish head.

Distribution. Common in dense thickets and aspen groves, usually near water.

Remarks. An insectivore.

WILSON'S WARBLER

Description. Small, yellow breast, olive brown back, black cap.

Distribution. Common in riparian thickets, shrublike conifers near timberline, and other similar habitats in GYE.

Remarks. Larger clutches found at higher elevations, presumably because of higher mortality rates in more severe climates.

WESTERN MEADOWLARK *page 213*

Description. Loud, bubbly song frequently heard in spring. Yellow breast, brown and black back, black necklace, large beak.

Distribution. Grassy valleys and foothills.

Remarks. Feeds by hopping along ground and picking up grasshoppers and other insects.

YELLOW-HEADED BLACKBIRD

Description. Black with bright yellow head.

Distribution. Marshes, particularly those with cattails.

Remarks. Utilizes different parts of marsh than the similar red-winged blackbird. Usually yellow-headed is in slightly deeper water (two to four feet). Males stake out territories; those with better sites typically attract more than one mate. Others may have one or no mates.

RED-WINGED BLACKBIRD *page 213*

Description. Black with red epaulettes.

Distribution. More abundant than yellow-headed. Almost anyplace there are cattails.

Remarks. The red shoulder patch can be concealed and is used to signal social intentions. A bird trying to defend its territory prominently displays patch, while foraging bird will usually keep patch hidden to avoid antagonizing rival male. Male defends territories, often breeding with more than one female if he controls a food-rich area.

BREWER'S BLACKBIRD

Description. Male has purple green sheen on head with a bright yellow eye, which distinguishes it from cowbird. Female brownish.

Distribution. Shrubby areas and aspen groves, especially near water.

Remarks. Insect eater. Has increased range as agriculture has spread. Nests in colonies of three to a hundred birds.

BROWN-HEADED COWBIRD

Description. Males greenish black, similar to Brewer's blackbird, but with shorter bill and brown head.

Distribution. Mostly open country.

Remarks. Is a brood parasite, laying eggs in nest of other birds, who raise the young as if they were their own. Scientists have recorded cowbird eggs in nests of more than 220 species, but not all are appropriate hosts. Some recognize different eggs and remove them. Others abandon nest and build another. Some hosts never notice unwanted young and simply exhaust themselves trying to feed them. Particularly true of small warblers, hummingbirds, and other tiny birds that are often smaller as adults than the cowbird chicks.

If undetected, young cowbird often gets more than its fair share of food. Sometimes will even kick out nest mates. Despite aggressive tactics, only about 3 percent of cowbirds hatch and survive to maturity. To compensate, eggs are produced almost continuously during breeding season, perhaps forty a year. Each goes into a different host nest.

Range has expanded greatly from earlier Great Plains habitat, due to clearing of forests and farming in many areas. A bird of open country, it often uses road and clearcut corridors to invade territory of forest dwellers. As a consequence, brood parasitism threatens many songbirds, particularly some warblers and vireos.

PINE GROSBEAK

Description. Male red with white wing bars. Both sexes have stout, seed-crushing bill.

Distribution. Common in higher-elevation coniferous forests. Typically seen in small flocks.

Remarks. Lives on seeds of spruce, alder, mountain ash, snowberry, and others. Doesn't migrate; merely moves to lower elevations in winter.

ROSY FINCH

Description. Stocky, small, gray cap, black forehead, rosy tinge to rump and wings.

Distribution. Alpine tundra.

Remarks. Wanders in small flocks eating seeds. Develops pouch in throat to carry loads of seeds back to nestlings.

PINE SISKIN

Description. Common, small, brown with streaks over body, yellow wing bars, yellow on rump.
Distribution. Conifer forests, woodlands.

VESPER SPARROW

Description. White-edged tail feathers, heavily streaked breast.
Distribution. Among most common sparrows in GYE, found at lower elevations in open grasslands.
Remarks. Forages on ground for seeds and insects.

DARK-EYED JUNCO   *page 213*

Description. Gray with brown back and white outer tail feathers, flashed when bird takes to flight.
Distribution. Common from lower elevations to timberline.
Remarks. Some say this is most abundant bird in ecosystem. Flits through conifers but feeds on seeds and insects from ground.

CHIPPING SPARROW

Description. Brown, streaked back, gray breast, brownish red cap delineated by white and black eye stripe.
Distribution. Conifers.
Remarks. Frequent cowbird host.

WHITE-CROWNED SPARROW

Description. White cap, black and white stripes on head.
Distribution. Thickets and shrubby vegetation up to timberline.
Remarks. Some males are polygamous; females are hostile to other females, singing to defend space within their male's territory.

LINCOLN'S SPARROW

Description. Brown, heavily streaked breast.

Distribution. Riparian thickets. Though common in GYE, this secretive bird is seldom seen by casual observers.

Remarks. Nests on ground. If disturbed, female will run away while faking broken wing to distract predators. Has an unusual habit of using both feet to scratch at ground to expose insects and seeds.

SONG SPARROW

Description. Brown, heavily streaked breast, prominent black breast spot.

Distribution. Habitat overlaps that of Lincoln's sparrow; both found in riparian thickets.

Remarks. Sings beautifully. In some areas, male tends young while female begins second clutch elsewhere, so one pair may produce two broods in a season.

MAMMALS

Compared with the rest of the United States, Yellowstone has a relatively intact mammal fauna. Ninety-four species are found in the GYE. The status of some, such as the fisher and lynx, is unknown; they may already be extinct or close to it. The numbers and distribution of bats, shrews, voles, and other small mammals are based on extremely limited data. For some species, there are only one or two records for the entire ecosystem! Despite this limited knowledge, most biologists consider greater Yellowstone to be one of the premier wildlife sanctuaries in the nation.

Mammals are warm and furry. Fur provides insulation and warm-bloodedness permits activity year-round, day or night. Mammals display relatively complex behaviors, particularly in learning ability. Young are born live and nursed.

Small Mammals

Small mammals are abundant in the ecosystem. There are seven species of shrews, ten bats, two rabbits, two hares, a pika, eight voles and mice, nine members of the squirrel family, ten small carnivores, and the porcupine, woodrat, and muskrat. However, except for a few squirrels, chipmunks, and the marmot, you're not likely to see most small mammals, since they tend to be nocturnal. Identification is complicated by similarities. A glimpse of a mouselike creature may not tell you whether it is a vole, a mouse, or a shrew. Even field guides are not particularly useful, since variation in color, size, and other features sometimes makes identification difficult.

Warm-bloodedness has advantages and drawbacks. It means these creatures can live, breed, and forage in cold weather. But their small bodies have relatively large surface areas that radiate heat. Since most small mammals tend to be very energetic, they have a tremendous need for food to stoke their "furnaces." A masked shrew's heart may beat as many as 1,300 times per minute, and it will starve if deprived of food for just eleven hours!

In cold weather, most small mammals remain in burrows, under snow, or in nest cavities to stay warm. Some bats go into a torpor when roosting, bringing their body temperature closer to the air temperature, which conserves energy. Marmots and some ground squirrels simply hibernate. Pikas and red squirrels cache food in summer to carry them through the long winters.

Small mammals are a major part of the diet of most predators. Adolph Murie, who studied the coyote in Yellowstone during the 1940s, examined thousands of droppings and noted that voles made up 34 percent of its diet while pocket gophers constituted 22 percent.

Shrews

There are seven shrews in the GYE. They are among the more primitive mammals and largely eat spiders, larvae of moths and beetles, slugs, snails, earthworms, and carrion.

All are similar. They have small brown or gray mouselike bodies with tiny, nearly functionless eyes; long-whiskered, pointy noses; red-tipped teeth; and more or less naked tails. They are the smallest mammals, which is a good thing for they are incredibly pugnacious.

Active year-round, shrews remain under snow in winter, constantly searching for food. They must eat every three or four hours and consume their weight daily. Probably due to their energetic lifestyle, shrews burn themselves out in a year and a half. Mating is in the spring and fall; young are born in eighteen days with four or five per litter. They mature in four months.

Territories are defended. The pygmy shrew emits a strong musky odor, perhaps to mark its realm. Because of their pinhole eyes, shrews feel their way around. They make rapid, twittering squeaks that help them locate themselves, much in the way bats do.

WATER SHREW (Sorex palustris)

Description. Only shrew you are likely to see often. Gray. The largest shrew, up to seven inches.

Habitat and Distribution. Near streams and creeks with lots of boulders and roots for cover, usually subalpine or alpine. Found throughout ecosystem.

Remarks. Tiny air bubbles in fur give it tremendous buoyancy. To dive, shrew must paddle furiously. Can remain submerged for up to forty-eight seconds. Among other aquatic adaptations are stiff guard hairs, plus slight webbing between third and fourth toes on hind feet. Sometimes appears to run on water. Air trapped in fur also insulates and helps keep shrew dry. Besides usual shrew diet, also eats fish eggs, mayflies, stoneflies, and an occasional small fish.

VAGRANT SHREW (Sorex vagrans)

Description. Reddish brown in summer, nearly black in winter. Four inches long with tail.

Habitat and Distribution. Found throughout West. Associated with swamps, bogs, streamsides with grass or shrubs as cover. Ranges into alpine zone.

DUSKY SHREW (Sorex monticolus)

Description. Dull brown. May grow to nearly five inches. Tail is dark above and light below.

Habitat and Distribution. Mountainous areas, occasionally ranges into alpine. Found in boggy habitats and forests. Habits and range similar to vagrant shrew.

MASKED SHREW (Sorex cinereus)

Description. Four inches with tail. Grayish brown, naked tail. Long, whiskery nose. Pink feet.

Habitat and Distribution. Damp meadows, forests at timberline, occasionally in sagebrush areas.

Remarks. Most common shrew in GYE.

DWARF SHREW (Sorex nanus)

Description. Dwarf and pygmy shrews are smallest mammals in North America. Dwarf reaches 3.3 to 4.2 inches. Greenish brown on back, fading to smoky gray on belly.

Habitat and Distribution. Prefers rocky outcrops in subalpine and alpine areas.

Remarks. Very rare; only eighteen dwarfs caught in United States from 1895 to 1966. Only thirty-seven taken in ecosystem since first was trapped in 1954, all in Beartooth Plateau along the Montana-Wyoming line between 8,000 and 10,500 feet or at one location (10,500 feet) in Grand Teton park.

MERRIAM'S SHREW (*Sorex merriami*)

Description. Length is 3.5 to 4.3 inches; gray brown above with whitish belly. Tail bicolored.

Habitat and Distribution. Sagebrush and grassland. Never recorded in Yellowstone, it has been found in nearby areas of all three states, so it is in GYE.

Remarks. Exceedingly rare throughout range.

PREBLE'S SHREW (*Sorex preblei*)

Description. Length: 3.4 to 3.8 inches. Bicolored tail.

Habitat and Distribution. Drier areas than other shrews, mostly sagebrush and grasslands.

Remarks. Almost nothing known about Preble's shrew, since only thirty-five have been collected in United States. Only one ever found in Wyoming was in Lamar Valley. A few locations in Montana, mostly in southwest, including Hebgen Lake area near West Yellowstone.

PYGMY SHREW (*Sorex hoyi*)

Description. Smallest mammal in North America, only 3 to 3½ inches. Body greenish brown above and grayish below. Nearly naked tail.

Habitat and Distribution. Subalpine meadows and rocky areas. Prefers drier meadows than other shrews and has been found in sagebrush-grass habitats.

Remarks. Never found in GYE, but well documented in northwest Montana and has been found in nearby Beaverhead County and south in Medicine Bow Mountains of Wyoming.

Bats

There are more species of bats than any other animal except rodents. Most are in tropical or subtropical climates, but ten are known or suspected to be in the GYE.

These are the only mammals that can truly fly (flying squirrels glide). Bats have thin membranes stretched between the long finger bones to form a wing and a membrane between the legs and tail. They have evolved to take over the nighttime niche of insect-feeding birds like swallows and are extremely maneuverable.

Bats have the most developed echolocation system of any animal. As they fly, bats emit high-frequency squeaks (too high to hear, though they do make sounds that humans can detect) that bounce off of objects or prey. Bats determine distance and general outlines by the length of time from the emission of sound to when the echo is received. They can not only find their way around but also locate insects. Some moths have developed a "jamming" system that emits sounds that foil the bat's radar.

In the GYE, bats prey mostly on insects, including moths, mosquitoes, beetles, and flies. A bat will eat nearly 10,000 mosquitoes in a night. Smaller bats eat up to a third of their weight daily. Insects are caught in a special pocket on the wing that is shaped like a baseball mitt. The bat will then bend its wing over and swallow the prey, or, if it is a large catch, it will fly back to the roost and eat it there.

Most bats produce only one young per year. Some mate in the late summer and females store the sperm and conceive the following spring. A baby will cling to its mother's chest, even while she is flying. At other times, it will be left hanging in the roost. If it loses its grip, it likely will perish. If the baby survives the impact, the mother often will try to rescue it. A young bat can fly and find food after three or four weeks.

In northern climates like the GYE, bats live outdoors for about six months before cold and lack of food drive them into hibernation or force migration. Bats usually hibernate in large caves, clustering for warmth, though their body temperature drops close to freezing. During this time, bats are extremely vulnerable to human disturbance because they have so little fat with which to make it through the winter. If agitated, they can burn up valuable calories. Since there's nothing for them to eat in winter, they can starve or freeze to death before spring.

During the summer, all bats roost during the day. Some enter caves, but many others roost under loose bark on large snags or in tree cavities (another reason dead trees are a valuable resource). Cracks in buildings and rocks also are daytime roosts.

Bats are declining in many areas. Loss of habitat, poison buildup in insects, and many other factors are responsible. Some species live up to thirty years and are good barometers of environmental changes. If bat numbers decline, which they are for nearly all species, that probably means that environmental quality is deteriorating.

BIG BROWN BAT (Eptesicus fuscus)

Description. Four to five inches, pale brown, wingspan of thirteen to fifteen inches. Large size is distinguishing.

Habitat and Distribution. Throughout North America. First specimen collected in Yellowstone park near Mammoth in 1984. Often roosts in barns and buildings.

Remarks. Takes more beetles than any other bat; also eats flies and ants. Upon start of hibernation, a third of its weight is fat. Hardier than most bats, perhaps because of its size. Starts hibernating late, comes out earlier in spring.

LITTLE BROWN BAT (Myotis lucifugus)

Description. Dark brown with lighter belly; dark face, ears, wings, and feet. Three to four inches long.

Habitat and Distribution. Common across North America. In GYE, gathers in large colonial roosts in buildings, tree cavities, caves.

Remarks. Female carries baby while foraging. Youngster matures in three weeks. Feeds primarily on aquatic insects, so is common by ponds, marshes, and streams.

SMALL-FOOTED MYOTIS (Myotis leibii)

Description. Distinctive black mask, black wing membrane. Otherwise, tan to brown. Length is 2 to 3½ inches.

Habitat and Distribution. Throughout much of West but sparse in GYE. Found near water, where it feeds on insects, particularly moths and beetles. Winters in caves.

LONG-LEGGED BAT (Myotis volans)

Description. Dark brown or reddish with lighter belly. Lacks black mask of small-footed myotis but has black wing membrane. Body 3.7 to 4.2 inches.

Habitat and Distribution. Widespread but uncommon. Not reported in Yellowstone park, but found in Park County, Wyoming, as well as nearby areas of Montana. Found near water up to timberline, particularly near coniferous and aspen forests.

Remarks. Flies higher than other bats; often forages near treetops. One of first bats to appear in evening.

SILVER-HAIRED MYOTIS (Lasionycteris noctivagans)

Description. Frosty outer hairs over dark brown or black fur; face is black. Body 3.7 to 4.5 inches.

Habitat and Distribution. Migratory tree-roosting bat, hiding under bark or in cavities. Normally found in coniferous forests; generally feeds over lakes and meadows. Fairly common in western Montana and has been seen in Wyoming, but not in Yellowstone park.

LONG-EARED MYOTIS (Myotis evotis)

Description. Longest ears of any bat in North America. Brown on back, pale belly, black wings. Body 3.5 to 3.9 inches in length.

Habitat and Distribution. Coniferous forests and small lakes. Particularly fond of beetles.

TOWNSEND'S BIG-EARED BAT (Plecotus townsendii)

Description. Ears like the long-eared myotis, but also has prominent bumps on snout. Gray brown on back, light gray belly. Body 3½ to 4½ inches.

Habitat and Distribution. Custer and Gallatin national forests, Grand Teton and Yellowstone parks. Roosts mostly in caves; not migratory. Feeds mostly in meadows along edge of forests.

Remarks. Sensitive to disturbance. Human intruders in caves can cause adults to abandon young. Has been in decline recently and is a candidate for endangered status.

HOARY BAT (*Lasiurus cinereus*)

Description. White-tipped hairs with light underhairs give it a hoary appearance. Largest bat in GYE, up to 5.8 inches long.

Habitat and Distribution. Throughout United States; recorded in Grand Teton park and Montana, but not in Yellowstone. Almost certainly lives there, however.

Remarks. Strong flyer, making annual migrations between southern United States and Mexico and ranges in northern United States and Canada. Tree rooster; seldom seen around buildings. Feeds primarily over water on moths and larger prey.

SPOTTED BAT (*Euderma maculatum*)

Description. Three large white spots on dark background on shoulders and rump. Belly whitish. Huge pink ears. Body 4.3 to 4.6 inches.

Habitat and Distribution. Drier environments like juniper-shrub, sage-grasslands. Forages in open fields and forests. Roosts in remote high cliffs. Reported in northeastern GYE, but likely found elsewhere, too.

Remarks. You're lucky if you see this one; only thirty-five reported from 1891 to 1965. U.S. Fish and Wildlife Service is considering listing species as endangered. Prefers undisturbed, remote sites. Forages for moths high above trees and fields.

FRINGED MYOTIS (*Myotis thysanodes*)

Description. Light brown, lighter belly; large, dark ears. Distinctive fringe of stiff hairs along tail membrane.

Habitat and Distribution. Dry coniferous forests. Roosts in caves and buildings. Has never been collected in ecosystem, but has been found in southwest Montana and parts of Wyoming, so it probably lives in GYE.

Remarks. Feeds mostly on moths, crickets, and beetles; hovers to capture insects on branches. Forms nursery colonies.

Pikas, Rabbits, and Hares

The order *Lagomorpha* includes rabbits and rabbitlike animals. There are two families—*Leporidae* (rabbits and hares) and *Ochotonidae* (pikas). Pika, mountain cottontail, desert cottontail, snowshoe hare, and white-tailed jackrabbit are found in the GYE.

Rabbits and hares look alike, but there are many subtle differences. Rabbits are born blind, hairless, and helpless; hares are born with hair and can move around almost immediately. Mature hares have longer legs and larger ears than rabbits. Hares rely upon speed to evade predators, while rabbits are more likely to dodge or seek cover.

During the breeding season, males fight for dominance like bull elk. Once a hierarchy is established, dominant males do most of the breeding. Pikas, rabbits, and hares eat their own feces in order to capture vitamins produced by bacteria in the intestines.

PIKA (Ochotona princeps)

Description. Sometimes called rock rabbit. Six to eight inches long with small ears, no tail.

Habitat and Distribution. Rocky slopes often at or near timberline, occasionally in boulder piles in lower forested valleys. Found throughout higher Rockies and Cascades and into Alaska. Common throughout GYE.

Remarks. Often heard before seen, it emits a loud, distinctive "eek," a warning whenever an intruder ventures too close. Caller may dart into a crack in rocks, only to reappear suddenly from behind another stone.

Each pika belongs to a loose colony but except for mating season lives a solitary life, defending its territory. A litter of three is produced in May and another usually in July. Since pika remains active all winter, it stores food in summer. Gathers grass and flowers, then spreads them on a rock to dry. After curing, "hay" is stashed under rocks. Stacks are fiercely defended.

MOUNTAIN COTTONTAIL (Sylvilagus nuttallii)

Description. Smaller version of more familiar eastern cottontail rabbit, with small, stubby ears. Body fourteen to sixteen inches. Tail dark above, white below.

Habitat and Distribution. Arid habitats with cover, such as sagebrush or thickets along streams. Widespread in West but only found sporadically at lower elevations around GYE. Look along the Gardner River between Mammoth and Gardiner, Montana.

Remarks. Hides in burrows in thickets or crevices. Does not dig, but occupies squirrel or fox holes. Eats buds, sagebrush bark, grass.

DESERT COTTONTAIL *(Sylvilagus audubonii)*

Description. Looks like mountain cottontail. Slightly larger, 15½ to 17½ inches, and generally lighter in color.

Habitat and Distribution. Grasslands and shrublands. Where ranges of desert and mountain cottontail overlap, desert species inhabits drier, more open country. Both favor dense vegetation for cover. Not found in Idaho, but common in Wyoming and Montana along eastern borders of GYE and near Gardiner on northern end of Yellowstone.

SNOWSHOE HARE *(Lepus americanus)*   *page 213*

Description. Up to twenty inches long. Large hind feet act like snowshoes, making it nimble over deep, powdery snow. Winter coat is white, matching its environment. Ears tips stay black; in summer, coat turns brown.

Habitat and Description. Probably most widely distributed rabbitlike animal in ecosystem. Found mostly in forests up to timberline, up to 12,000 feet in Wyoming.

Remarks. Active year-round. Several adaptations to cold include highly insulated coat and lower metabolism in winter to reduce food needs. Snowshoe has cyclic existence, with numbers peaking every ten or eleven years. No one knows why, but may be influenced by disease, stress, and nutrition. Snowshoe is important food for lynx, wolverine, great horned owl, coyote, and goshawk.

WHITE-TAILED JACKRABBIT *(Lepus townsendii)*   *page 213*

Description. Similar to snowshoe except for longer legs and larger body, up to twenty-six inches. Brown in summer, white in winter, with long, black-tipped ears.

Habitat and Distribution. Open country, usually grasslands, but roams into alpine.

Remarks. Remarkably swift; will even take to water to evade a predator. Still, many become dinner for coyotes, whose diet may be up to 75 percent jackrabbit.

Rodents

This is the largest group of mammals in Yellowstone. Most are nocturnal, and though they are abundant, you won't see many different types even after numerous visits. Rodents have upper and lower incisors that grow continually. If not worn down, the teeth will grow until they eventually curve back into the mouth. Most rodents are vegetarians, though some will occasionally eat meat. A few prey on grasshoppers and other insects. Some are active year-round, but many hibernate in winter.

Rodents are critical to the ecosystem. They convert plants, seeds, and insects into meat, and so are needed for the survival of species from raptors to coyotes and from pine martens to snakes.

DEER MOUSE *(Peromyscus maniculatus)*

Description. Gray to reddish above with white belly, chin, legs, and feet and a long tail, dark on top, white below. Relatively large ears and eyes. Up to seven inches, including tail.

Habitat and Distribution. Most abundant and widespread mouse in West. Lives in nearly every habitat, but seems to avoid wet meadows and riparian areas.

Remarks. Active year-round; doesn't store much food. Forages under snow. Nest composed of fur and other material placed under rocks and logs. As many as four litters per year. Many become snacks for everything from hawks to weasels.

WESTERN JUMPING MOUSE *(Zaphus princeps)*

Description. Cream-colored beneath, gray or brown above, long tail, large hind legs. Up to nine inches, including tail.

Habitat and Distribution. Wet meadows, riparian and streamside areas, where it feeds on insects and seeds.

Remarks. In kangaroo fashion, will catapult into the air as high as three to six feet. After putting on fat in fall, hibernates in a burrow, not stirring until May. If it has insufficient fat, may die in burrow. Mates in spring; young mature in two months. Few live longer than a year.

BUSHY-TAILED WOODRAT *(Neotoma cinerea)*

Description. Squirrel-size, gray, fourteen- to eighteen-inch body with lighter belly. Long, bushy tail; white feet; large eyes and ears.

Habitat and Distribution. Throughout ecosystem in cliffs, crevices, and abandoned cabins from lowest elevations to timberline.

Remarks. Signs include a pile of wood and other debris under a rocky ledge, sludgy deposits of black feces, and orange lichen on a cliff face (courtesy of fertilizing urine). Because it carts off bright objects such as bottle caps and other bits of metal, it's sometimes called pack rat. These are deposited in and around nest. Territorial and usually solitary, except when young are present. During mating season, males leave scents on rocks and seek out females. Young take almost a year to mature, a long time for rodents. Also lives longer than most mice, up to four years. Eats conifer leaves, seeds, fruit, other vegetable matter. Active all winter; sometimes leaves snow tracks.

GAPPER'S RED-BACKED VOLE (*Clethrionomys gapperi*)

Description. Body up to seven inches, including tail. Back reddish, belly whitish to gray. Tail short, bicolored.

Habitat and Distribution. Across southern Canada into Rockies. Prefers moisture, usually coniferous forests.

Remarks. Forages for seeds, berries, and buds, but will eat carrion. Active all year; maintains nests and tunnels beneath snow. In summer, nests built beneath logs and other debris in old-growth forests. Prey to nearly everything, particularly weasel and marten, vole maintains itself by producing two to four litters each summer.

HEATHER VOLE (*Phenacomys intermedius*)

Description. Body four to six inches. Grayish, light gray belly, white feet.

Habitat and Distribution. From alpine tundra in Beartooths to sagebrush valleys of Grand Teton park, but seldom reported in ecosystem.

Remarks. Active all winter, sometimes eating from caches left during previous summer.

MONTANE VOLE (*Microtus montanus*)

Description. Body 5½ to 7½ inches, brown to gray brown, silver belly, and short, bicolored tail.

Habitat and Distribution. From valley floor to alpine tundra, but usually moist meadows, riparian areas, grassy sagebrush.

Remarks. Breeds year-round; three-week-old female can produce a litter, compensating for high predation losses. Territorial, with both sexes maintaining areas, though male's will overlap several females'.

MEADOW VOLE (Microtus pennsylvanicus)

Description. Body 6½ to 7½ inches. Dark gray to nearly black, lighter belly, short, slightly bicolored tail.

Habitat and Distribution. Marshes to wet meadows and riparian areas, from valley bottoms to timberline.

Remarks. Has two- to four-year population cycles, reaching densities of up to 400 animals per acre. Can breed at four to six weeks; mates continually. Single pair could have a million descendants in one year if nearly 90 percent didn't die in first month. Sometimes swims to safety, but then falls prey to trout and other fish.

RICHARDSON'S WATER VOLE (Microtus richardsoni)

Description. Body up to eleven inches, making it largest vole in GYE. Gray-brown on back, short tail. Resembles small muskrat.

Habitat and Distribution. Stream or pond edges; even has underwater burrow entrances. Higher elevations.

Remarks. Spends a lot of time swimming and diving. Nests on ground beneath snow, connecting subterranean resting spots with tunnels. Seen in spring when ridges of soil are exposed after snow melts (pocket gopher leaves such ridges, too).

LONG-TAILED VOLE (Microtus longicaudus)

Description. Tail makes up 30 percent of overall length of 8½ inches. Brown back, light belly.

Habitat and Distribution. Alpine tundra to aspen groves; favors moist locations.

SAGEBRUSH VOLE (Lemmiscus curtatus)

Description. Very light gray body, whitish belly; five to six inches long with one-inch tail.

Habitat and Distribution. Dry sagebrush; only vole found there. Not well documented in GYE, but reported in Jackson Hole area.

Remarks. Unlike other voles, nests underground.

MUSKRAT *(Ondatra zibethicus)* page 214

Description. Dark brown or gray on back, silver gray on belly. Body up to twenty-five inches, including long, naked tail. Small eyes and ears on large head.

Habitat and Distribution. Wetlands, marshes, swamps, slow-moving rivers and creeks.

Remarks. Not a rat, but largest vole in ecosystem. *Zibethicus* means "musky-odored" in Latin, refers to smell from glands near base of tail. In water, whips its ratlike tail and uses webbed hind feet. Dives for as long as seventeen minutes. Builds low lodges of vegetation and mud. Underwater entrances allow use even when pond is frozen. Active year-round but does not store food or build dams. Eats cattails, tubers, reeds, and sedges.

NORTHERN POCKET GOPHER *(Thomomys talpoides)*

Description. Body ten inches, cylindrical with stubby tail. Brownish gray. Short, dense fur and large front claws.

Habitat and Distribution. Throughout ecosystem from lowlands to alpine. Needs deep soil.

Remarks. Only type of pocket gopher in GYE. Rarely surfaces from burrows. Even if you don't see it, you'll spot sinewy piles of dirt on surface 400 to 500 feet long. Evident after snow melts. Territorial; only one gopher per tunnel system. Eats roots and bulbs; caches food in chambers. Grizzlies will sometimes raid these stores.

GOLDEN-MANTLED GROUND SQUIRREL
(Spermophilus lateralis)

Description. Eleven to twelve inches long. Looks like a big chipmunk with bold black and white stripes on flanks. Unlike chipmunk, there are no stripes on head. Generally golden red over rest of body.

Habitat and Distribution. Found throughout ecosystem in rocky, open areas from valleys to forest meadowlands up to alpine.

Remarks. Not only looks like a chipmunk but has chipmunk habit of gathering food in cheeks and then caching it in burrow. Hibernates from October, becomes active again in March or April. Breeds shortly after emergence in spring.

UINTA GROUND SQUIRREL (Spermophilus armatus)

Description. Looks like Richardson's ground squirrel, except tail is completely gray. Body eleven to twelve inches with grayish back sprinkled with white spots. Nose and shoulders reddish brown.

Habitat and Distribution. Idaho, Utah, Montana, and Wyoming, but distribution is spotty. Found in disturbed grasslands, meadows, and sagebrush flats up to timberline.

Remarks. Lives in colonies. Active in summer, but hibernates much of year. One study in Utah found it was active only eighty-five days a year. Male emerges from burrow first and may be seen in March. July heat drives the Uinta ground squirrel underground and hibernation begins again. Eats mostly leafy material but will partake of other vegetation such as mushrooms, along with carrion, including its own road-killed relatives. Some believe it is in decline.

YELLOW-BELLIED MARMOT (Marmota flaviventris)

Description. This cousin of eastern groundhog is reddish brown on back, golden on stomach. Chunky body with short legs. Waddles. May reach twenty-eight inches long and twelve pounds.

Habitat and Distribution. Only marmot known in GYE. (Hoary marmot is found further north and west and does not reach this part of Rockies.) Lives mostly in rock piles or burrows, can be found from lowest valleys up to alpine zone.

Remarks. Lives in small colonies, with a dominant male and several females and young. Male waves tail slowly as sign of dominance. If a member spots something amiss, it rises on its haunches and whistles.

Active only in summer; may hibernate eight months of the year. If it can't fatten up properly during summer, it may starve in burrow the following winter. Predators from grizzly bear to golden eagle eat marmots; may constitute up to 71 percent of golden eagle's diet.

WHITE-TAILED PRAIRIE DOG (Cynomys leucurus)

Description. Cousin of ubiquitous black-tailed prairie dog. Tan body, white tip on tail.

Habitat and Distribution. From central Wyoming with small ranges into Montana, Utah, and Colorado. Generally higher elevations than black-tailed. Reported along eastern edge of ecosystem in drier lowland valleys and basins like Clark's Fork valley.

Remarks. Hibernates much of year, active between April and August. Lives in colonies, preferring overgrazed sites because reduced cover allows easier detection of predators. Though range abuse encourages spread of prairie dogs, many ranchers dislike them because they compete with cattle for forage. Many prairie dog colonies have been poisoned; one authority says species is at 2 percent of former numbers.

Ecological effects have been tremendous. Prairie dogs are eaten by many other animals, and species from burrowing owls to snakes use their burrows. Near-extinction of ferret and fox as well as declines in others like burrowing owl are partly related to prairie dog losses.

UINTA CHIPMUNK (Tamias umbrinus)

Description. Golden with striped back and face. Ten inches long, including five-inch tail. Largest chipmunk in ecosystem.

Habitat and Distribution. Higher-elevation forests, usually above 8,000 feet; reaches northernmost range in GYE.

Remarks. Hibernates much of year, occasionally awakening to eat food stored in burrow. Largely vegetarian, it will eat insects and carrion.

LEAST CHIPMUNK (Tamias minimus)

Description. Less than nine inches long, including tail; smallest of three chipmunks found in GYE. Two white stripes line face; back has four gray lines backed with black.

Habitat and Distribution. Widest range of any chipmunk in West. Found in many habitats, but appears to prefer surroundings drier than does Uinta chipmunk.

Remarks. Distinguished by carrying tail straight up when running. Feeds more on seeds than other chipmunks. Like most members of squirrel family in region, it hibernates, usually reappearing in March or April, depending on elevation.

YELLOW PINE CHIPMUNK *(Tamias amoenus)*

Description. Yellowish, though telling it from least chipmunk is difficult. Black and white stripes on back and sides distinct. Sides tawny.

Habitat and Distribution. Throughout Pacific Northwest, with range extending into GYE, where it's found in open lodgepole or Douglas fir forests and burned areas. Prefers drier habitat than least or Uinta chipmunk.

RED SQUIRREL *(Tamiasciurus hudsonicus)*   *page 214*

Description. Reddish brown, sometimes almost chocolate brown. Underparts white. White eye ring. Length up to fifteen inches, including tail.

Habitat and Distribution. *Hudsonicus* refers to affinity for boreal forests. Distribution includes Canada, ranging south along mountains of East and West. Common in conifer forests throughout ecosystem.

Remarks. Unlike most small mammals, doesn't mind letting you know it's around. Chatters excitedly when disturbed. Scampers about trees and forest floor gathering cones, seeds, mushrooms, and other food to cache in middens. Some contain as many as 20,000 discarded cones.

Whitebark cone middens are raided by grizzlies, which also relish the large, meaty seeds. Red squirrel also hangs mushrooms in trees to dry or impales them on a sliver of bark. Aggressively defends caches. Though it is active all winter, spends much time curled in a burrow beneath snow or hollow log.

Breeds in spring; a litter of five or so is born naked and helpless. Remains with mother for up to eighteen weeks.

NORTHERN FLYING SQUIRREL *(Glaucomys sabrinus)*

Description. Grizzled brown with light grayish belly; large eyes. Membrane stretches from each leg, front to back, acting as gliding wings. Large, flattened tail has dark tip.

Habitat and Distribution. Old-growth forests. Nests in tree cavities and feeds on fungi, which are abundant in old growth.

Remarks. Glides, doesn't fly. With folds of skin stretched between its front and back legs, the squirrel is able to jump from a high perch and glide to another tree or the ground. It is fond of fungi and is important for dispersal of spores, which it excretes. Unlike the territorial red squirrel, northern flying squirrel lives in families. In winter, they snuggle in a nest cavity to keep warm.

BEAVER *(Castor canadensis)*   *page 214*

Description. Largest rodent in West. May reach a length of 4½ feet and weigh up to 100 pounds. Dark brown with webbed hind feet and a broad, flat tail.

Habitat and Distribution. Waterways and ponds. Trappers nearly drove beaver to extinction. In many parts of country, beaver had to be reintroduced, which is ongoing in Absaroka-Beartooth Wilderness. Lives in areas with abundant willow, aspen, and cottonwood; will eat leaves, twigs, even bark. In some parts of Yellowstone, yellow pond lily is a major food.

Remarks. When alarmed, it slaps its tail on water. This alerts others to possible danger. Aquatic adaptations include translucent eyelids that allow underwater vision and ear and nose openings that can be closed when diving.

Beaver constructs dams to create ponds as protection against predators and allow easy movement of food and materials. Lodges are built of mud and sticks amid streams, ponds, and marshes. Beaver enters via underwater entrances; this is where kits are born, usually in April, and extra food is stored for winter. In larger rivers like the Yellowstone, beaver digs burrows into banks.

A colony consists of a mature male and female mated for life, plus other family members, including one- to two-year-old adolescents. Young usually live with parents for about two years.

Considered a keystone species in West because it benefits many others. Ponds provide forage or nesting habitat for duck, moose, and others. Damming of small streams helps to regulate late-season flows and reduces flooding from rapid early summer snowmelt. This benefits downstream fisheries as well as animals dependent on fish like otter, mink, and bald eagle. By moderating floodwater, beaver dams reduce bank erosion and sloughing. Silt is trapped behind dams and eventually creates wet meadows. Many smaller forest openings and meadows in West are attributable to beavers.

Beaver is rare in much of GYE, particularly in Yellowstone park. A survey of 275 miles of park waterways in 1988–89 found only twenty-seven, and sign of perhaps several dozen more. Most were concentrated in Thorofare region, Bechler River, and Gallatin and Madison drainages.

PORCUPINE (Erethizon dorsatum)

Description. Second-largest rodent, up to forty pounds and fifty inches long. Blunt, black face surrounded by yellow and black quills; flat, quill-filled tail. Poor eyesight but good senses of hearing and smell.

Habitat and Distribution. Throughout forests in GYE, though it will wander into treeless areas.

Remarks. Slow-moving; discourages attack with thousands of barbed quills (actually modified hairs), which are difficult to remove if embedded in skin.

In summer, eats roots, leaves, and twigs. In winter, almost exclusively the inner bark of trees. Tends to stay in one grove for weeks, girdling the trees. Ever see a group of trees where bark has been removed at about the same height? Chances are it was a porcupine feeding in winter—the scars indicate snow levels.

In colder weather, "porky" will hole up in a dead log or under rocky ledges, culverts, or other cover. Produces one offspring in April or May. Unlike most rodents, young porcupine has full hair and can see.

Carnivores

There are five major groups in the GYE: cats (felids), dogs (canids), weasels (mustelids), bears (ursids), and raccoons (procyonids). A carnivore's pointy teeth are a telling feature, used for shredding, tearing, and cutting flesh. Long, sharp claws, with which prey is captured, held, and ripped open, are another. Many predators have superb hearing, sight, and sense of smell. A mountain lion can see well with less than one-sixth the illumination needed by humans. A wolf can hear another wolf howling up to six miles away and locate prey by odor several hours old.

Meat is easier to digest than the vegetation consumed by rodents and hooved animals, so carnivores have a simple system that processes food quickly. A carnivore's life is often feast or famine and is full of risk. Hunting can result in a broken leg or fractured skull. Even a minor injury can doom a predator because it isn't quite as good as it once was at obtaining food. Because of the danger, most predators do not kill more than they can eat.

Most young carnivores spend a lot of time learning survival skills. They are less "programmed" than other animals and must be able to exploit new opportunities. Usually, a carnivore's family teaches it how to survive. A bear will show her cubs what to eat and where to find it at each season. Grizzlies in Yellowstone may feed on spawning cutthroat in June, cutworms on high peaks in July, and whitebark pine nuts in September. Knowing where to find these foods is an important part of bear "culture" passed from generation to generation.

Predators must range widely to support themselves and by necessity be sparser than their prey. Wolves and coyotes have fairly definite territories, identified by scents and howling. Mountain lions, though solitary, also signal their presence by scraping the ground or defecating or urinating in these spots. Other lions tend to avoid the occupied territory.

Weasels

There are ten mustelids in the GYE. They tend to be long and lean, though the badger is chunky. Most are solitary adults and have an anal scent gland used for defense and marking territory. The skunk's is most highly developed.

Most mustelids, like bears, feature "delayed implantation." After mating, development of the fertilized egg is postponed. Pregnancy and birth are delayed until the most favorable time. The pine marten mates in midsummer, but the eggs are not implanted in the uterus until winter. The young are born in early spring.

Many weasels are known as furbearers because of their beautiful pelts. Pine marten is sold as sable and wolverine pelts are prized for parka collars because they don't collect frost. Most weasels are easily trapped, and in many states, they were essentially wiped out. By the 1930s, the wolverine was extinct in Montana except for Glacier National Park. The fisher, never abundant to begin with, was exterminated. It has been reintroduced to some areas. Though better regulated today, trapping still removes animals from the ecosystem, depriving the public of the opportunity to enjoy its creatures in the wild.

SHORT-TAILED WEASEL *(Mustela erminea)*   *page 214*

Description. Long, skinny, pink nose, black beady eyes. In summer, dark to reddish brown with white underside; all white in winter except for black-tipped tail. Between eight and thirteen inches long; males 20 to 30 percent larger.

Habitat and Distribution. Subalpine forests and meadows; also occasionally found at lower elevations. Throughout ecosystem.

Remarks. Long, sinewy body allows weasel to enter burrows for mice, voles, shrews, and chipmunks. Also will take prey much larger than itself, including snowshoe hare and cottontail. Large body surface costs it a great deal of heat. To compensate, needs to eat nearly a third of its body weight daily.

LONG-TAILED WEASEL *(Mustela frenata)*

Description. Largest North American weasel, reaching up to twenty-two inches, counting four- to six-inch-long tail. Dark brown in summer, belly tan or buff. Chin may be white. White in winter with black-tipped tail; hard to tell it from short-tailed weasel except by size.

Habitat and Distribution. Open country, but found elsewhere too. More widely distributed than short-tailed weasel, particularly at lower elevations in sagebrush and grasslands.

Remarks. Has same basic diet as short-tailed weasel, but larger size means long-tailed preys on larger animals, like hare and rabbit, more regularly.

PINE MARTEN *(Martes americana)*   *page 214*

Description. Longish, but not quite as tubular as a weasel. Larger ears and catlike face. Thick, dark brown fur marked by orange on throat. Does not change to white in winter.

Habitat and Distribution. Forests, particularly old growth with plenty of dead and dying trees. I also have seen it on alpine tundra, and even once on a glacier in Canadian Rockies.

Remarks. Active year-round; has furry feet that make it easy to travel over snow. Will search every blowdown and log for prey—voles, mice, squirrels, rabbits. Will eat berries. Dependent on dead and downed timber for shelter. Vulnerable to cold weather; will dig a nest in rotten logs, using loose chips as extra insulation. Extremely curious; displays little caution around traps. One marten was live-trapped seventy-seven times by biologists in Glacier National Park.

FISHER *(Martes pennanti)*

Description. Catlike; up to forty-eight inches long, including long, bushy tail. Slightly larger than marten, but generally darker, with chocolate fur over entire body and no orange throat patch.

Habitat and Distribution. Boreal forests of Canada; reaches southern limit in GYE. Only a few reports of fisher in Yellowstone area; probably absent from much of ecosystem.

WOLVERINE *(Gulo gulo)*

Description. Dark brown, white throat, tan sides. Reaches forty-two inches and sixty pounds. From a distance, looks like a small bear cub. Loping gait is distinctive.

Habitat and Distribution. Dense forests. In winter, often travels above timberline on wind-swept ridges.

Remarks. A tireless wanderer in search of food. Research in northwest Montana found wolverine traveling as far as one hundred miles in a single week.

A strong, tough animal with powerful jaws, wolverine regularly takes down prey much larger than itself, especially when deep snow makes animals like deer more vulnerable. Researchers have found that wolverine can chew through trap doors made of cyclone fencing. Eats snowshoe hare, porcupine, grouse, smaller mammals, and carrion. Relatively rare in GYE; only forty-nine reports of this animal in Yellowstone park from 1970–87, fewer than three a year. Dens built in log jams. Young born in April; female raises the litter of two to four by herself.

MINK *(Mustela vison)*   *page 214*

Description. Twenty to twenty-eight inches long; lustrous, chocolate brown fur with white chin patch. Semiaquatic with partially webbed feet. Is almost as at home in water as on land.

Habitat and Distribution. Mostly rivers and lakeshores throughout ecosystem.

Remarks. Eats fish, crayfish, frogs, ducks, muskrats, voles, mice, snakes, and almost anything else that runs, swims, or flies. Takes 100 pelts to make a full-length mink coat.

RIVER OTTER *(Lutra canadensis)*   *page 214*

Description. Long, lanky, cylindrical body up to fifty inches with long, thick tail, short legs, webbed feet.

Habitat and Distribution. Throughout ecosystem in larger rivers and lakes, but not abundant. Will travel overland between water courses.

Remarks. While diving, otter's heart slows, allowing it to remain submerged for up to two minutes. Fur is dense, trapping air as protection against cold when animal dives. Young usually born in dens in abandoned beaver burrows or root tangles beneath stumps and trees. Helpless at birth, young grow rapidly. Despite aquatic adaptations, young must learn to swim, with mother forcing them reluctantly into water. Fish eater, though salamanders, ducks, and anything else are fair game.

BADGER *(Taxidea taxus)*   *page 214*

Description. Up to thirty-four inches, black and white facial markings, grizzled coat, squat body, stubby legs.

Habitat and Distribution. Arid grasslands and sagebrush, but can be found in coniferous forests and subalpine meadows. Throughout GYE.

Remarks. Fierce, confrontational. If pursued, snarls and hisses while digging hole for itself in ground. Eats ground squirrels, prairie dogs, pocket gophers that it digs out of burrows.

SPOTTED SKUNK *(Spilogale putorius)*

Description. White spots dot black coat; large, irregular black and white stripes. The smaller of two skunks found in GYE, spotted is seldom more than twenty-two inches long and weighs less than two pounds.

Habitat and Distribution. Rare in ecosystem. Active year-round; usually nocturnal. In cold weather, generally remains in den, usually in a hollow log, culvert, or under an old building.

Remarks. Main defense is irritating, foul-smelling musk emitted from glands near the hind legs.

STRIPED SKUNK *(Mephitus mephitus)* *page 214*

Description. Larger than spotted skunk, reaching thirty inches and four to ten pounds. Mostly black with thin white strip from nose to nape of neck. From neck to tail, a broad white stripe marks each side.

Habitat and Distribution. Near water in brushy habitat throughout GYE.

Remarks. Eats grains, berries, insects, carrion, small rodents, snakes, and birds.

BLACK-FOOTED FERRET *(Mustela nigripes)*

Description. Weasellike, light brown, black mask and feet.

Habitat and Distribution. Never numerous. Almost always found around prairie dogs, its chief prey. Poisoning of millions of prairie dogs by ranchers not only severely reduces ferret's food supply but also kills many ferrets outright.

Remarks. Probably extinct in the wild. The last known group of wild ferrets were captured near Meeteetse, Wyoming, just east of ecosystem. Captive breeding program, with releases of young into wild, may bring ferret back from the edge.

RACCOON *(Procyon lotor)* *page 215*

Description. Twenty-five to thirty-six inches long, up to forty pounds. Distinguishing feature is the black mask; otherwise, grizzled gray with reddish tints. Bushy tail has black stripes on brown.

Habitat and Distribution. Recent immigrant to GYE. Has spread into Yellowstone since turn of century and is relatively common along low-elevation rivers and riparian areas.

Remarks. Primarily nocturnal. Forages for crayfish, fish, ducks, snakes, carrion, and garbage. Not a true hibernator, but usually dens up for winter. Pulse rate remains high and it is easily roused. Occasionally, will forage on warmer winter nights.

Cats

There are three members of the *Felis* family in the GYE: the mountain lion, bobcat, and lynx. They are almost exclusively meat eaters and surprise prey rather than running it down. Their teeth are designed for puncturing and slicing, and sharp claws grasp prey securely. They usually kill by biting into the base of the neck. Since all cats have retractable claws, they usually just leave paw prints with four toes.

LYNX (Felis lynx)

Description. Mid-sized cat weighing up to forty pounds. Grayish brown, pointed ears, short, black-tipped tail. Feet are outlandishly large, for walking on snow.

Habitat and Distribution. Boreal forests of Canada with extensions into similar areas. Only a few reports in the GYE.

Remarks. Feeds on rodents, small birds, and grouse, but snowshoe hare is the staple; a lynx may eat more than 200 a year. Lynx numbers will even follow hare population cycles.

BOBCAT (Felis rufus)

Description. A smaller lynx, weighing up to thirty pounds. Often identified as a lynx, though it's browner and has light spots. Stubby tail like lynx, but only top is black; bottom is white.

Habitat and Distribution. Open, broken country, generally at lower elevations in GYE.

Remarks. Eats rabbits, rodents, and birds. Remarkably tame. At the rare times a human encounters a bobcat, it often will sit and stare back.

MOUNTAIN LION (Felis concolor)

Description. Tawny. Reaches more than 200 pounds and a length of up to nine feet, including long tail.

Habitat and Distribution. Throughout GYE, particularly in rocky, broken, semiopen areas.

Remarks. Known also as cougar, panther, and puma, was once the most widely distributed mammal in Western Hemisphere, found from East to West coasts and from the Yukon Territory throughout western United States to tip of South America. Now nearly extinct in East but safe in West. Largely nocturnal and secretive, so it's seldom seen even where common.

Except during breeding season, males remain separate. Females and kittens have smaller territories than males, and territory of dominant male may overlap those of several females. Biologists speculate there are thirty lions, including young of the year, between Yankee Jim Canyon and Cooke City, Montana.

Regularly kills large animals like elk and deer, sneaking up and taking them in a rush with a bite on the neck or a swipe at the head, which snaps the neck. Will eat its fill, then cover the carcass with duff and leaves, to return to feed again.

Mates in late winter and early spring; two or three kittens born about three months later. Young are spotted and have gray-blue eyes. Female teaches young to hunt after about six months. Young stay with mother for about a year. Females sometimes remain in mother's territory or settle in one nearby, but young males wander widely. One lion born and captured near Bear Creek by Gardiner, Montana, eventually established territory on Stillwater River on north side of Beartooth Mountains. Another born near Soda Butte in Yellowstone park moved into Crandall Creek in North Absaroka Wilderness.

Lion was once indiscriminately killed throughout ecosystem, even in Yellowstone park. One 1914 park report mentions the killing of nineteen lions with use of dogs. From 1904–25, when last was killed, 121 were slain in Yellowstone. For many years, there were no confirmed sightings within park, but gradually cats began to recover. Lion still hunted outside park; according to ongoing study, two-thirds of deaths of park lions attributed to humans.

Dogs

There are three wild canids—the coyote, swift fox, and red fox—in Yellowstone. The largest member, the wolf, is endangered and was not in the ecosystem in 1991, though it may soon return naturally from northern Montana or be reintroduced.

This family tends to rely more on speed than stealth to hunt. The wolf particularly has long legs that help it hunt and get around its large territories. Wolves have traveled as far as forty-five miles in a day, and some radio-collared animals have traveled more than 450 miles between release and recapture.

Canids defend territories marked by excrement. Usually, one breeding pair is found per territory and both parents raise the young, unusual

Coyotes are frequently trapped or killed on private and public lands, even when no livestock are threatened. Research has shown that in protected areas like Yellowstone, unhunted populations are more stable and produce fewer young than hunted populations.

among mammals. The den is constructed in the ground or beneath tree roots and occasionally in a hollow log.

COYOTE (*Canis latrans*)

Description. Light gray brown, thirty to fifty pounds, brushy tail. Face narrower than a wolf's and legs not as lanky.

Habitat and Distribution. Most abundant canid in GYE; found in nearly every habitat, though typically in grasslands and sagebrush meadows.

Remarks. Eats pocket gophers, rabbits, jackrabbits, ground squirrels. Coyote often "mouses" in meadow, pouncing on small rodent with front paws. Does take larger prey when possible, such as bighorn sheep, antelope, deer, even elk.

Though protected within Yellowstone park today, coyote was once vigorously hunted there, as it was considered destructive to young game. From 1904–35, when predator control in park ceased, 4,352 were killed.

Outside Yellowstone and Grand Teton, coyotes are still killed by ranchers, trappers, and government agents working for taxpayer-supported Animal Damage Control program. In 1989, ADC killed 76,000 coyotes in West, primarily to benefit ranchers.

In face of persecution, coyote usually forms small family of parents and year's young. In the few places where it is protected, coyote forms packs and sets up territories. Birth rates are low compared with persecuted coyotes, and young from previous year or two stay with packs, probably helping to care for current pups.

RED FOX *(Vulpes vulpes)*   *page 215*

Description. Not always red. May be silver, black, or brown. Bushy,

The wolf has been missing from the GYE's fauna since the animal was extirpated to make the region safe for domestic animals. As predators of wild game, however, wolves cull excess numbers, help disperse animals, and remove the sick and injured.

white-tipped tail. Rather small, weighing ten to fifteen pounds.

Habitat and Distribution. Numbers and range have increased tremendously throughout GYE. However, areas with many coyotes tend to have fewer foxes. Appears always to have been rare in higher elevations of ecosystem.

Remarks. Omnivorous, eating small mammals, birds, frogs, insects, and berries. Enlarges existing burrows or uses hollow logs or other natural shelters where one to ten young are born helpless and sightless. Both parents rear pups.

SWIFT FOX (*Vulpes velox*)   *page 215*

Description. Small, tan.

Habitat and Distribution. Previously much of short- to mid-grass high plains of North America. Distribution and numbers are now greatly reduced.

Remarks. Preys upon small rodents and birds. Nearly extinct over much of range due to trapping and poisoning aimed at coyote. Nearly extinct in Montana, though one was trapped in 1978 near Billings. Numbers growing in Wyoming, with a big increase when the poison 1080 was banned. Greatest concentration now is in Nebraska, Colorado, and nearby states. At least one swift fox recently trapped in Green River drainage, which proves it exists at least on fringes of ecosystem.

WOLF (*Canis lupus*)

Description. Large, somewhat resembles German shepherd or malamute, with bushy tail, long legs, large feet. Adult may weigh 125 or more pounds. Males larger than females.

Habitat and Distribution. Extinct in GYE, but if wolf recovers, it will almost certainly be found in big-game wintering areas.

Remarks. Studies in northern Montana and Canada show that elk and deer are main prey, though moose, antelope, bison, and bighorn sheep also are taken.

To bring down such large animals, wolves hunt in packs. It is often said that wolves only take young and old. This is generally true, because trying to pull down a healthy, mature elk or moose is dangerous. Most wolves test prey, looking for weakness, before moving in for kill. Wolves will take a healthy animal if they can surprise it or if they have no other choice.

Most packs consist of dominant male and female who do most of the breeding, while younger members help raise pups. Young are born in dens in spring and begin to follow parents on hunting expeditions by late summer. Dens are often located under tree roots or rocks or are dug into well-drained gravels.

The first historical reference to wolf comes from Osborn Russell on August 18, 1836. He was hunting elk at outlet of Yellowstone Lake and heard a wolf howl. Beginning in 1850s, wolf was systematically poisoned throughout West for hides. Pelts became secondary when states and ranchers offered bounties. Wolves were plentiful in Yellowstone according to first official exploration parties in 1870, but poisoning instituted in 1872 shortly after park's establishment was devastating. Though private wolfers and soldiers took wolves through early 1900s, systematic extermination throughout West (including park) didn't begin till 1915. From 1915–26, 136 wolves were killed in Yellowstone.

In 1973, Northern Rocky Mountain wolf was listed as endangered. Under law, U.S. Fish and Wildlife Service must help all listed species recover; GYE was selected as potential wolf haven. Most people in Montana, Wyoming, and Idaho support this effort, but some ranchers, outfitters, and hunters have stalled action for more than a decade.

Bears

It could be that no animal is more irresistible to people than the bear, perhaps sheerly because of its size—grizzlies in coastal Alaska can weigh more than 1,500 pounds, and the largest ever weighed in the GYE was more than 1,100.

There are two types in the region, the black and the grizzly. Telling them apart is not always easy, even for experienced people. A grizzly has long front claws; a broad, dishlike face; and a shoulder hump. It generally is the larger, with blond or brown fur. Black bears have a narrower snout, shorter claws, and no shoulder hump and are usually black. There are many exceptions. Some black bears have brown, blond, or cinnamon coats, and a few grizzlies are almost black. Sometimes, a black bear seems to have a hump.

Black bears tend to stay in forests, while grizzlies are more common in meadows or alpine basins, though never far from cover. Ninety percent of radio-collared bears were in timber too dense to observe them. Because of their longer claws, grizzlies usually do not climb trees, but black bears can. Although neither seems to have good vision, hearing and smell are well developed. Bears can sense humans several hundred yards away by scent alone.

Bears eat almost anything—carrion, ground squirrels, marmots, fish, beetles, large mammals, and even picnic basket goodies. They love meat but the average bear is mostly a vegetarian, eating pine nuts, berries, grasses, sedges, roots, and leafy plants.

Because of reduced food availability in winter, bears retreat to dens for a prolonged "sleep." They don't really hibernate, but can be roused if disturbed. Relying on layers of fat for energy and insulation, the bear does not eat, drink, or excrete for five or six months. It gradually falls into a deep sleep over several weeks. In midwinter, its temperature drops several degrees and its heart rate decreases from forty to eight beats per minute.

Dens can be under rock ledges, holes dug in the ground, or inside large trees. Trees are used less often in the West than in the East. Bears usually select north slopes for den sites since the snow lasts longer and provides better insulation. Bears enter their dens as early as the first of October and sometimes as late as the first week of December. Most dens are abandoned between mid-March and early May. Fat stored during the summer and fall also supplies energy well into the spring. Bears do not eat immediately upon leaving their dens, and once they begin foraging, they commonly eat low-value food, so they continue to lose weight for months after emergence. Loss of a major autumn food source like whitebark pine nuts or the rare find of an early spring high-protein food like carrion can often make the difference between death and survival.

Bears have one of the lowest reproductive rates of any land mammal. A female grizzly may be six or seven years old before she has her first cubs and may not have another litter for three or four years. Black bears typically breed at four and a half years. It is what makes bears so vulnerable to overhunting and loss of habitat. Breeding in both species is in the late spring or early summer (late May to early July in Yellowstone). Due to delayed implantation, the egg does not grow for six or seven months. The squirrel-size cubs are born blind and helpless while the female is sleeping in her den. The male plays no role in the rearing and may kill the cubs if he can.

Bears are intelligent. The cubs are curious, rambunctious, and playful. Grizzly cubs will slide down snowfields, then race back up and slide down again. Cubs also play hide-and-seek, racing out from behind some willows to "attack" Mom, then diving back and waiting to ambush her again.

The ability to learn is essential to survival. Sows teach their cubs where to find food in specific seasons, what is edible, and how to avoid conflicts with other bears or humans. This is passed down from generation to generation. One of the reasons small populations of bears are more vulnerable to extinction is the possible loss of "cultural" knowledge.

Bears communicate with sounds, postures, and facial expressions. A "woof" is often a sign of surprise and is sometimes heard before a bear attacks or flees. A charging bear is not necessarily attacking; most charges are bluffs, signalling that another bear or human has overstepped its bounds. Given the ability to learn and overall intelligence, it follows that bears used to human foods are much more likely to attack people than bears with no knowledge of humans. Research shows there are few "nuisance" bears, just nuisance people who don't keep their food away from bears.

The two Yellowstone bears probably evolved from one ancestor. The forest-dwelling black bear crossed into North America from Asia on the Bering Sea land bridge 250,000 to 300,000 years ago. The open-country grizzly arrived much later, after the last major glacial advance 10,000 years ago.

Habitat preferences may explain behavior differences. When a black bear is threatened, it runs for a tree. Black bear sows will even drive their cubs up trees to protect them while they are foraging. Sow grizzlies have no trees in much of their range, so they evolved to defend their cubs in the open. Over time, the more aggressive mothers were most successful, so this trait was passed on. The environment of the grizzly favored its fearsome personality.

BLACK BEAR (Ursus americanus) page 215

Description. Adult usually no more than thirty-two inches tall at shoulder and less than six feet from tail to snout. Most females weigh no more than 200 pounds; males about 250. Largest black bears in Yellowstone weigh less than 500 pounds.

Habitat and Distribution. Distributed throughout GYE and in peripheral areas where there are no grizzlies. One estimate is as many as 600 black bears in Yellowstone park and about 100 in Grand Teton park.

Remarks. The five front claws are usually less than 1½ inches long.

Black bear eats mostly vegetation, though it also enjoys a meal of meat or carrion. One study found an 81 percent vegetation diet, including 47 percent grasses and sedges. Because of this, black bear tends to stay in mixed forests, where open meadows provide forage. In spring, bear relies on bulbs like spring beauty and wild onion, plus rodents and carrion. Also likes sweet cambium layer beneath outer bark on trees. Will strip bark to get to surgery sap. There are few berries in GYE, but it does eat strawberries, grouse whortleberries, chokecherries, and others when available. In fall, black bear relishes whitebark pine nuts.

Black bear avoids more aggressive grizzly. Both will scratch trees, apparently to indicate presence to other bears. Neither species has strictly defended territories.

GRIZZLY BEAR *(Ursus arctos)*

Description. Named for grizzled coat. However, color varies considerably, from blond to nearly black. Sometimes a silver gray band on shoulder, leading to name "silvertip." Male may weigh up to 1,000 pounds, but 400 to 600 more common. Females 250 to 300. Erect bear may be eight feet high.

Habitat and Distribution. Open country, near cover—mountain meadows, riparian areas, open forests. GYE doesn't seem to be too hospitable; two well-known bear researchers, the Craighead brothers, calculated one grizzly per thirty-four square miles here compared with one per eight square miles in Glacier National Park in northwest Montana and one per 0.75 square mile on Kodiak Island in Alaska.

Heart of grizzly distribution in GYE is Yellowstone park and nearby areas, particularly northern Teton Wilderness, eastern portions of North Absaroka and Washakie wildernesses, and southern portions of Absaroka-Beartooth Wilderness, Gallatin Range, Lee Metcalf Wilderness, Lionhead area, and adjacent portions of Targhee National Forest. Grizzlies also seen on very northern fringes of Grand Teton park, but since 1930s there have been only forty-three sightings, all north of Jackson Lake.

Remarks. Oldest grizzly reported from Yellowstone was a 25½-year-old captured by Craigheads. Female from Cabinet Mountains in northwest Montana was more than thirty-four years old, oldest wild bear ever captured.

Grizzly eats grasses, dandelions, clover, spring beauty, yampa, horsetail, ants, rodents, and carrion. Whitebark pine nuts are choice in autumn, as are elk calves in early summer. Unlike grizzlies elsewhere, Yellowstone bears do not eat many berries, from lack of a crop. Spawning cutthroat are an increasing food source.

Once found from Mexico to the Arctic, from Great Plains to California coast, grizzly has declined in much of former range, primarily from persecution by livestock industry. Other factors include habitat destruction, increased access due to logging roads, and oil and gas drilling. Odds of encountering a grizzly are low. Car accidents, drownings, avalanches, even lightning are far greater threats to Yellowstone visitors than being mauled by a bear. Estimates vary, but a minimum of 175 to 250 grizzlies are thought to roam GYE.

Ungulates

Ungulates are hooved mammals, of which there are three families in the GYE. The deer family (Cervidae) is represented by the moose, white-tailed deer, mule deer, and elk. The Bovidae in the ecosystem are bison, mountain goat, and bighorn sheep. The pronghorn antelope is the sole member of Antilocapridae.

Ungulates have four-part stomachs to help them digest cellulose in woody material and grasses. Break apart a winter moose dropping and it will look like sawdust, which is exactly what it is. It is difficult to live on sawdust. Protozoa and bacteria in the stomachs ferment the woody material, producing fatty acids, vitamins, proteins, and minerals.

Deer shed their antlers each year, and only males have them. Male and female bovids have permanent horns, though the males' are larger, particularly in bighorn sheep. Horns grow throughout life. Horns and antlers are useful for defense, but in many animals they are much more important as indicators of status within the herd—much as big houses and expensive cars indicate wealth and prestige among humans. This is because growing horns or antlers takes energy, and only animals of superior size and foraging abilities can afford to grow these "accessories." The pecking order reduces conflict by lessening the need for constant testing and battling to establish rank within the herd. The males with the largest horns or antlers usually do the most breeding and thus pass on their genes.

Another almost universal characteristic of ungulates is their precocious young. Most can stand within a few minutes of birth and run within a few days. This is critical to animals that must outrun predators. However, in the youngest, the safest strategy is usually to avoid detection. Baby deer, antelope, and other ungulates have no scent and will lie down and remain motionless. A predator can walk within yards of these youngsters and never detect them.

Though all are plant eaters, each ungulate uses resources in different ways. These niches do overlap, particularly when food is low, so competition can be severe.

Bighorn sheep, elk, and bison are grazers. Bighorn has the smallest body and the highest protein needs of the three and must be pickier about what it eats when possible. Because of its larger size, the bison needs bulk and is less selective. The elk falls somewhere in between.

The bighorn can graze on steeper terrain than elk and avoid some of the competition. Because the elk is not tied to rugged country as a defense, it can forage where sheep would not. The bison will eat coarse material that the elk ignores. When these chomped-on grasses send up tender shoots, the elk will seek them out. This is sort of a forage rotational system.

Because of its size, the bison is mostly immune to predation and can wander widely in search of food. This is fortunate considering its massive intake. The smaller bighorn is much more vulnerable and uses cliffs as escape terrain. Because of this, it tends to use traditional locations year after year.

The antelope is the smallest and most selective ungulate in the ecosystem. It tends to eat high-protein forbs and less grass during the spring and summer, and its winter diet is largely sagebrush, also high in protein. Since speed is its main defense, the antelope forages in the open, where it can see far and wide.

Mule deer, white-tailed deer, and moose are primarily browsers, eating more shrubs than grass, particularly in winter. (Elk also eat shrubs, but prefer grass.) Deer and moose will eat grass when it is tender, such as in the spring. Moose and deer largely avoid competition through timing and different habitats. In winter, the moose can live in greater snow depths than the deer, so that when food is least available, these animals occupy different areas.

WHITE-TAILED DEER (*Odocoileus virginianus*)   *page 215*

Description. Long tail (brown on top, white underneath) is waved when alarmed and in flight. A delicate body with reddish coat in summer, changing to gray in winter. Buck sports antlers with main beam and additional points; mule deer has forked antlers.

Habitat and Distribution. Most widely distributed ungulate in North America, but limited in GYE. Associated with brushy riparian areas or other dense cover along low-elevation water courses. A few whitetails summer in Yellowstone and Grand Teton parks, but most habitat is on fringes of GYE. Area north of park in Paradise Valley has seen big whitetail increase in recent years. Whitetails also found along South Fork of Snake. Only 1,700 whitetails are thought to live on federal lands in ecosystem.

MULE DEER (*Odocoileus hemionus*) *page 215*

Description. Named for large, mulelike ears. Tail is white on top and bottom with black tip, giving it its other common name—black-tailed deer. Most of year, mule deer is grayish with white rump and tan lower legs; tends to reddish brown in midsummer. Has stiff, jumping escape movement. Instead of running, it bounces along like a pogo stick.

Habitat and Distribution. Widely distributed throughout GYE. Some 88,000 estimated to live on federal lands in region in 1990, with largest number, 25,000, in Gallatin National Forest, followed by 21,500 in Bridger-Teton National Forest, 17,000 in Beaverhead National Forest, and 12,000 in Shoshone National Forest.

Remarks. Buck usually begins growing antlers in second year and antlers become larger with each year. Covered with blood-vessel-rich "velvet" during growing stage; velvet is sloughed off by fall. Mates in November and December. During rut, neck of male swells and he becomes more aggressive. May search widely for receptive doe. Unlike elk, which retains antlers through most of winter, buck drops antlers in January. Young are born in May and June in GYE and have spotted camouflage coats.

Unlike reclusive whitetail, mule deer is at home in the open, preferring grasslands, sage-covered slopes, and even alpine habitats. In winter, may retreat to dense cover, particularly old-growth stands.

ELK (*Cervus elaphus*) *page 215*

Description. Also called wapiti. Looks like a small, long-necked, tan horse. Bull will reach 1,100 pounds; cow half as large. Head and neck are dark brown, sides tan with buff rump patch. In fall, bull sports immense, spreading antlers that give him a regal look.

Habitat and Distribution. Most numerous large ungulate in GYE, estimated at 95,000. Found everywhere from grasslands to alpine.

Remarks. Bull begins growing antlers in April, shortly after shedding previous year's. A one-year-old's are merely spikes a foot or two long. By second year, antlers may have three or four points each. Third set may have five points, while older bull sports six or seven tines per side.

Rutting is earlier than for deer—starting in August, peaking by September. Male rattles antlers on shrubs and small trees to rub off velvet, paws, urinates, then rolls around in whole mess. This apparently pleases the cows, because they gather around some of the more mature bulls. These try to keep other potential suitors away. In late August, male will bugle; more like a high whistle than a horn, this tells other bulls to stay away. During breeding, bull concentrates on keeping females together and, of course, mating as much as possible. By early winter, he is so exhausted and has lost so much fat that he is frequently the first to die in harsh winter. Being top stud has its costs.

Depending upon where it lives, elk may be a browser or grazer. In the ecosystem, grasses and sedges are primary diet, but will eat shrubs and saplings like aspen. In harsh winters, it gnaws aspen and cottonwood, leaving lower trunks scarred with hard, black bark.

Though now thought of as a Western animal, elk once ranged as far east as Virginia, North Carolina, and Pennsylvania. Disappeared from these areas with advancing settlement and was even eliminated by over-hunting over vast areas of West. By late 1800s, Yellowstone was one of last strongholds for elk in West. Yellowstone elk were used to reintroduce stock from Gila Wilderness of New Mexico to Canadian Rockies. Elk numbers are higher now across West than at any time since the turn of the century in spite of road building, logging, and oil and gas development.

Because of deep snows, elk must migrate out of GYE. Older cows lead herds, which may summer at up to 11,000 feet or more, down to lower elevations in fall. Elk prefer areas where snow is less than two feet deep. Wind-blown ridges and south-facing slopes are important sites.

There are a number of major herds in GYE, particularly in and around Yellowstone park, where 50,000 elk spend summer. These animals separate into different herds in winter. The largest is the 20,800 (1990 estimated population) herd that winters in northern Yellowstone and on lands just outside the park, along the Yellowstone River. Some migrate twenty-five miles north of the park to the Emigrant Peak area.

The Jackson herd (11,000 elk) summers south of Yellowstone Lake and winters thirty to forty miles away in the Gros Ventre River valley and in the National Elk Refuge in Jackson Hole. Studies have shown approximately 40 percent of the elk that winter in the National Elk Refuge summer in Yellowstone or the Teton Wilderness. Migrating elk take approximately three weeks to move between ranges.

The Sand Creek herd (4,900 elk) usually summers on the Madison and Pitchstone plateaus in western Yellowstone and in the Targhee National Forest. They winter near Sand Creek, north of Rexburg, Idaho. More elk used to spend summer outside of the park on Targhee forest lands, but stopped because of heavy timber harvest.

The North Fork of the Shoshone winters 2,600 animals, most from eastern Yellowstone or higher elevations in the Shoshone National Forest.

The 3,180 elk in the Clarks Fork herd winter at upper Clarks Fork and Sunlight Basin in Wyoming. These animals summer along the divide between the headwaters of tributaries to the Clarks Fork and the upper Lamar River and Mirror Plateau in Yellowstone.

The Gallatin herd in Montana (2,500 elk) spends its summers at the headwaters of Gallatin River in the park, as well as the Gallatin and Madison ranges.

The Carter Mountain elk herd (2,550 elk) summers near the headwaters of the South Fork of Shoshone River in the Washakie Wilderness, as well as the upper Thorofare River area in the Teton Wilderness. The herd winters on Carter Mountain, southwest of Cody, Wyoming.

The Madison-Firehole herd (800 elk) is nonmigratory. It survives Yellowstone winters primarily by using snowfree areas around the thermal features between Old Faithful and West Yellowstone.

MOOSE (*Alces alces*)   *page 215*

Description. Largest member of deer family in GYE. More than seven feet high at shoulder and can weigh more than 1,000 pounds. Looks like a dark brown (almost black) horse with long legs and long, odd-looking muzzle. Appears ungainly, but it isn't. Male has wide, palmate antlers up to six feet across.

Habitat and Distribution. Throughout GYE from sagebrush to timberline, often in willows and aspen. Long legs good for getting around in deep snow; will winter at 9,000 feet or higher.

Remarks. Mature spruce-fir forest helps winter survival. Tight canopy serves as an umbrella, reducing snow depth so that foraging animals don't tire so quickly. Opening canopy by logging can alter moose wintering range significantly. Least social among deer family, moose is usually solitary, except for females with young. However, on winter ranges can be seen in groups.

Eats shrubs, including willow, gooseberry, buffaloberry, and aspen. In spring, frequently seen on knees grazing fresh grass shoots. In winter, diet includes a lot of conifers like subalpine fir, lodgepole pine, and Douglas fir. Antlers begin growing in April and velvet dries by August. The rut begins in September, when bull becomes aggressive and occasionally will attack hikers. Female bellows to attract male. Mates in September and early October, with one or two calves born usually in May. Young remain with mother until chased away when new calf is born.

Originally very scarce in GYE and Rockies in general. Early trappers didn't mention moose; later Yellowstone explorers noted no sightings. May have entered area around 1870s. Not recorded in northern Yellowstone or south-central Montana until 1913. Now entrenched, with 6,000 in GYE. There are 200 year-round moose in Grand Teton park alone, with as many as 800 in winter. Recent research in northern ecosystem indicates a decline during 1980s.

BISON *(Bison bison)*   *page 215*

Description. Large, dark brown, cattlelike with large shoulder humps sloping to lower hindquarters. Both sexes have horns; bull's are bigger. Head, forelegs, shoulders covered with long hair, while back and hindquarters have shorter coats.

Habitat and Distribution. Grasslands, though seen in forests of Yellowstone. Now found only in Yellowstone and Grand Teton parks, though some occasionally wander outside these preserves. Has been seen along upper Green River and near West Yellowstone, Montana.

Remarks. Female sexually mature at four years, though some younger ones do breed. During rut from mid-July to mid-August, bulls shove, push,

Bison can efficiently digest low-quality forage. In winter, they use their heads like bulldozers to expose plants beneath three feet of snow.

and bellow. Dominant animals do most breeding. Usually a single calf is born in May or early June. Calves are a delight to watch as they gambol.

Primarily a grazer, with grasses and sedges making up more than 90 percent of diet in all seasons. Less selective than elk; will eat rougher, drier forage. Bison grazing may help stabilize grasslands in ecosystem.

Because of diet, bison concentrates in summer in larger meadows in the park. Herds are likely to be seen in Hayden Valley, along Madison and Firehole rivers, on Mirror Plateau and upper Lamar River, in Pelican Creek, and on Madison Plateau. In winter, normally move to lower elevations such as northern winter range along Madison River, or areas with thermal features such as Old Faithful Geyser Basin. In deep snow, some animals tough it out by swinging their large heads back and forth to uncover grasses.

Many people have suggested that domestic cattle are similar to bison, but there are a number of differences. Bison move more frequently, almost never staying in the same place for more than two or three days, so they are less likely to overgraze. They also need less water than domestic stock, and thus spend less time in riparian zones.

Yellowstone bison are descendants of the only continuously wild herd in the United States, though some claim bison were driven to the mountains after being wiped out on the plains. Bison *were* far more numerous on the plains, but there is evidence they were always native to the high valleys and mountains of the region.

Osborn Russell, who trapped the area from 1834–43, reported bison in Pierre's Hole by Driggs, Idaho; in Montana's Centennial Valley and upper Ruby River; in the Salt River Valley near Afton, Wyoming; and in Jackson Hole, Wyoming. Walter DeLacy, a miner who traveled with other prospectors through southern Yellowstone in 1863, commented on the many bison trails he found around Shoshone Lake. Bart Henderson, a miner who explored the area around Cooke City in 1870, reported seeing thousands of bison (this may be an exaggeration) on the Buffalo Plateau along what is now the northern border of Yellowstone park.

Clearly, bison were always found in the GYE. However, the 1870s were a time of uncontrolled market hunting throughout the West. When the Army began regular park patrols in 1886, market hunting first came under regulation. Even then, poaching was such that by 1901, the superintendent reported, "I do not believe that there are more than twenty-five buffalo left in the park."

In 1902, bison from several captive herds were transplanted to the park. They were kept semicaptive, corraled at night and herded during the day. Until 1938, park bison were fed each winter. The Lamar ranger station was once "Buffalo Ranch," and winter feed was grown each summer along the Lamar River. Bison were regularly removed (killed or given away) until the 1960s, when natural processes were allowed to control numbers.

Beginning in the harsh winter of 1975–76, bison began to wander outside Yellowstone regularly, particularly near Gardiner on the northern border and West Yellowstone on the west. The increased use by snowmobiles out of West Yellowstone may be responsible; they compress snow, making easy bison migration routes.

As bison began to move outside the park, ranchers in Montana demanded that they be controlled, fearing an outbreak of brucellosis, a disease that causes abortions in bison and cattle. A hunting season began in Montana in 1985. During the harsh winter of 1989, more than 560 of the 2,700 bison in Yellowstone were killed by hunters as they crossed park borders. Hunters continued to shoot bison in 1990–91 amid growing nationwide outrage. A new policy is being considered.

The Jackson Hole bison herd began in 1969 when eight animals were released in Grand Teton park. The herd grew slowly, summering in the park and wintering among the elk in the National Elk Refuge. It now numbers around 100. Cattle owners brought pressure upon the government to reduce the number, and in 1988–89, sixteen were shot, followed by nineteen in the winter of 1989–90. Bison are seen increasingly outside of Jackson Hole—in the upper Gros Ventre River, upper Green River, and even the northern edges of the Wind River Range.

BIGHORN SHEEP (*Ovis canadensis*)   page 215

Description. There are four major subspecies of sheep in North America; Rocky Mountain bighorn is the largest. Both sexes have horns, but the male's are larger and curling. Shorter than deer, but stockier, with a tan coat and large white rump patch. Mature ram may weigh 300 pounds or more; ewes 20 percent smaller.

Habitat and Distribution. Mountainous country. However, before the white man brought guns, wild sheep also ranged out into prairies and badlands along major river courses like the Missouri and Yellowstone. Bighorn is primarily a grazer, though it will eat shrubs. Normally avoids forests. Found on alpine plateaus, wind-swept ridges, and south-facing grassy hills. Common on drier, grassier, eastern side of ecosystem, which lies in a rain shadow. Most grazing is near steep or rocky terrain that sheep retreats to when in danger. Fire suppression has allowed forest to take over some bighorn sites, reducing habitat.

Remarks. Very loyal to home ranges, though it may migrate between summer and winter pastures. Since it lives in groups in limited habitat, bighorn has developed complex behavior and organization, with strict ranking within herd. Both sexes are found together in winter, but rams form bachelor herds in summer, grazing at higher elevations than ewes and lambs. May move more than ten miles to get to summer or winter range.

Has largest horns of any ruminant in proportion to body size. Ram's may make up as much as 12 percent of total weight. Mature males have large, curling horns, while ewes and immature rams have daggerlike ones. Since horns are not shed annually, they grow until the animal dies. Most horn growth stops during cold weather. Alternating ridges and dips in horns indicate periods of rapid and slow growth and can be counted to determine animal's age.

In bighorn society, horns indicate social status. The larger the horn, the more dominant the individual. Rams with horns of nearly equal size will engage in ritualistic head-battering contests. Though battles look deadly, injury is rare because skulls are made to absorb shock. Fights help determine ranking, and dominant males usually get to do most breeding. These individuals pay for privilege by often being in poorer shape to survive winter than other rams.

Osborn Russell reported thousands of sheep in the Absaroka Mountains, but numbers declined significantly once white man arrived. Market hunters found the sheep easy prey; many herds were wiped out. Ranges were overrun by domestic sheep, and introduced diseases spread by domestic stock took their toll. Despite losses, GYE probably contains the greatest concentration of bighorn in the United States, with about 7,700 in the Shoshone, Bridger-Teton, and Gallatin national forests.

In Montana, the largest sheep herds are in the Tom Miner and Hyalite Peak areas of the Gallatin Range; the Lionhead area; along the crest of the Madison Range by Hilgard and Taylor Peaks, as well as the Spanish Peaks along the Gallatin Canyon; and around the headwaters of Mill Creek, Boulder River, West Boulder River, Stillwater River, Rosebud Creek, Rock Creek, and Clarks Fork River.

In Yellowstone park, most sheep are along Specimen Ridge, on Mt. Washburn, Mt. Everts, and in the Gallatin Range. They are occasionally seen in the Heart Mountain area in southern Yellowstone.

Other Wyoming sheep ranges include the upper Clarks Fork near Trout Peak and Wapiti Ridge and Younts Peak on the South Fork of the Shoshone and Wood rivers. Another major herd lives south of Dubois in Wind River Range. Smaller herds are found near Jackson in the Gros Ventre and Hoback river valleys, as well as the west slope of the Tetons.

The only bighorns in the Idaho portion of the GYE live along the continental divide in the Lionhead area, northeast of Henry's Lake.

MOUNTAIN GOAT (Oreamnos americanus)

Description. Stockier than bighorn with long coat, usually white year-round. Horns are short (up to thirteen inches), black, and daggerlike.

Male and female have similar horns, except billy's tend to be slightly larger. Standing 2½ feet at shoulder, male weighs up to 275 pounds; female 75 to 150 pounds.

Habitat and Distribution. Rugged terrain, usually near timberline. No goats native to GYE; closest native relatives are in Beaverhead Mountains along Idaho-Montana line and in Pioneer Mountains northwest of Dillon, Montana.

Goats are found in Madison Range, along the divide between West Boulder and Yellowstone, in headwaters of Mill Creek, around upper Boulder River, along upper Rosebud and Rock creeks in the Absaroka-Beartooth Wilderness, and in high alpine plateaus northeast of Cooke City. Goats from the Beartooths have also moved into the Clark Forks canyon. They are colonizing the Gallatin Range, moving west from the Absarokas across Yankee Jim Canyon. The only goats in the Idaho segment are in the Snake River Mountains (Palisades) on the Targhee National Forest. Goats have also been sighted in Yellowstone, apparently moving in from Montana, and in Grand Teton National Park.

Remarks. Eats grasses and forbs year-round, but in winter sometimes resorts to conifer needles and branches. Snow restricts foraging either to cliff faces swept clear by avalanches or to wind-blown ridges. Is somewhat social and forms small herds. Female, especially with young, is aggressive and selects best cliff habitat, which she defends against other goats, including males. During November rut, males attempt to round up females. Sparring matches between billies can be lethal due to sharp, short horns.

The recent sightings of goats in Yellowstone and Grand Teton parks pose some real problems for park service. Parks are supposed to be managed for native species; expansion into either park may harm native bighorn and fragile alpine flora unaccustomed to goat grazing.

PRONGHORN ANTELOPE (*Antilocapra americana*)   *page 215*

Description. Not a true antelope or a goat, the pronghorn is in a family all its own. Delicate looking with large eyes, generally tan with white on sides and rump. Winter hairs are hollow, which helps to trap heat. Both sexes have horns, but buck's are larger. Horn sheaths are shed each November, leaving bony core.

Habitat and Distribution. Grasslands and plains. Restricted in ecosystem to grass and sage flats of major river valleys. Antelope avoids forests, but I have seen them passing through timbered draws on Specimen Ridge and in upper Gros Ventre River Valley.

There are about 5,500 antelope on federal lands in GYE: Beaverhead National Forest (1,400), Shoshone forest (1,147), Bridger-Teton forest (950), Red Rock Lakes National Wildlife Refuge (600), and Targhee National Forest (500). Some 125 and 360 pronghorn are reported for Grand Teton and Yellowstone national parks, respectively. Best places to see antelope in summer include Yellowstone park between Gardiner and Lamar River Valley; Centennial Valley, including Red Rock Lakes; upper Madison River Valley area; Baseline Flats in Grand Teton; and Gros Ventre and upper Green river valleys.

Remarks. Main defense is speed; has been clocked at 45 mph. Youngster remains motionless, relying on lack of scent to protect it from detection. Fences are a major obstacle, since antelope cannot jump them and often cannot crawl under. Fences block migration and predators use them to trap pronghorn.

Selective feeder. Prefers succulent, high-protein food and more shrubs and forbs than grasses. Domestic stock, particularly sheep, competes directly with antelope for food where ranges overlap. Sagebrush is major portion of winter diet. In winter, many antelope in Jackson Hole migrate up the Gros Ventre River and into the Green River Valley by Pinedale and beyond. Antelope in upper Yellowstone used to migrate into Paradise Valley and mix with animals from plains beyond, but housing development, ranching, and highways have all but blocked this. Antelope in northern end of park are now isolated, raising concern of inbreeding and genetic defects.

THE FUTURE OF
GREATER YELLOWSTONE

The idea of managing the Greater Yellowstone Ecosystem for its natural-ness, ecological integrity, and features is new. A variety of organizations and individuals manages lands within it, including seven national forests, two national parks, three wildlife refuges, the BLM, three state govern-ments, three fish and game departments, Indian reservations, twelve county governments, and private landowners. Often these are at odds over how to best protect the ecosystem, and there is little coordinated effort. For instance, though wolverines are protected in the Wyoming portion, just across the line in Montana, it is perfectly legal to trap them. This hodgepodge is destroying the qualities that make greater Yellowstone unique.

Managing the GYE from an ecological, instead of a political, perspec-tive will require new thinking. As heirs of an international treasure, we must treat these lands with a special respect for their real values. We need to ask, What does this region do best?

It is well established that preservation of the region's unique qualities fuels the local economies. Mining, logging, and grazing, which many people believe support local growth, actually account for fewer than 8 percent of the jobs derived from public lands. Recreation and tourism account for 80 percent. Furthermore, this is the only portion of the regional economy that is growing. That doesn't even include people who relocated their businesses or retired in the region based upon the per-ceived quality of life. The new jobs may not directly depend upon serving tourists, but they provide greater economic diversity nevertheless. Pro-tecting the ecosystem makes good business sense.

Sure, you can harvest timber here and the trees will grow back, but the high elevation and dry, cold climate keep the GYE from being a particularly good timber producer. It is not the nation's woodpile. For the same investment of public dollars on wood production, far more lumber would be produced in Georgia or Wisconsin. The same argument applies to livestock production. We allow ranchers to graze their cattle and sheep at subsidized rates on public lands that could otherwise support wildlife. We spend tax dollars to kill predators to protect the stock while we divert water from our famous trout streams to irrigate hay for it. Is this really the best use of our precious water, forage, and wildlife?

You can raise trees in Georgia and cows in Texas, but you can't grow grizzlies in Georgia or produce blue-ribbon trout streams in the Lone Star State. There are plenty of opportunities to produce timber and livestock in the private sector; we don't have to spend taxpayer money to degrade public property to coax out a meager amount of some commodity that is easily produced elsewhere. We can let grizzlies and trout thrive with almost no investment, just by leaving things alone.

What the public lands in the ecosystem are rich in are scenic, wildlife, geological, ecological, and historical values. It is our obligation as a nation to protect, enhance, recover, and repair our natural integrity, and there is no better place to start than in the Greater Yellowstone Ecosystem.

◆

WILDERNESS AND ROADLESS AREAS

The Greater Yellowstone Ecosystem is one of the largest wilderness complexes in the lower forty-eight states. Only central Idaho, which includes the River of No Return and Selway Bitterroot wildernesses, has a larger roadless area complex.

Designation of land as a public wilderness is a legal step authorized by Congress that prohibits mining, logging, road building, and motorized vehicles in that area. Fishing, hunting, camping, hiking, skiing, canoeing, and other recreational uses are usually permitted. Wilderness areas are increasingly recognized for their preservation of biological diversity, watershed, and scientific controls to be compared with more developed areas. The following brief descriptions include not only designated wildernesses but also significant roadless lands that could and should be protected as such.

Montana

Absaroka-Beartooth Wilderness
(Gallatin and Custer national forests)

This 920,310-acre wilderness is the second largest in Montana and the largest in the ecosystem. It is the northern border of Yellowstone park. Gardiner, Montana, is at its southwest corner; Livingston is on the northwest; Red Lodge is to the northeast; and Cooke City is on the south-central flank. The Absaroka and Beartooth ranges account for the name. This is Montana's high country, with twenty-nine peaks of more than 12,000 feet and the state's highest, Granite Peak (12,799 feet). Although heavily glaciated with rugged, deep granite canyons reminiscent of the Yosemite Valley, much of the wilderness consists of rolling plateaus with lyrical names like Silver Run, Hellroaring, and Boulder, each dotted with

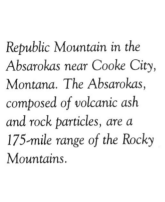

Republic Mountain in the Absarokas near Cooke City, Montana. The Absarokas, composed of volcanic ash and rock particles, are a 175-mile range of the Rocky Mountains.

dozens of lakes. Nearly three-fourths of this mountain mass is above the timberline, and alpine areas run on for miles.

The western portion, the Absaroka Mountains, consists of volcanic rocks overlain with basement granitics that make up the rest of the Beartooth Range. Due to their softer texture, these mountains are highly eroded and overall gentler in relief with beautiful flowered basins and more timber. Wildlife is particularly diverse and includes bighorn sheep, moose, grizzly and black bears, elk, and introduced mountain goats. Bison were once common in several parts, including the appropriately named Buffalo Plateau.

Several significant roadless areas border the wilderness and are proposed additions to it. Beginning at Gardiner and circling clockwise, there is Dome Mountain, an important winter range for elk; Emigrant Peak, a dramatic landmark; the 12,000-acre Chico Peak roadless area, another scenic backdrop to Paradise Valley; Paradise Face, bordering Paradise Valley between Mill Creek and Suce Creek near Livingston; Tie Creek, a spectacular foothill area; and the Line Creek Plateau, a 20,000-acre alpine area east of the Beartooth Highway.

Lee Metcalf Wilderness (BLM lands, Beaverhead and Gallatin national forests)

The 254,944-acre Lee Metcalf Wilderness is just northwest of Yellowstone park with its southern boundary near West Yellowstone, Montana. It is broken into four segments that straddle the Madison Range for fifty miles. These lands, along with the 36,752-acre Cabin Creek Wildlife Management Area and adjacent roadless lands, total 352,936 acres. The wilderness is named for Montana Sen. Lee Metcalf, a staunch wilderness supporter who died in 1978.

From the whitewater rapids of the Beartrap Canyon to the alpine summits of the Spanish Peaks, this wilderness contains some of the most spectacular scenery in the state, with several peaks exceeding 11,000 feet.

The abrupt face of the Madison Range, in Beaverhead National Forest, Montana, is an example of uplift along a fault. The Madison River flows 183 miles from Wyoming to Montana, where it joins the Jefferson and Gallatin rivers.

Hilgard Peak at 11,316 feet is the second highest in Montana outside of the lofty Beartooth Range. High peaks are clustered in five groups: the Spanish Peaks in the north; the Lone Mountain-Cedar Mountain-Sphinx Mountain group; and Taylor, Hilgard, and Monument peaks farthest south. Glaciated cirques, seventy alpine lakes, and rugged mountains with large meadows and parks puncture the forested slopes and valleys of this area. Grizzlies are common in the southern portion of the range, and there have been unconfirmed reports of them as far north as Beartrap Canyon. Elk, moose, and deer can be found throughout. Bighorn sheep and introduced mountain goats roam the higher terrain.

The proposed 26,000-acre Cowboy's Heaven addition lies between Beartrap Canyon and the Spanish Peaks. Formal designation would protect the connecting corridor.

Red Rock Lakes Wilderness (Red Rock Lakes Wildlife Refuge)

This 32,350-acre wilderness is predominately wetlands within Red Rock Lakes Wildlife Refuge. The refuge was created in 1935 to protect the lakes and ponds of the remote Centennial Valley, which were considered critical to the survival of what was then thought to be the last flocks of trumpeter swans. The refuge is home to moose, antelope, red fox, deer, and hundreds of bird species. It is a particularly good place to see the endangered peregrine falcon. The waters of the refuge are also one of the last places where the arctic grayling, extinct over most of its former Montana range, can still be found. Access is restricted during the nesting season of the swans.

Gallatin Range Proposed Wilderness (Gallatin National Forest)

The spectacular Gallatin Range, with many peaks topping 10,000 feet, runs south from Bozeman, Montana, into Yellowstone park's northwest corner. It is one of the largest unprotected roadless areas in Montana and a proposed wilderness area. Many consider these mountains among the better wildlife areas of the state, with large herds of elk as well as moose, grizzly bears, bighorn sheep, and deer. There are many wildflower meadows, particularly at higher elevations.

Lionhead Proposed Wilderness (Gallatin National Forest and Targhee National Forest, Idaho)

The area, named for 10,180-foot Lionhead Peak, lies just west of West

Yellowstone on the Continental Divide. It is the southern continuation of the Madison Range, separated from the range to the north by the Madison River where it flows through Quake Lake. The area has relatively open alpine ridges. There are nearly 50,000 roadless acres (32,000 on the Montana side) that are home to bighorn sheep, moose, grizzlies, elk, and deer.

Gravelly Range Proposed Wilderness (Beaverhead National Forest)

Lying east of the Ruby River and west of the Madison River Valley, the Gravelly Range is a high, plateaulike upland featuring large meadows dotted with timber. Access is by the Gravelly Range Road, which travels the ridge for miles, offering fantastic views, hiking, and camping. There are more than 300,000 roadless acres here, but they are fragmented into nine units. The largest are the 95,000-acre Freezeout Mountain area and the 39,000-acre Black Butte area. Though outside of the normal area for grizzlies, a bear was killed after being trapped by Animal Damage Control program officials in 1986, and there were twenty-nine confirmed grizzly sightings as of November 1990, including one as far north as Granite Mountain.

Snowcrest Range Proposed Wilderness (Beaverhead National Forest and BLM lands)

The 110,000 roadless acres in the Snowcrest Range make it one of the larger proposed wildernesses in the GYE, yet it is relatively unknown. The Snowcrests are gentle mountains with many broad, open ridges and only an occasional glacial cirque basin. Higher peaks and ridges exceed 10,000 feet. Patches of aspen and conifers are found on north slopes and in wet basins. Meadows are abundant; so are cattle and domestic sheep, and many of the meadows are "stock burnt" (overgrazed). There are no lakes, and clean water can be scarce because of the cattle.

Centennial Mountains Proposed Wilderness (BLM lands, Beaverhead National Forest, and Targhee National Forest, Idaho)

There are nearly 100,000 roadless acres in the Centennial Mountains, which straddle the Continental Divide in an east-west ridge between Henry's Lake, Idaho, and where Interstate 15 crosses Monida Pass. The fact that it's east-west is one of the area's major values, as it provides a continuous corridor for the migration of wildlife between the ecosystem and areas farther west in Idaho. The higher peaks are 9,000 to 10,000 feet. Hellroaring Creek is one of the most distant sources of the Missouri River. Grizzlies are reported, while moose and elk are common. The south slope, mostly managed by the Targhee National Forest, is gentle with broad meadows and patches of timber, while the north face, which looks over the Centennial Valley in Montana, is steep with glacially carved cirques. Much of the Montana side is managed by the BLM, with only small areas under Beaverhead National Forest management.

Idaho

There are no GYE designated wildernesses in this state. In addition to the proposed wildernesses listed here, portions of some proposed Montana wilderness areas are in Idaho.

Garns Mountain Proposed Wilderness (Targhee National Forest)

The 78,000-acre Garns Mountain roadless area lies in the Big Hole Mountains and forms the western backdrop to Pierre's Hole (around Driggs, Idaho). The South Fork of the Snake River is the more southerly border of this area. These gentle mountains barely rise above 9,000 feet, but their parks and meadows are spectacular. There are many trails as well as elk, mountain goats (introduced), black bears, and moose.

Palisades Proposed Wilderness (Targhee National Forest)

The Snake River Mountains, better known as the Palisades, are on the Wyoming-Idaho line just north of Palisades Reservoir and the Snake River. These rugged, steep, heavily glaciated mountains rise to more than 10,000 feet and contain over 200,000 roadless acres almost equally divided between the two states. The area has many streams and a few lakes. Many of the trails are short but steep, offering quick access to the higher ridges and peaks. There are moose, elk, bighorn sheep, mountain goats (introduced), and deer. As part of the Overthrust Belt, the area has drawn the attention of oil and gas companies.

Bear Creek Proposed Wilderness (Targhee and Caribou national forests)

The 107,000-acre Bear Creek roadless area lies just west of Palisades Reservoir and is the most northerly of three major roadless areas in the Caribou Range. There are many parallel ridges, with the highest peaks little more than 9,000 feet. Aspen groves and meadows make for outstanding views. This region also is part of the Overthrust Belt.

The Northern Wyoming Range, near the head of Cliff Creek, Bridger-Teton National Forest, is part of the Overthrust Belt, thought to hold large reserves of oil. Consequently, much of this range is threatened by development.

Caribou Proposed Wilderness (Targhee and Caribou national forests)

There are 89,000 acres in this area. Like the adjacent Bear Creek, the Caribou area has many parallel ridges; Caribou Mountain is the high point. The Caribou City mining district once was here and there are new proposals for gold mining on Caribou Mountain. Several streams are critical habitat for fine-spotted cutthroat trout.

Stump Creek Proposed Wilderness (Caribou National Forest)

The 100,000-acre Stump Creek roadless region is the most southerly of the three roadless areas in the Caribou Range. Like the proposed Bear Creek and Caribou wildernesses, this area is part of the Overthrust Belt. It also has numerous parallel ridges separated by linear canyons. Stump Creek has one of the highest concentrations of elk in Idaho. The South Fork of Tincup Creek and Stump Creek are critical habitat for fine-spotted cutthroat trout.

Wyoming

Jedediah Smith Wilderness (Targhee National Forest)

The 116,535-acre Jedediah Smith Wilderness covers the western flank of the Teton Range—only the areas east of the range divide are actually part of Grand Teton park. Although it's in Wyoming, nearly all access is from Idaho. The wilderness has spectacular glaciated scenery. About 115,000 acres in adjacent Grand Teton park have been proposed as wilderness. Domestic sheep grazing continues to degrade the alpine and subalpine meadows for which this area is famous.

Salt River Range Proposed Wilderness
(Bridger-Teton National Forest)

The extremely glaciated and rugged escarpment of this 245,000-acre area is just west of Afton, Wyoming. Its 11,000-foot peaks form the dramatic backdrop for the Star Valley on the Idaho-Wyoming line. The area has many streams but few lakes. Still, the open nature of the forest cover, with its many aspen groves and meadows, provides excellent views and cross-country hiking. The area has elk, moose, bears, and deer. Again, this area is part of the Overthrust Belt, which interests oil drillers. Almost unknown except to oil and logging companies, this area is coming under increasing development threats.

Wyoming Range Proposed Wilderness
(Bridger-Teton National Forest)

This 225,000-acre roadless region, sometimes called Grayback Ridge, lies directly south of the Hoback River Canyon, east of the Greys River, and west of the Green River. Like the adjacent Salt River Range, the Wyoming Range is steep, glaciated country, but with ridges and slopes that offer superb views. Aspen groves with lush meadows make this an attractive but little-known hiking area. The Wyoming Range Recreation Trail runs the length of the crest. This area is experiencing greater oil exploration, development, and logging. Sheep and cattle continue to trample the mountains to dust.

Fritzpatrick, Popo Agie, and Bridger wildernesses
(Shoshone and Bridger-Teton national forests)

Many people consider the Wind River Range to be the nation's most spectacular mountains. If you want solitude, this is probably not the place to go. If you don't mind sharing the trails, the Winds can't be beaten for sheer visual intensity. Studded with more than 1,000 lakes, dozens of waterfalls, and hundreds of granite peaks and cirques (including Wyoming's highest point, 13,804-foot Gannett Peak), the range offers a grand scale. In its 100-mile length, there are forty-five peaks topping 13,000 feet. It is not surprising that the Winds also contain the largest glaciers in the Rocky Mountains south of Canada.

Between South Pass, where the range jumps from sagebrush deserts in Wyoming's Great Basin to Whiskey Mountain near Dubois, the Wind River Range contains more than a million acres of roadless lands that straddle the Continental Divide. There are more than 700,000 acres in three wilderness areas, plus nearly 200,000 roadless acres on the Wind River Indian Reservation in the middle eastern slope of the range. The Bridger Wilderness, at 428,169 acres, is the largest and takes in most of the western slope. The Popo Agie and Fritzpatrick wildernesses are on the eastern side of the divide and are separated by the Wind River Reservation. The Whiskey Mountain bighorn sheep herd by Dubois has more than 1,000 head and is the largest in Wyoming. Livestock grazing continues to degrade fragile mountain meadows in the wildernesses. Acid rain is also increasingly tainting many of the range's waters.

Gros Ventre Wilderness (Bridger-Teton National Forest)

This 287,000-acre wilderness is just east of Jackson and forms the eastern escarpment of the Jackson "hole." It is primarily limestone and has many glaciated peaks but few lakes. Despite the glaciation, there are many broad, flat alpine ridges. The limestone weathers to form deep, rich soils that support relatively lush alpine meadows.

This area is important for the Jackson Hole elk herd and also supports a healthy number of bighorn sheep. An additional 160,000 roadless acres border the wilderness and offer an outstanding wildland corridor between the Wyoming Range south of the Snake River and the Yellowstone country north of the Gros Ventre.

Mount Leidy Highlands Proposed Wilderness
(Bridger-Teton National Forest)

At 10,326 feet, Mount Leidy is the highest point in this area of rolling forested ridges and meadows north of the Gros Ventre River. Due to its gentler terrain, it was heavily exploited by logging and oil companies. The remaining roadless area of 100,000 acres is under new threats of oil exploration and development. These highlands are a critical migration corridor for the southern Yellowstone elk herds and are part of the grizzly's habitat.

Winegar Hole Wilderness (Targhee National Forest)
The 14,000-acre Winegar Hole Wilderness is the smallest in the ecosystem. Located near the southwest boundary of Yellowstone park, the Winegar Hole area is nearly level forest full of small lakes, swamps, and other wetlands. It is accessible from the Flagg Ranch-Ashton Road.

Teton Wilderness (Bridger-Teton National Forest)
This wilderness flanks the western side of the Continental Divide south of Yellowstone park and covers 586,468 acres. It is part of a two-million-acre contiguous wildland complex that includes the southern part of Yellowstone and adjacent portions of the Washakie Wilderness. As headwaters for the upper Yellowstone and Snake rivers, this is one of the major watershed divides in the West. The Teton wilderness also includes Two Ocean Pass, where Two Ocean Creek splits. The Upper Thorofare River within this wilderness is the farthest point from a road (twenty-two miles) in the United States outside of Alaska.

The area is diverse and rolling, but there are rugged glaciated peaks near the Continental Divide plus high alpine plateaus. This region is elk and moose heaven, with grizzlies thrown in for good measure. Most of the rock is loose Absaroka volcanics and thus easily weathered. There are few lakes, so this area is used more by hunters packing in by horse in the fall than by hikers in the summer.

Washakie Wilderness (Shoshone National Forest)
The 704,000-acre Washakie Wilderness borders southeastern Yellowstone park east of Cody and north of Dubois, Wyoming. It is made up of Absaroka volcanics, consisting of nearly horizontal layers of lava and breccia that weather to deep, rich soils supporting lavish wildflower displays. The area has extensive alpine plateaus, pinnacles like the Washakie Needles, and rugged glaciated mountains, including 13,140-foot Franc Peak. There is a lot of undesignated roadless country on the eastern edge of the Washakie, much of it essential to big game in winter. The 26,000-

acre DuNoir Area, a spectacular glacially carved basin just north of Dubois, is a proposed addition. Like the Teton wilderness to the west, the Washakie is exceptional big-game country with elk, grizzlies, bighorn sheep, and moose.

North Absaroka Wilderness (Shoshone National Forest)

This 350,538-acre area lies west and north of Cody, north of the Shoshone River, and borders eastern Yellowstone park. Glaciated peaks and alpine tundra plateaus make it a visual treat. The area is along the Absaroka volcanics belt, so it has few lakes but many rich, flowery meadows. Bighorn sheep commonly winter at the highest elevations on windswept peaks and plateaus. Grizzlies, elk, and moose also are found here. Much of this area burned during the 1988 fires.

Absaroka-Beartooth Wilderness (Shoshone National Forest)

Though most of this wilderness is in Montana, 23,700 acres lie in Wyoming. The rolling country is dotted with lakes and meadows. Just east of this addition is the 14,700-acre Wyoming High Lakes Wilderness Study Area, established by the 1984 Wyoming wilderness bill. This keeps the area roadless but does little toward achieving wilderness designation.

The 135,000-acre Deep Lake proposed addition is sandwiched between the Beartooth Highway and the spectacular Clarks Fork River Canyon. There are peat beds with permafrost as well as numerous lakes.

COMMUNITIES

Cody, Wyoming—At 5,093 feet elevation, Cody is just east of the Absaroka Mountains at the mouth of Shoshone Canyon on the Shoshone River. It was named for founder William F. Cody, or Buffalo Bill. He earned his nickname for slaughtering 4,280 bison—more than exist in Yellowstone and Grand Teton parks today—in just eighteen months. Cody held a variety of jobs, including guide and scout. During an expedition to the Bighorn Basin in the 1870s, he became enthralled with the beauty and abundant wildlife of the region. In 1896, he came back to the area as a land developer and founded the town.

Today, Cody has 7,838 people, and Park County has 22,727. The area still thrives off of its natural resources. Since it is the only major community along the road to the eastern entrance of Yellowstone park, tourism is a major business. Besides Yellowstone, there are many other attractions nearby, including Shoshone National Forest, which includes the spectacular Washakie and North Absaroka wildernesses. The recently designated Clarks Fork Wild and Scenic River protects the magnificent 1,200-foot-deep granite gorge.

Cody is home to the Buffalo Bill Historical Center, the Foundation for North American Wild Sheep, and several historical sites, including the Irma Hotel, built by Cody and named for his daughter; Old Trail Town, restored to appear like an old-time Western community; and the Wapiti ranger station, oldest in the United States. Heart Mountain just north of Cody was the site of a Japanese-American internment camp during World War II.

Despite the emphasis on tourism, government is still the largest employer in the Cody area. Among the major employers are Shoshone National Forest, the Bureau of Reclamation, the Bureau of Land Management, and state, county, and local agencies. Retailing, oil, mining, and agriculture are other parts of the economy.

Cody has more than 300 sunny days a year, a scenic setting, a small-town flavor, and an active arts community that includes an annual jazz festival.

Lander, Wyoming—Lander is along the Pogo Agie River on the east side of the Wind River Range at 5,357 feet. It has nearly 300 days of sunshine a year, and its average wind speed of 4.7 mph is one of the lowest in the nation. Winters are cold but sunny with low humidity, while summers are dry with cool nights. A total of 8,058 people call Lander home, with 36,798 in Fremont County. The town was incorporated in 1884 and became the county seat. The county, named for explorer John C. Fremont, is 150 miles from corner to corner, larger than any of the seven smallest states.

Lander is the gateway to the Pogo Agie Wilderness, a spectacular chunk of the Wind River Range with peaks towering up to 13,000 feet. Fremont County could be called the rooftop of Wyoming, with 40 peaks of more than 13,000 feet. Lakes dot the granite basins and cirques provide great fishing. Just as spectacular is the nearby Red Desert, a vast sage-covered area managed by the BLM that includes the largest unfenced region in the United States.

Sinks Canyon State Park is just outside of town. Here the North Fork of the Pogo Agie disappears into a hole in the limestone, only to reappear as a large spring a half-mile downstream. Large trout fin in the clear, icy waters. Bighorn sheep are also frequently seen in the canyon.

South of Lander is the restored ghost town of South Pass City. In the 1860s, this gold rush community had a population of 2,000. It is now a state historical site and many of the original buildings are open to the public. The Oregon Trail also passes over South Pass, the only nearly level crossing of the Continental Divide in the Rockies.

North of Lander on U.S. 287 lies the Wind River Indian Reservation, home of 6,000 people of Arapaho and Shoshone descent. Here is the grave of Sacagawea, who guided Lewis and Clark across Montana. Powwows and dances are held throughout the summer, and visitors are welcome.

Services are the largest employer in Fremont County, providing nearly 5,000 jobs. Government employers include the U.S. Forest Service, BLM, the Department of Environmental Quality, the Game and Fish Department, and the Wyoming State Training School, plus the county and city.

Aspen frames Jackson Lake and the Teton Range in Grand Teton National Range, Wyoming, created in 1929. Local citizens opposed the creation of the park, fearing it would destroy their livelihoods. Today the regional economy depends on tourism.

Serving the reservation, hospitals, and tourism are also important to the economy. Lander is home to the National Outdoor Leadership School, which leads major wilderness expeditions throughout the world.

Often neglected in economic analyses is the role of retirees. Many people with independent incomes live in Lander because of the climate and recreation. There is a program to help retirees settle and coordinate activities.

Pinedale, Wyoming—Pinedale lies at 7,175 feet in the upper Green River Valley between the Wind River Range on the east and the Wyoming Range on the west. It enjoys sunny skies and ten inches of precipitation annually. With a year-round population of only 1,000 and fewer than 5,000 in Sublette County, Pinedale swells in summer with thousands of visitors from across the nation. Though there still is some ranching in the upper Green River Valley, tourism feeds the local econ-

omy. In summer, people descend on the 400,000-acre Bridger Wilderness and its 1,300 lakes to fish, hike, camp, climb, and just soak in the peace and beauty. A scenic twenty-six-mile drive to Elkhart Park offers spectacular views of the Wind River Range and glacially carved Fremont Lake. The drive to Green River Lakes and the unforgettable view of Square Top Mountain is another local favorite.

Jackson, Wyoming—Located beneath the majestic Teton Range, Jackson is the seat of Teton County. The town sits at 6,209 feet at the south end of sixty-mile-long Jackson Hole. About 5,700 people live here, while the county has 13,140. Compared with Cody or Lander, Jackson is wet, with 17.42 inches of precipitation a year, including 150 inches of snow.

Jackson is the high-rent district, the premier tourist town in Wyoming. The average house in Teton County costs $202,000. Gaze upon the Teton Range on a sunny day and it's easy to understand why. With Grand Teton park outside the back door, there is no shortage of outdoor places to have fun. Jackson also is the jumping-off point for trips into the Gros Ventre and Teton wildernesses, and there are dozens of trails in other equally spectacular settings like the Salt River, Hoback, and Snake River ranges. There is rafting, kayaking, and canoeing on the Snake River, plus excellent fishing in the Snake, Gros Ventre, Hoback, and Grey's rivers.

The National Elk Refuge is just outside the city. In winter, thousands of elk here are fed hay to compensate for the winter range lost to housing tracts or livestock. Winter recreation includes the Grand Targhee, Jackson Hole, and Snow King skiing areas plus cross-country skiing, snowmobiling, and winter wildlife watching. Jackson Hole Ski Resort has the greatest vertical rise (4,139 feet) of any in the nation.

The economy is service oriented; the government has a large role as well. Jackson has the lowest unemployment rate in the state, recently around 3.5 percent. It has the supervisor's headquarters for the sprawling Bridger-Teton National Forest, the Wyoming Fish and Game Department district office, and other state, county, and city personnel.

Dubois, Wyoming—Dubois sits at 6,927 feet above sea level in the upper Wind River Valley. With the Wind River Range to the south and the Absaroka Range to the north, one could not find a more scenic setting. The community was established in the late 1800s, when loggers

came to cut railroad ties, which were floated down the Wind River to Riverton. Logging played a role until Louisiana Pacific closed its mill here in the late 1980s. Since then, Dubois has relied more and more on its scenery. The fishing, hunting, hiking, and wildlife watching are excellent. In particular, the Whiskey Mountain bighorn sheep herd south of town is the largest in the state, and it's easy to get to.

Driggs, Idaho—This town in the scenic Teton Valley is on the "other" side of the Tetons, which is just as scenic as the more famous Wyoming side. Still, this community has until lately been more of interest to potato farmers and ranchers than tourists. But the construction of Grand Targhee Ski Resort and the allure of the west slope of the Tetons has gradually turned it into a tourist base. The high cost of housing in Jackson has driven some commuters to Driggs.

The west slope of the Tetons is part of the Jedediah Smith Wilderness, with many trails leading up to the Teton Crest. There also is hiking in the Big Hole Mountains west of town. Fishing in the spring-fed Teton River is excellent, and other nearby waters include the South Fork of the Snake.

West Yellowstone, Montana—West Yellowstone lies at 6,666 feet at the west entrance of the park. Known for its winter chill, the high elevation means comfortable summer days. The town of 780 is almost entirely dependent upon tourism. It has recently spruced up its streets with pleasing signs, lamps, and boardwalks.

The town is surrounded by national park or forest lands. It is famous for Hebgen Lake and Quake Lake, created by the 1959 earthquake, which brought down part of a mountain to dam the Madison River. It also is a fly-fishing mecca along the Madison, Firehole, Henry's Fork, and Gallatin rivers and nearby lakes. In winter, most snowmobile trips into Yellowstone park originate from here. West Yellowstone is also one of the better cross-country skiing areas in the West. Both the U.S. Nordic and biathlon teams train here.

Bozeman, Montana—Named for wagon train guide John Bozeman, who pioneered the trail from Wyoming into Montana's fertile Gallatin Valley in 1864, Bozeman is at 4,793 feet and has 30,000 residents. It is the seat of Gallatin County and is the cultural and educational hub of the Greater Yellowstone Ecosystem.

One of the fastest-growing parts of Montana (nearly 17 percent over the last ten years), Bozeman has one of the lowest unemployment rates in Montana, less than 3.7 percent. It is seventy-five miles from Yellowstone park, but Bozeman has plenty to offer on its own. Within an hour or less from town are the Gallatin, Madison, and Bridger ranges, all equally impressive. Summer hiking, mountain biking, and camping abound. Fishing is good in the Madison, Gallatin, and Yellowstone rivers, and there is hunting in the fall. For winter buffs, there is skiing at nearby Bridger Bowl and Big Sky, plus miles of cross-country terrain.

Though the county was originally known for agriculture, farm and ranch employment now only makes up 5 percent of the jobs, and timbering accounts for even fewer, though you couldn't tell from the number of clear-cuts that scar the mountains. Bozeman's economy has grown on services, government, and education. One of the largest employers is Montana State University, where 10,000 study everything from nursing to philosophy. Also here are offices of the Gallatin National Forest, Soil Conservation Service, Montana Department of Fish, Wildlife, and Parks, and many other federal, state, and local agencies.

Livingston, Montana

Livingston, Montana—This is the seat of Park County. It has 7,000 people and was founded in 1879 as a tent camp during the construction of the Northern Pacific Railroad. For decades afterward, the railroad provided high-paying jobs for area workers. In 1979, the Burlington Northern, the descendant of the Northern Pacific, closed its shops, laying off nearly 1,000 employees. For a time, the community staggered under the loss, but its economy has been rebuilt because of retirement and tourism. Paradise Valley just south of here is one of the most attractive valleys in the Yellowstone ecosystem, drawing new well-to-do residents from around the country.

Only fifty-six miles away is Yellowstone park, an easy hour's drive. Livingston is less than twenty-three miles on an interstate from Bozeman with its university and shops.

But this Montana town is not a bedroom community. Livingston has a historic downtown and a reputation as an artistic center with perhaps more writers, photographers, and artists per capita than any other community in the region.

Livingston is tied with nearby Big Timber as the two windiest places in Montana. Chinooks sometimes kick up gusts of eighty mph, but the town also is one of the warmest places in the ecosystem in winter, with an average January temperature of twenty-six degrees, equal to New York's. Hiking is fine in the nearby Absaroka-Beartooth Wilderness, Gallatin Range, and Crazy Mountains, as is fishing in the spring creeks and Yellowstone River.

Gardiner, Montana—Located at the north entrance of Yellowstone park, Gardiner, population 700, is perhaps the best place in the ecosystem to see wildlife just outside your door. At 5,280 feet, the town is in the rain shadow of the Gallatin Range and gets less than ten inches annually. Mountains rise dramatically on all sides and there is plenty of blue sky and little snow, so a wide variety of wildlife winters here. Take a short stroll from downtown and you may see antelope, bighorn sheep, elk, bison, mule deer, coyotes, and white-tailed jackrabbits.

Gardiner is still largely a tourist town, but the new gold mine six miles away in Jardine has brought a boom of sorts. It is also a bedroom community for many employees of Yellowstone park. You can fish in the Yellowstone and Gardner rivers just a stone's throw from downtown, and there is hiking in the Absaroka-Beartooth Wilderness and Yellowstone park. Whitewater rafting is popular on the Yellowstone, particularly in Yankee Jim Canyon. In winter, there is good cross-country skiing on park and forest service lands.

Cooke City, Montana—Cooke City, elevation 7,600 feet, is the only community in the ecosystem that really sits up in the mountains. It is in a narrow valley with rugged peaks rising majestically on either side. Cooke City was a gold rush town that turned into a summer home and tourist community. Old mining claims near Fisher Mountain may soon be redeveloped.

Gold was discovered here in 1869 by Adam Miller (Miller Mountain bears his name) while it was part of the Crow Reservation. Naturally, that did not deter the miners. A town named Shoo-fly sprang up below Republic Mountain, but the name was changed to Cooke City in 1880 to honor Jay Cooke, who miners hoped would build a railroad to the town. By the mid-1880s, there were more than 1,000 people, thirteen saloons, three general stores, and two sawmills.

Today, Cooke City's 100 or so year-round residents stay alive by serving tourists on the Beartooth Highway or from Yellowstone park. Snowmobiling is a major sport, while backpacking, fishing, and horsepacking into the Absaroka-Beartooth and North Absaroka wildernesses are popular in summer.

Red Lodge, Montana—The area around Red Lodge was once part of the Crow Reservation. Legend has it that the Indians set up tepees painted with red clay, giving the location its name. After the area was removed from the reservation in 1882 (the third reduction in Crow lands), coal mining picked up and the town was founded in 1885 to serve the mines.

Sitting close to the mountains, Red Lodge receives a fair amount of orographic rainfall. Its annual precipitation of 22.35 inches makes it more than twice as wet as, say, Cody or Pinedale, Wyoming. Still, the climate is relatively mild, with a January average of 20.5 degrees and a July mean of 68.3.

Red Lodge is at 5,600 feet and straddles Rock Creek, which issues from the lofty Beartooth Mountains. Because of its scenic location, many of Red Lodge's 2,000 residents cater to the visitors who come to hike, fish, ski, and just gawk at the mountains. Red Lodge Mountain often has some of the latest skiing in the state. The Beartooth Highway, which crosses miles of alpine tundra from Red Lodge to Cooke City, Montana, is often called the most beautiful highway in the nation. Backpacking and horsepacking on the alpine lake-studded plateaus of the Absaroka-Beartooth Wilderness are major summer sports in the area.

With 110 workers, Red Lodge Mountain is the largest employer in the community, followed by Carbon County, which has eighty-four employees, and Crazy Creek Products, a manufacturer of sporting goods, with twenty. Other employers include the Red Lodge Ranger District, the Soil Conservation Service, and other federal agencies.

BIRD LIST

This bird list does not include every bird one might see in the GYE, but it contains the most common species or ones of significant interest. The abundance of species varies considerably, both seasonally and throughout the ecosystem. I have omitted many birds which are seen only occasionally during migration. The rating system for abundance goes from 1 to 5. The higher the number, the more common the species.

1. Rare: seldom seen either because of very low numbers or unusual occurrence.
2. Occasional: seen a few times a season or in small numbers.
3. Uncommon: present, but not certain to be seen.
4. Common: certain to be seen in appropriate habitat with some effort.
5. Abundant: seen without much effort in any appropriate habitat.

Most of these species have been recorded as breeders or are suspected of breeding somewhere in the GYE. Breeding may occur only in a particular location: for example, the only known breeding area for ferruginous hawks in the ecosystem is Red Rock Lakes National Wildlife Refuge. Although there are historic accounts of merlins breeding in the ecosystem, none have been recorded in recent years. Italicized type is used for those birds that are not believed to breed in the Yellowstone area.

Ducks, Swans, and Geese

____ Common loon (3)

____ Red-necked grebe (1)

____ Western grebe (4)

____ Horned grebe (1)

____ Eared grebe (3)

____ Pied-billed grebe (3)

____ White pelican (4)

____ Double-crested cormorant (3)

____ *Tundra swan* (3)

____ Trumpeter swan (4)

____ Canada goose (5)

____ *Snow goose* (1)

____ Mallard (4)

____ Northern pintail (3)

____ Gadwall (4)

____ American wigeon (4)

Ducks, Swans, and Geese (continued)

____ Northern shoveler (3)
____ Blue-winged teal (3)
____ Cinnamon teal (4)
____ Green-winged teal (4)
____ Redhead (3)
____ Canvasback (3)
____ Ring-necked duck (4)
____ Lesser scaup (4)

____ Common goldeneye (4)
____ Barrow's goldeneye (4)
____ Bufflehead (3)
____ Harlequin duck (1)
____ Ruddy duck (3)
____ Hooded merganser (1)
____ Red-breasted merganser (1)
____ Common merganser (4)

Hawks, Falcons, and Eagles

____ Northern goshawk (3)
____ Cooper's hawk (3)
____ Sharp-shinned hawk (3)
____ Northern harrier (4)
____ *Rough-legged hawk* (4)
____ Ferruginous hawk (1)
____ Red-tailed hawk (4)
____ Swainson's hawk (4)

____ Golden eagle (4)
____ Bald eagle (3)
____ Osprey (3)
____ Prairie falcon (4)
____ Peregrine falcon (2)
____ Merlin (1)
____ Kestrel (4)
____ *Turkey vulture* (2)

Grouse

____ Blue grouse (3)
____ Ruffed grouse (4)

____ Sage grouse (2)

Turkey

____ Turkey (3)

Wading Birds and Dabblers

____ *Snowy egret* (1)
____ Great blue heron (4)
____ Black-crowned night heron (1)
____ American bittern (2)
____ *White-faced ibis* (2)
____ Sandhill crane (3)
____ *Whooping crane* (1)
____ Virginia rail (2)
____ Sora (3)
____ *Yellow rail* (1)

____ American coot (5)
____ American avocet (4)
____ *Black-necked stilt* (1)
____ *Semipalmated plover* (1)
____ Killdeer (4)
____ Marbled godwit (2)
____ Long-billed curlew (2)
____ *Greater yellowlegs* (1)
____ *Lesser yellowlegs* (1)
____ *Solitary sandpiper* (2)

Wading Birds and Dabblers (continued)

_____ *Upland sandpiper* (2)   _____ Common snipe (4)

_____ Willet (4)   _____ *Semipalmated sandpiper* (2)

_____ *Long-billed dowitcher* (3)   _____ *Western sandpiper* (2)

_____ Wilson's phalarope (4)

Gulls and Terns

_____ California gull (5)   _____ Forster's tern (3)

_____ Ring-billed gull (3)   _____ Black tern (3)

_____ Franklin's gull (3)

Doves

_____ Mourning dove (3)

Owls

_____ Great horned owl (4)   _____ *Burrowing owl* (1)

_____ Long-eared owl (2)   _____ Northern saw-whet owl (1)

_____ Short-eared owl (2)   _____ Northern pygmy owl (1)

_____ Great gray owl (2)   _____ Boreal owl (1)

Nighthawks

_____ Common nighthawk (4)

Swifts

_____ White-throated swift (3)

Hummingbirds

_____ Broad-tailed hummingbird (2)   _____ *Black-chinned hummingbird* (2)

_____ Calliope hummingbird (3)   _____ Rufous hummingbird (3)

Kingfishers

_____ Belted kingfisher (4)

Woodpeckers

_____ *Pileated woodpecker* (1)   _____ Red-naped sapsucker (4)

_____ Flicker (4)   _____ Williamson's sapsucker (3)

_____ *Lewis's woodpecker* (1)   _____ Hairy woodpecker (4)

Woodpeckers (continued)

____ Downy woodpecker (4)
____ *Black-backed woodpecker* (1)

____ *Three-toed woodpecker* (2)

Flycatchers

____ Eastern kingbird (2)
____ *Western kingbird* (1)
____ *Say's phoebe* (1)
____ Willow flycatcher (3)
____ Dusty flycatcher (4)

____ Hammond's flycatcher (3)
____ Western flycatcher (2)
____ Western wood peewee (3)
____ Olive-sided flycatcher (3)

Larks

____ Horned lark (4)

Swallows

____ Barn swallow (4)
____ Cliff swallow (5)
____ Violet-green swallow (4)
____ Tree swallow (4)

____ Bank swallow (3)
____ Northern rough-winged swallow (3)

Jays and Crows

____ Stellar's jay (3)
____ Gray jay (4)
____ Black-billed magpie (4)

____ Clark's nutcracker (4)
____ Common raven (5)
____ American crow (1)

Dippers

____ Dipper (4)

Chickadees, Nuthatches, Creepers

____ Black-capped chickadee (4)
____ Mountain chickadee (5)
____ White-breasted nuthatch (3)

____ Red-breasted nuthatch (4)
____ Pygmy nuthatch (1)
____ Brown creeper (1)

Wrens

____ House wren (4)
____ Rock wren (3)

____ Marsh wren (3)

Thrashers

_____ Sage thrasher (3)

Thrushes

_____ American robin (4)   _____ Swainson's thrush (4)
_____ Townsend's solitaire (4)   _____ Veery (1)
_____ Hermit thrush (3)   _____ Mountain bluebird (5)

Kinglets

_____ Golden-crowned kinglet (3)   _____ Ruby-crowned kinglet (4)

Pipits

_____ Water pipit (4)

Waxwings

_____ Bohemian waxwing (3)   _____ Cedar waxwing (3)

Shrikes

_____ *Northern shrike (3)*   _____ *Loggerhead shrike (1)*

Starlings

_____ European starling (4)

Vireos and Warblers

_____ *Solitary vireo (1)*   _____ Townsend's warbler (1)
_____ Warbling vireo (4)   _____ Common yellowthroat (4)
_____ *Red-eyed vireo (1)*   _____ MacGillivray's warbler (4)
_____ Orange-crowned warbler (2)   _____ Wilson's warbler (4)
_____ Yellow warbler (4)   _____ American redstart (1)
_____ Yellow-rumped warbler (5)

Weaver Finches

_____ House sparrow (4)

Blackbirds and Orioles

_____ Western meadowlark (4)   _____ Brewer's blackbird (4)
_____ Yellow-headed blackbird (4) _____ Brown-headed cowbird (4)
_____ Red-winged blackbird (4)   _____ Northern oriole (1)

Tanagers

_____ Western tanager (4)

Grosbeaks, Finches, Sparrows, and Buntings

_____ Evening grosbeak (3)
_____ Lazuli bunting (2)
_____ Cassin's finch (4)
_____ Pine grosbeak (4)
_____ Rosy finch (4)
_____ *Common redpoll* (3)
_____ Pine siskin (4)
_____ American goldfinch (2)
_____ Red crossbill (3)
_____ Green-tailed towhee (2)

_____ Savannah sparrow (3)
_____ Vesper sparrow (4)
_____ Lark sparrow (3)
_____ Dark-eyed junco (4)
_____ Chipping sparrow (4)
_____ Brewer's sparrow (4)
_____ White-crowned sparrow (4)
_____ Lincoln's sparrow (4)
_____ Song sparrow (4)
_____ *Snow bunting* (3)

FIELD GUIDE
TO PLANTS AND ANIMALS

alder leaves
and catkins

bebb willow

red-osier
dogwood

black cottonwood

wood rose

serviceberry

shrubby cinquefoil

Douglas fir

ninebark

thimble berry

aspen leaves
and catkins

lodgepole pine

Englemann spruce

subalpine fir

whitebark pine

bog kalmia

dryas or Mt. Avens

Yellowstone cutthroat trout

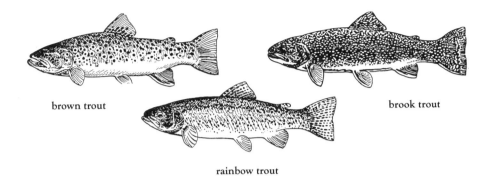

brown trout

brook trout

rainbow trout

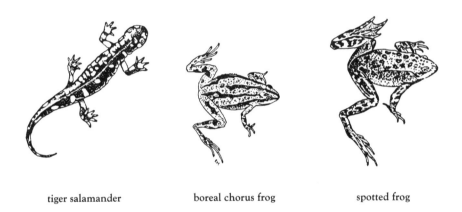

tiger salamander

boreal chorus frog

spotted frog

rubber boa

garter snake

common loon

western grebe

trumpeter swan

white pelican

Canada goose

mallard

Barrow's goldeneye

common merganser

great blue heron   killdeer   Wilson's phalarope

whooping crane

sandhill crane

northern harrier

red-tailed hawk

American kestrel

bald eagle

golden eagle

great horned owl

ruffed grouse

dipper   belted kingfisher   nighthawk

violet-green swallow   gray jay   black-billed
                                                        magpie

Clark's nutcracker   common raven

black-capped
chickadee

American robin   Swainson's thrush   yellow-rumped
warbler

common yellowthroat   western meadowlark   red-winged blackbird

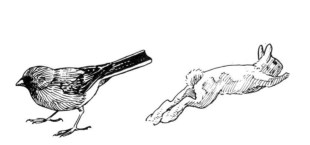 

dark-eyed junco   showshoe hare   white-tailed jackrabbit

muskrat   red squirrel   beaver

marten   mink

short-tailed weasel

badger   striped skunk

river otter

raccoon

fox   black bear   white-tailed deer

mule deer   elk   moose

bison   bighorn sheep   pronghorn antelope

INDEX